AF614854

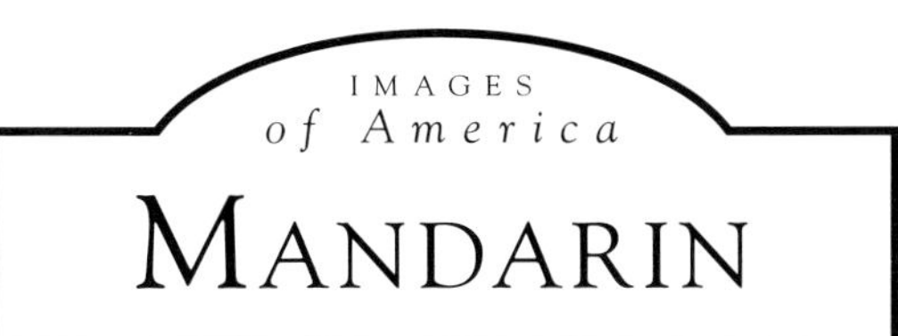
IMAGES
of America
MANDARIN

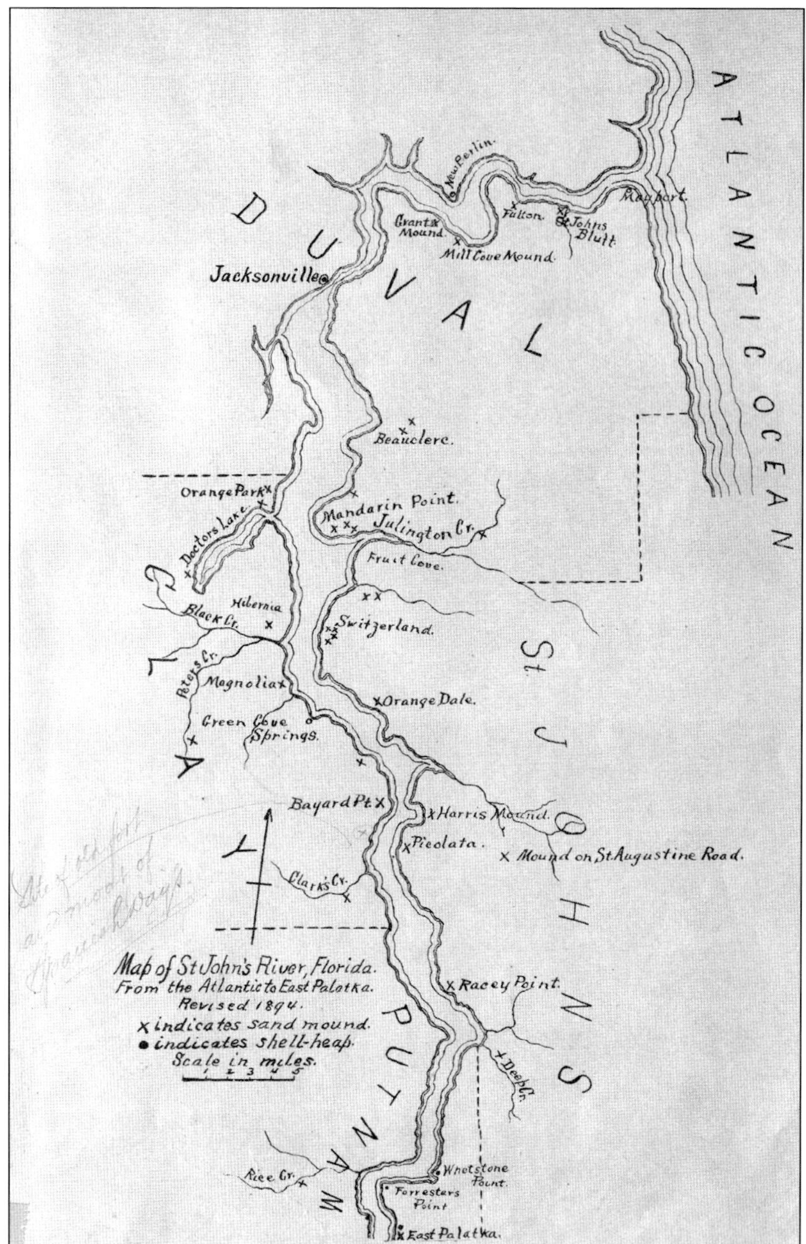

This map of the St. Johns River is from the book *Certain Sand Mounds of the St. Johns River, Florida, Part 2* by Clarence Bloomfield Moore, published in 1894. Since the St. Johns flows north, this view illustrates the course from just south of Orangedale in St. Johns County, past Mandarin Point, through Jacksonville and to the Atlantic Ocean on the east side. On the left of the map are Clay County and Duval County's west side. The "x" markings indicate the locations of discovered mounds of the now-extinct Timucua population. (Courtesy of Jacksonville Public Library, Florida Collection.)

On the Cover: It is believed this photograph was taken on the William W. Webb property, which is now the City of Jacksonville's Walter Jones Historical Park. The men appear to be leaning against a railcar that Webb had fashioned to move his citrus from packing to the wharf for steamboat pick-up. The men represent the workforce of Mandarin in the late 19th century: Black and White laborers provided the muscle for citrus production, farming, building, and lumbering—typical work available in Mandarin for men during this time. (Courtesy of the Mandarin Museum & Historical Society.)

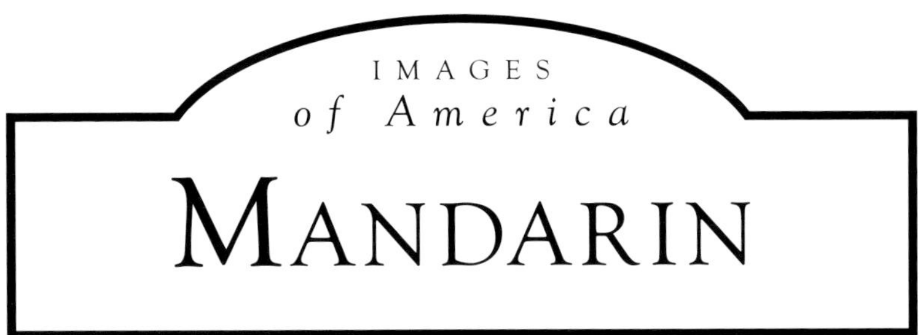

Susan Ford and
the Mandarin Museum & Historical Society

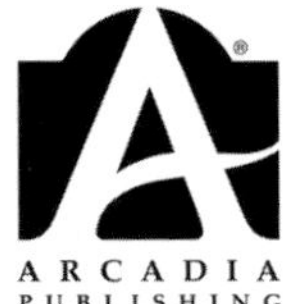

ISBN 978-1-4671-0819-5

Published by Arcadia Publishing
Charleston, South Carolina

Printed in the United States of America

Library of Congress Control Number: 2021949109

For all general information, please contact Arcadia Publishing:
Telephone 843-853-2070
Fax 843-853-0044
E-mail sales@arcadiapublishing.com
For customer service and orders:
Toll-Free 1-888-313-2665

Visit us on the Internet at www.arcadiapublishing.com

Contents

Acknowledgments 6

Introduction 7

1. "Always the River" 9
2. Harriet Beecher Stowe 25
3. The *Maple Leaf* 33
4. Historic Houses 39
5. Untold Stories of Black Mandarin 49
6. Community Life 69
7. Mandarin Artists 79
8. Businesses 95
9. Churches and Schools 113
10. The Beauty of Mandarin 121

About the Mandarin Museum & Historical Society 127

Acknowledgments

Although this book is a joint effort of the author and the Mandarin Museum & Historical Society (MMHS), several individuals must be thanked for their assistance and inspiration.

Many years ago, I met a lovely woman who had collected Mandarin history. At the time, many considered her to be "Mandarin's historian." Her name was Jean Morrow. We spent hours together talking about Mandarin, and with each visit, I became more and more interested in the history of the area. She touched my mind, but also my heart, and I started collecting and studying everything I could find about Mandarin. Sadly, she is no longer with us today, but she was my mentor, and I will be forever grateful to her for her encouragement and inspiration to keep Mandarin's stories alive.

Sandy Arpen, a fellow board member of MMHS, worked tirelessly typing, editing, and helping choose the photographs for the book. Leann Arndt, an MMHS volunteer with professional experience in museum publications and archives, was a great help with scanning photographs and submitting all the material to Arcadia in the required format. Bob Nay, former MMHS board member and a published author himself, offered encouragement and support from the very beginning of the project. I thank him also for writing the introduction.

Unless otherwise noted, photographs are from the collection of the Mandarin Museum & Historical Society. However, many "Mandarinites" and others shared family photographs that helped us tell the story and we are grateful to them.

It is my hope that this book will help people connect with the deep and rich history of Mandarin. I invite all to learn more by visiting the Mandarin Museum & Historical Society, 11964 Mandarin Road, Jacksonville, Florida, 32223.

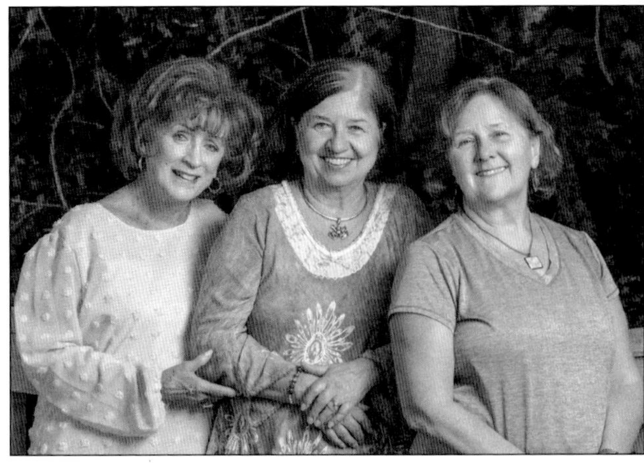

Pictured from left to right are Susan Ford, Sandy Arpen, and Leann Arndt. (Courtesy of Olis Garber.)

INTRODUCTION

Mandarin Point, which lies along the St. Johns River about 15 nautical miles south of Jacksonville, Florida, is a focal point on a map of Mandarin in northeast Florida. The original inhabitants of this land were native indigenous populations including the Timucua. People have lived here under the rule of Spain and Great Britain, during Territorial times, and finally under the State of Florida (1845). In the mid-1800s, Mandarin was a small agricultural community. Back in those days, it was defined as the peninsula of land that is surrounded on three sides by the St. Johns River and Julington Creek. Other communities that were in the area, like Plummer's Cove, Loretto, Sunbeam, and Greenland, eventually became part of a much larger area called Mandarin today—St. Johns River on the west, Goodby's Lake on the North, US Route 1 on the east, and Julington Creek on the south.

Prior to the Civil War, Mandarin was primarily a cotton, lumber, and citrus area supported by a few wharves and a few steamships along the St. Johns River and a few families along the river. The economy was supported by the labor of enslaved Africans.

After the Civil War, Mandarin attracted a diversity of newcomers to its expanding geographical borders. From the north came families to start a new beginning with farming and orange groves. Before the railroads, visitors and winter residents became attracted to northeast Florida for its pleasant climate and natural beauty. Also, many formerly enslaved families in Mandarin stayed in the area, developed their own farms and businesses, and were a big part of the workforce. Other African American families came to Mandarin from South Carolina for farmland and better living, introducing Gullah Geechee heritage to the area.

For Mandarin, its most important advocate, beyond its own natural beauty, was Harriet Beecher Stowe and her husband, the Reverend Calvin Stowe. Harriet was a major influence along with other newcomers, including immigrants from England. New churches supported the educational and religious needs of both its White and Black populations. Harriet wrote many articles and a book, *Palmetto Leaves*, highlighting the beauty of Mandarin, the climate, the friendliness of people in the small community, and its opportunities as a place to vacation in the winter months or to live the entire year.

Maj. W.W. Webb, a retired Army officer from New York, purchased a riverfront farmhouse on 30 acres along the St. Johns River in 1875 and built Webb's Wharf extending 1,000 feet into the river, where steamers stopped to pick up boxes of his oranges, vegetables, and strawberries. Later, the Walter Jones family owned this property for almost a century.

Mandarin became known for its large oak trees lining Mandarin Road, its cypress trees hugging the St. Johns River, its many orange groves and produce, its abundance of natural flowers, its boardwalk along the river, and its small but growing population of diverse peoples, from farmers to artists.

Mandarin continues to provide (even with urban sprawl and growth), a similar feeling of being among its natural beauty and serenity. The river still provides a boundary, and the beautiful drive along Mandarin Road with a canopy of live oaks is unsurpassed in the area. Mandarin's parks, especially the Walter Jones Historical Park, which is home to the Mandarin Museum & Historical Society, can take one back to the late 1800s. Mandarin in many ways has kept its charm. Though much has changed, there is a timelessness in the giant oaks with their moss and the St. Johns River flowing by, connecting the past and the present.

It is our desire that after viewing the images within this book you will visit Mandarin and experience for yourself the peaceful spirit it brings to all its visitors—residents and strangers alike.

Bob Nay
Former board member of the Mandarin Museum & Historical Society
Author of I Am a Full-fledged Floridian Now: The Life and Times of Major William Wirt Webb of Mandarin, Florida

One

"Always the River"

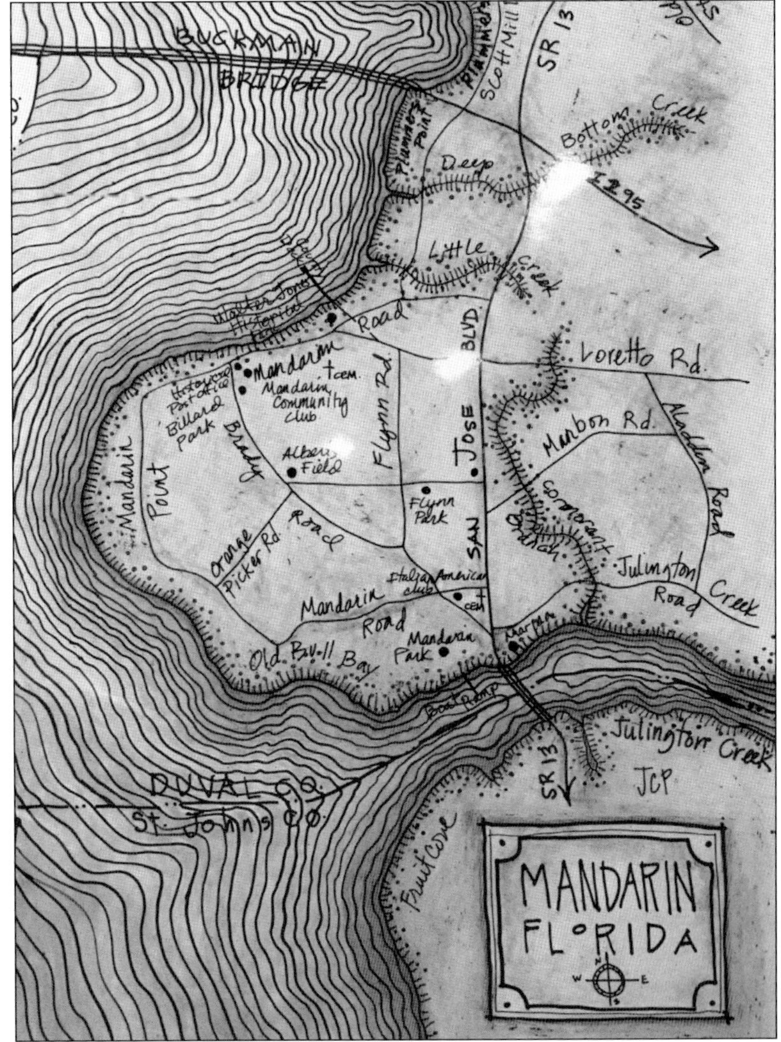

Throughout time, Mandarin's historic and economic development has been tied to its location on the St. Johns River. The river took its current form 5,000–7,000 years ago, flowing north from central Florida and passing Mandarin on its 310-mile route to the Atlantic. This drawing was done by local and contemporary artist, Julie Fetzer. It clearly illustrates Mandarin as a peninsula in the St. Johns. (Courtesy of Julie Fetzer.)

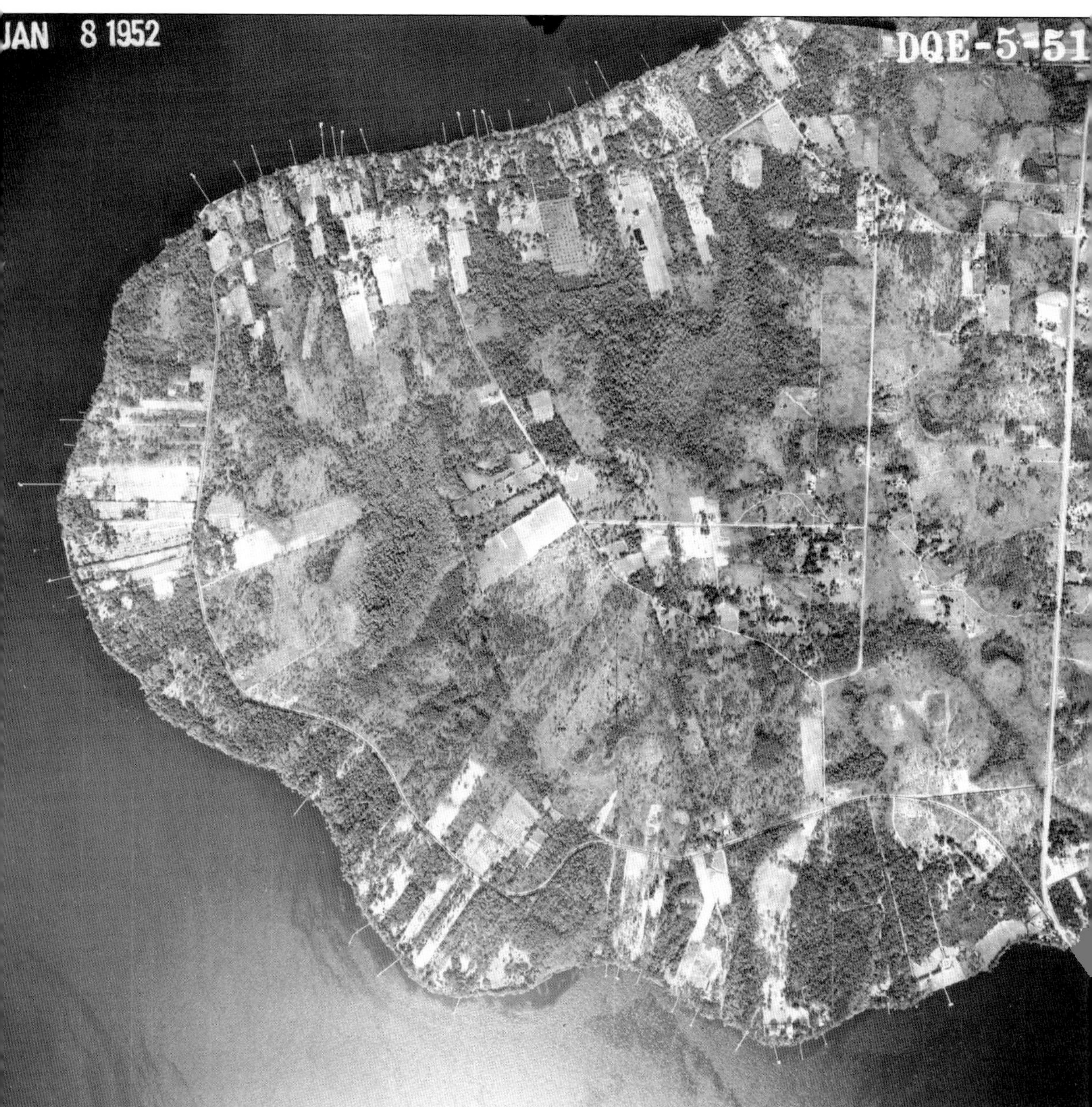

Timucua-speaking Native Americans lived along the St. Johns prior to the arrival of Europeans. They called the river Welaka ("River of Lakes") and used it for food, transportation, and safety. French, Spanish, and British settlers sailed the St. Johns as a primary mode of transportation. The French named it La Riviere du Mai ("May River") after arriving in May 1562. The Spanish called it several names in different periods: Rio de Corrientes ("River of Currents"), San Mateo ("St. Matthew"), and finally, Rio de San Juan, which the British later anglicized to St. Johns River. This image was captured in 1952. (Courtesy of Florida Department of Transportation.)

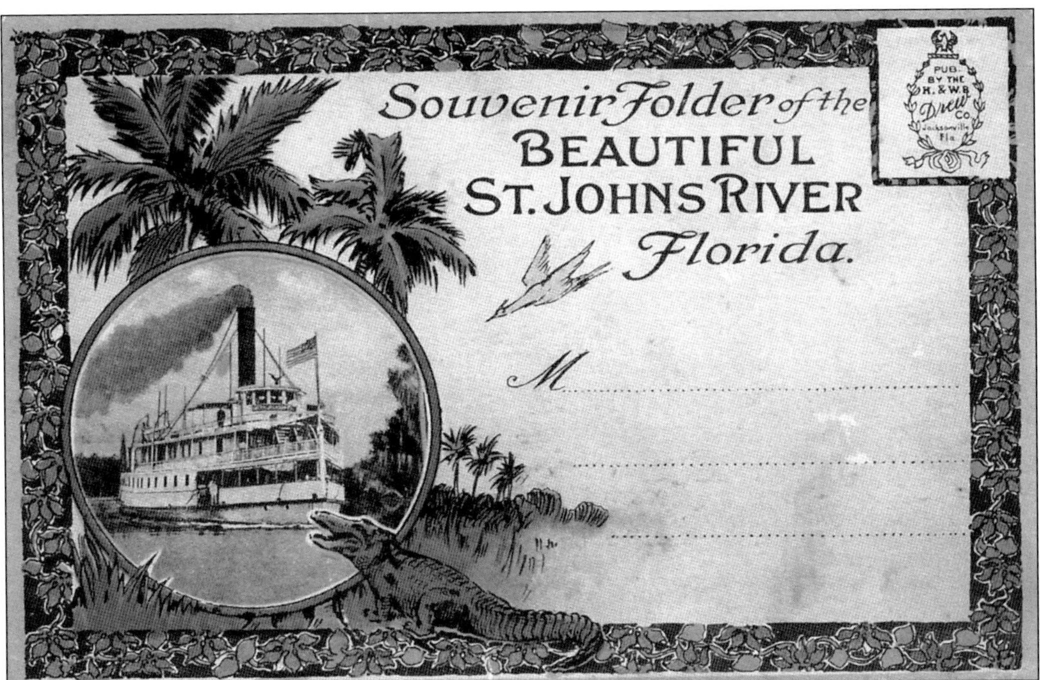

The river was a pathway to the world for early Mandarin residents in the 19th and early 20th centuries. They depended on it for transportation, mail, and import and export of goods. In 1874, Harriet Beecher Stowe reported northerners could catch a steamship in New York City for $27, transfer in Charleston or Savannah, and arrive in Jacksonville in about four days. Visitors came, as northerners were enticed by Florida's beauty, climate, and opportunities. They came by steamboat.

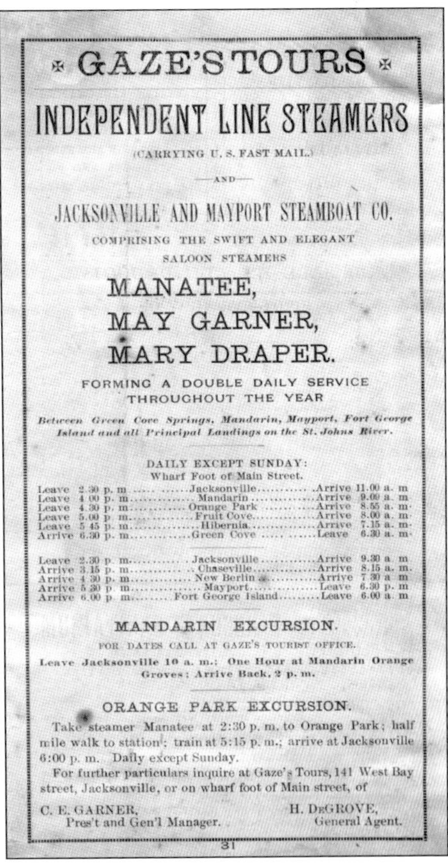

GAZE'S TOURS

INDEPENDENT LINE STEAMERS

(CARRYING U. S. FAST MAIL.)

—AND—

JACKSONVILLE AND MAYPORT STEAMBOAT CO.

COMPRISING THE SWIFT AND ELEGANT SALOON STEAMERS

MANATEE,
MAY GARNER,
MARY DRAPER.

FORMING A DOUBLE DAILY SERVICE THROUGHOUT THE YEAR

Between Green Cove Springs, Mandarin, Mayport, Fort George Island and all Principal Landings on the St. Johns River.

DAILY EXCEPT SUNDAY:
Wharf Foot of Main Street.

Leave 2.30 p. m. .... Jacksonville .... Arrive 11.00 a. m
Leave 4.00 p. m. .... Mandarin .... Arrive 9.00 a. m
Leave 4.30 p. m. .... Orange Park .... Arrive 8.55 a. m
Leave 5.00 p. m. .... Fruit Cove .... Arrive 8.00 a. m
Leave 5.45 p. m. .... Hibernia .... Arrive 7.15 a. m
Arrive 6.30 p. m. .... Green Cove .... Leave 6.30 a. m

Leave 2.30 p. m. .... Jacksonville .... Arrive 9.30 a. m
Arrive 3.15 p. m. .... Chaseville .... Arrive 8.15 a. m.
Arrive 4.30 p. m. .... New Berlin .... Arrive 7.30 a. m
Arrive 5.30 p. m. .... Mayport .... Leave 6.30 p. m
Arrive 6.00 p. m. .... Fort George Island .... Leave 6.00 a. m

MANDARIN EXCURSION.

FOR DATES CALL AT GAZE'S TOURIST OFFICE.

Leave Jacksonville 10 a. m.: One Hour at Mandarin Orange Groves; Arrive Back, 2 p. m.

ORANGE PARK EXCURSION.

Take steamer Manatee at 2:30 p. m. to Orange Park; half mile walk to station; train at 5:15 p. m.; arrive at Jacksonville 6:00 p. m. Daily except Sunday.

For further particulars inquire at Gaze's Tours, 141 West Bay street, Jacksonville, or on wharf foot of Main street, of

C. E. GARNER,
Pres't and Gen'l Manager.

H. DEGROVE,
General Agent.

31

Many ships would stop in Mandarin, with names like *Sarah Spaulding*, *General Clinch*, *City Point*, *Port Royal*, and *Manatee*. But the three that were remembered most by Mandarin residents were the *May Garner*, the *Magnolia*, and the *Mary Draper*, all of the Independent Line (later called the St. Johns River Day Line) operated by Capt. Charles Edward Garner and also by Captains Henry D. DeGrove Sr. and Jr. and Bob Townsend.

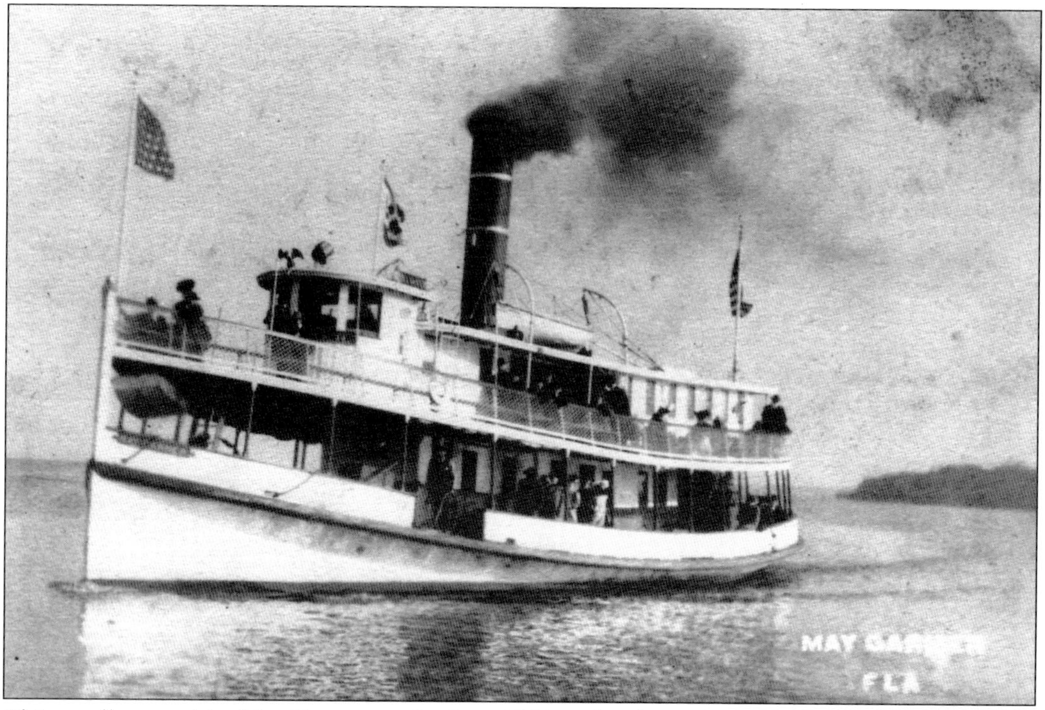

This small steamship, *May Garner*, was built in 1891 and is the most mentioned ship that came to Mandarin. It was a double-decker with lounging space on the inside and deck chairs on the outside. In her personal papers, Mary J. Brown described it: "It docked in Mandarin at nine AM, picking up the outgoing mail, passengers and freight. . . . when Jacksonville was on fire in 1901, the *May Garner* carried people to safety in Mandarin."

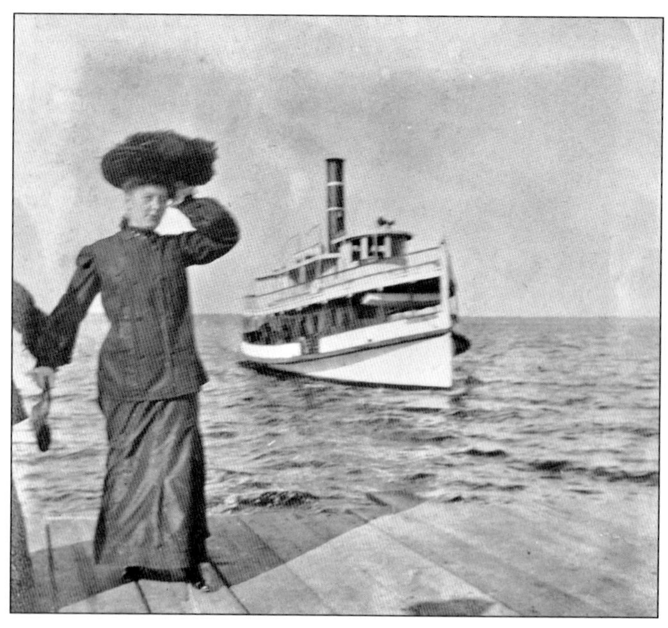

The woman waiting at the wharf is said to be "Mrs. Belote." The *May Garner* is coming to bring passengers, mail, and needed products and to take citrus and other crops to market, as well as the outgoing mail and passengers who want to go to Green Cove Springs or Jacksonville. The ship also carried the schoolchildren from Mandarin to Jacksonville once they reached the ninth grade and planned to continue their education since there was no high school in Mandarin at the time. The children would stay with family or friends or in a boarding house during the week, returning home on Friday.

Capt. Charles Edwin Garner (1853–1915) was born in Indiana and came from a family who studied river transportation His father was captain of the *Belle Creole*, a ship that traveled from Cincinnati to New Orleans. Moving to Jacksonville in 1881, Captain Garner had a successful career with the DeBary Line and the Independent Line, of which he was president. (Courtesy of Green Cove Springs Historical Society.)

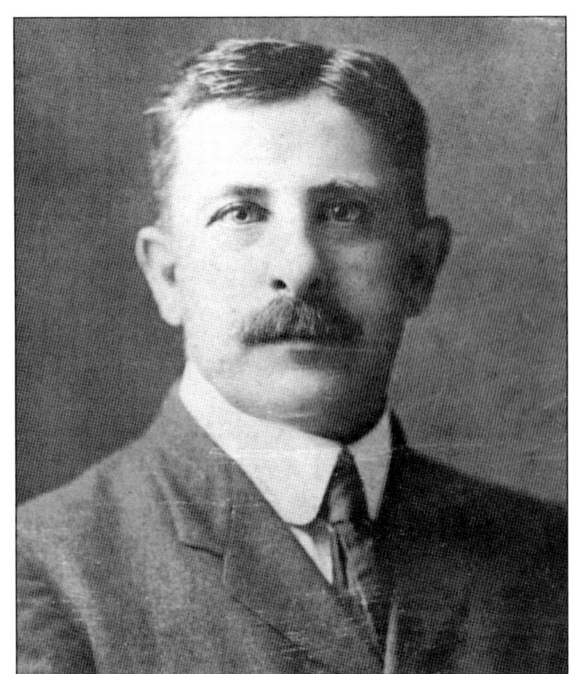

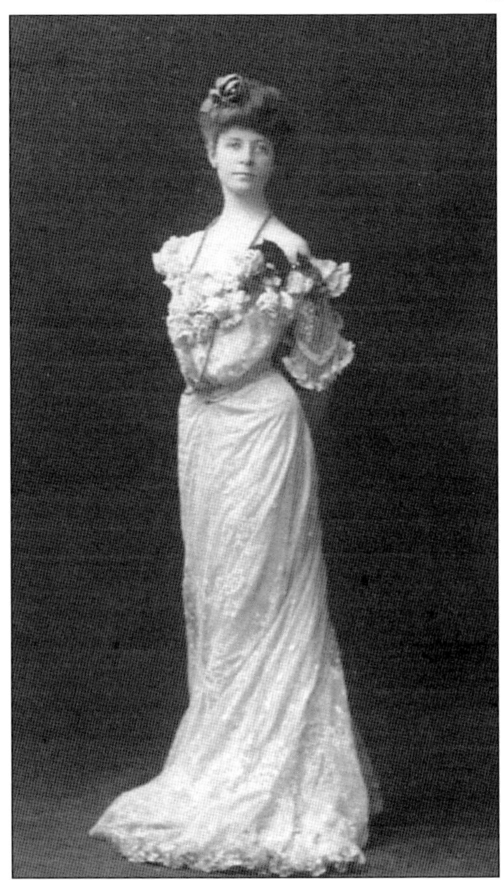

Florida May Garner (1885–1951) was the daughter of Charles E. Garner. The ship was named after her when she was eight years old. (Courtesy of the Garner family.)

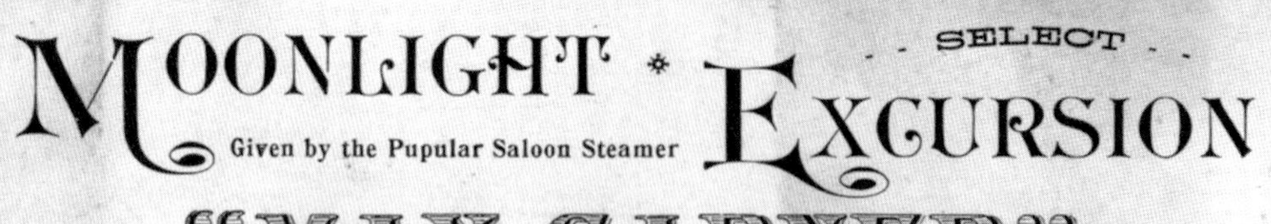

"Moonlight Excursions" were a popular steamboat outing from downtown Jacksonville to Mandarin.

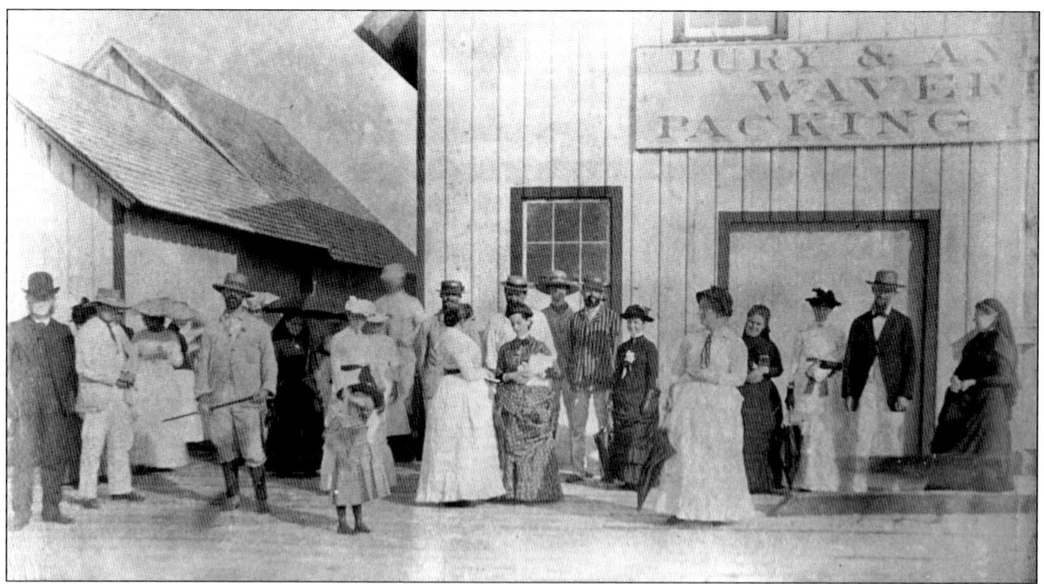

Waverly Dock was one of three major steamboat landings. Besides shipping a lot of citrus, fruits, and vegetables out of Bury & Anderson's packinghouse, there was also a community center building where special events could take place. These Mandarin citizens were clearly about to do something special either at the center or waiting to board a ship. (Courtesy of the Mary Graff Collection, Jacksonville Historical Society.)

Capt. Henry D. DeGrove Sr. (1860–1952) is pictured here sitting on the deck of the *May Garner*. There were two Captain DeGroves involved in steamboating, tugboating, and ferrying on the St. Johns: H.D. DeGrove Sr. and H.D. "Hal" DeGrove II. Captain DeGrove II died in 1972 and was considered the "last of the steamboat captains of old on the St. Johns River," per Ed Mueller, legendary steamboat historian. (Courtesy of the Green Cove Springs Historical Society.)

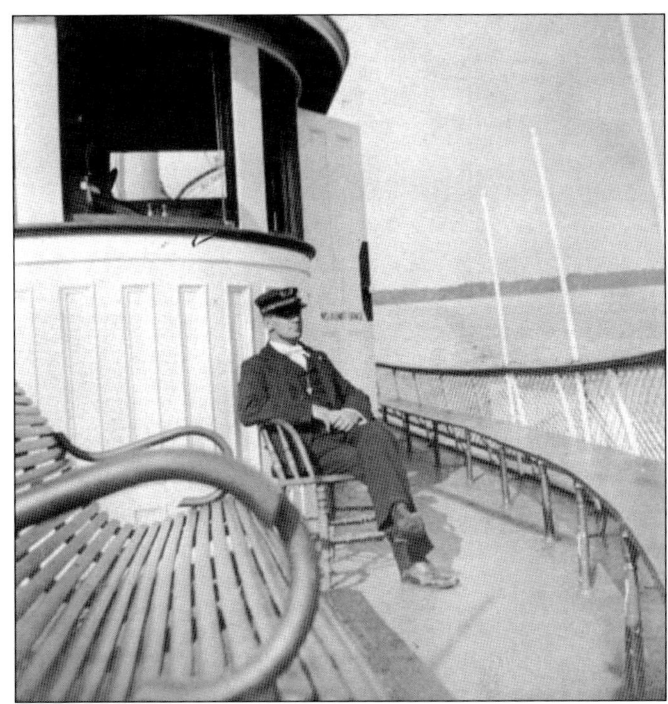

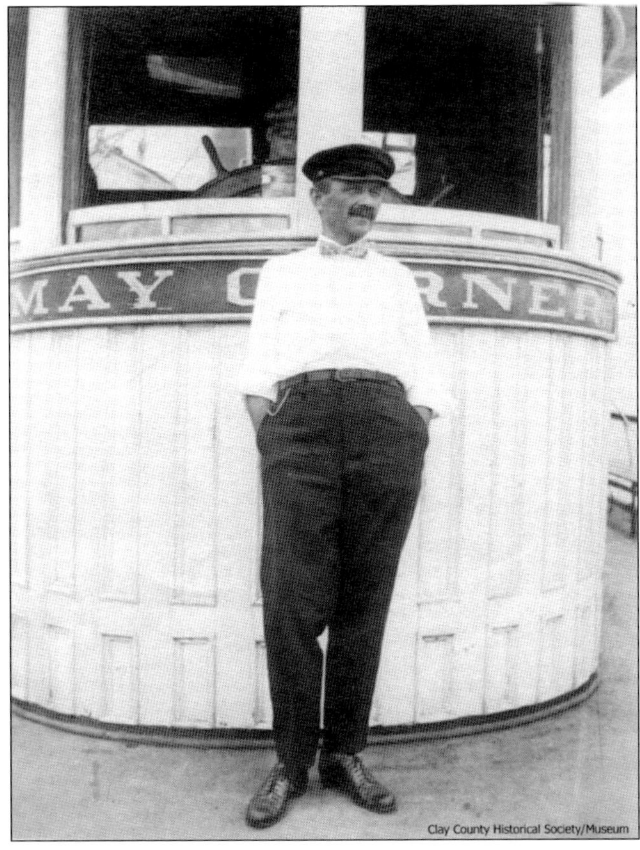

Capt. Robert Lee "Bob" Townsend (1879–1956) lived his entire life in Green Cove Springs, where the May Garner berthed at night. His occupation is identified as "steamboat captain" in the 1910 and 1920 censuses. (Courtesy of the Green Cove Springs Historical Society.)

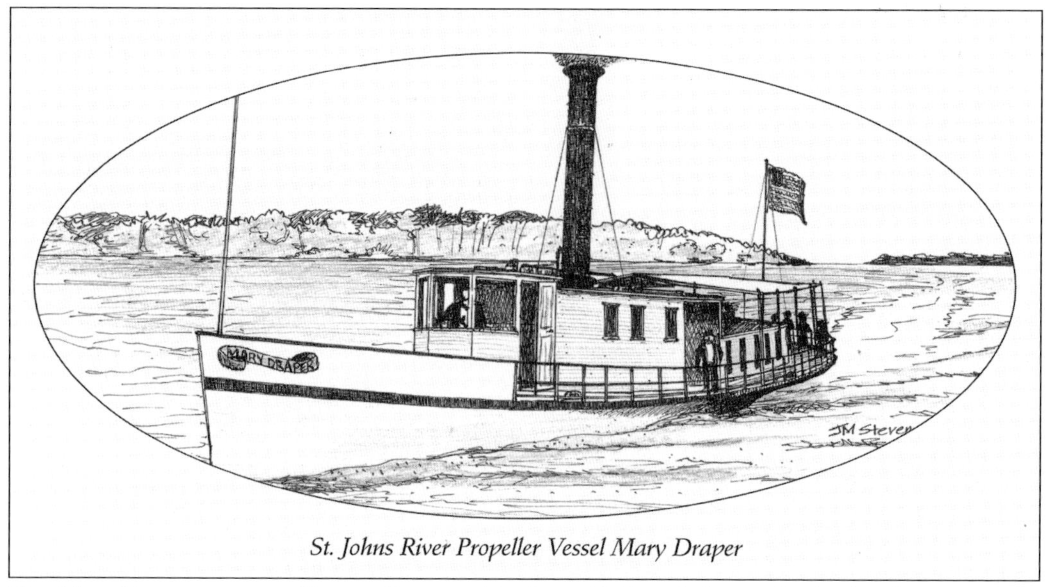

St. Johns River Propeller Vessel Mary Draper

The *Mary Draper* was a small propeller vessel built in 1869 in Jacksonville for local service from Jacksonville to Green Cove Springs. She ran until 1947, being rebuilt several times. She was also known for daily 75¢ excursions to Mandarin during the winter season, bringing tourists to see Harriet Beecher Stowe's home. In the off-season of May 1872, Stowe took the steamboat across the river, referring to it as "a little thimble of a steamer."

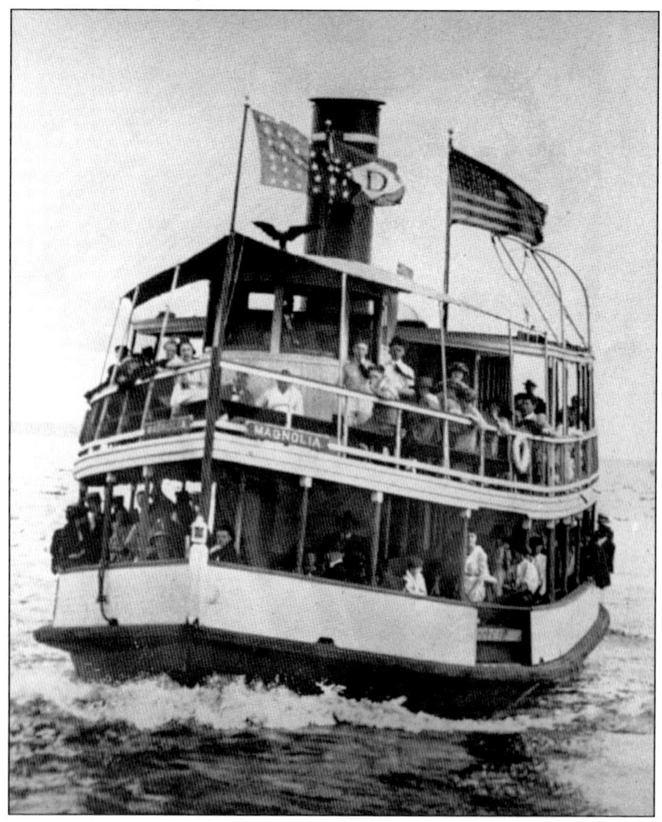

The *Magnolia*, also a frequent visitor to Mandarin, was built locally in 1918 by the Anderson Drydock and Repair Yards, which was located on the south bank of the river near the Main Street Bridge today. She was about 67 feet long and made of oak and heart cypress. She was sold to a party in Georgia and eventually destroyed by fire.

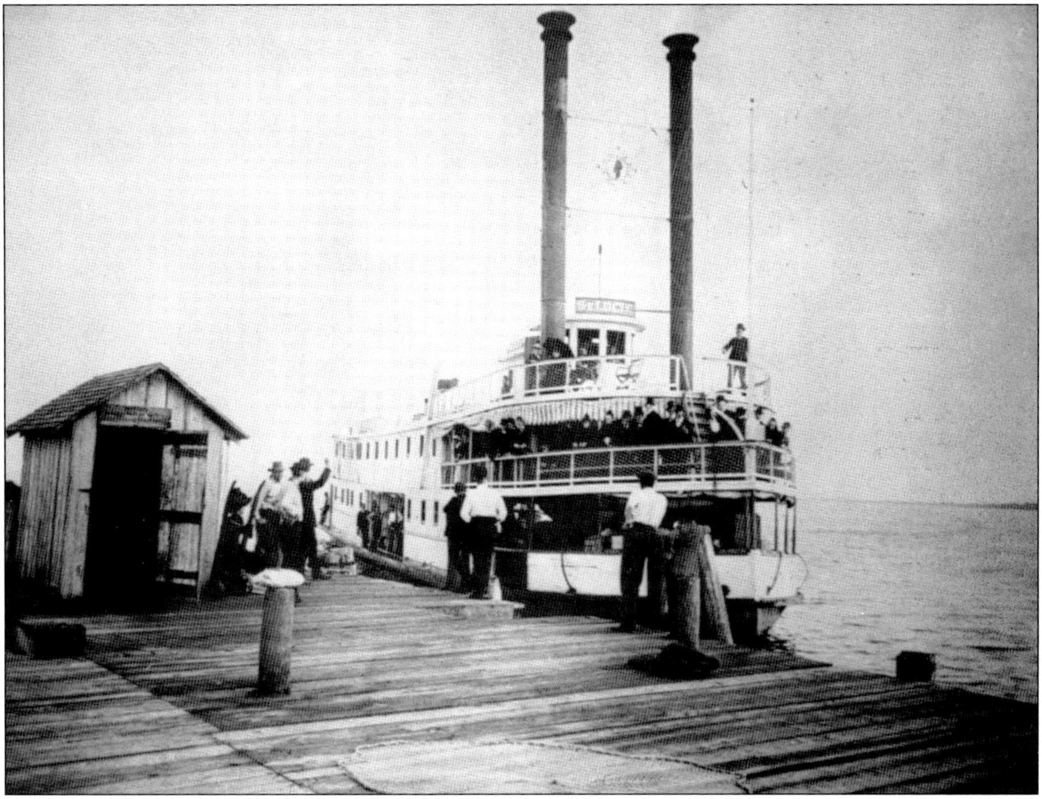

Some of the ships entering Mandarin Wharf were larger. The *St. Lucie* with two smokestacks is seen here. It may have been going south to Enterprise.

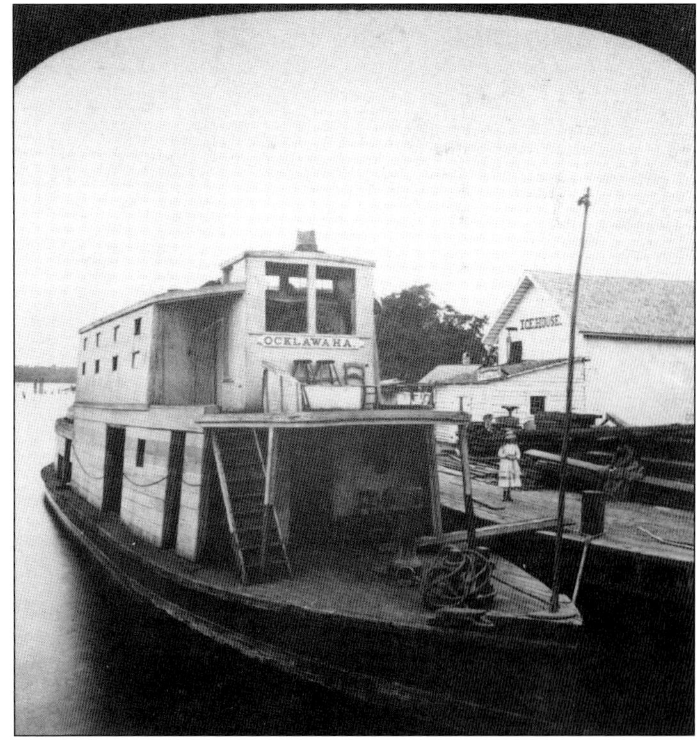

The *Ocklawaha* was a small no-frills ship built to navigate the narrow and snakelike river of the same name, going into Silver Springs. The first time Harriet Beecher Stowe saw the ship from her Mandarin home, she described it as a "coffin in twilight." Stowe's account of her voyage to Silver Springs is full of wonderful descriptions of the birds, alligators, trees, flowers, and crystal waters. (Courtesy of the State Archives of Florida.)

A DAY'S OUTING

ON BEAUTIFUL ST. JOHNS RIVER

YACHT "ALBERT M. IVES"

LEAVES FOOT OF LAURA STREET DAILY AT 10 A. M., STOPPING AT MANDARIN, THE LATE HOME OF HARRIETT BEECHER STOWE, AMONG THE BEAUTIFUL ORANGE GROVES

ROUND TRIP, ONE DOLLAR.

(OVER)

According to *Merchant Steam Vessels of the United States*, the yacht *Albert M. Ives* was built in Mandarin in 1905. It was named for Albert Mackey Ives (1849–1929), who was born in Lake City to Edward R. Ives and Mary Jane Hogan (connected with early Jacksonville pioneers). Albert came to Jacksonville in 1871 and worked his way up from a grocery clerk to clerk for the Plant Railway to Jacksonville city treasurer to director of Florida National Bank. This small vessel was clearly an excursion yacht in the early 1900s, but little else is known about its history.

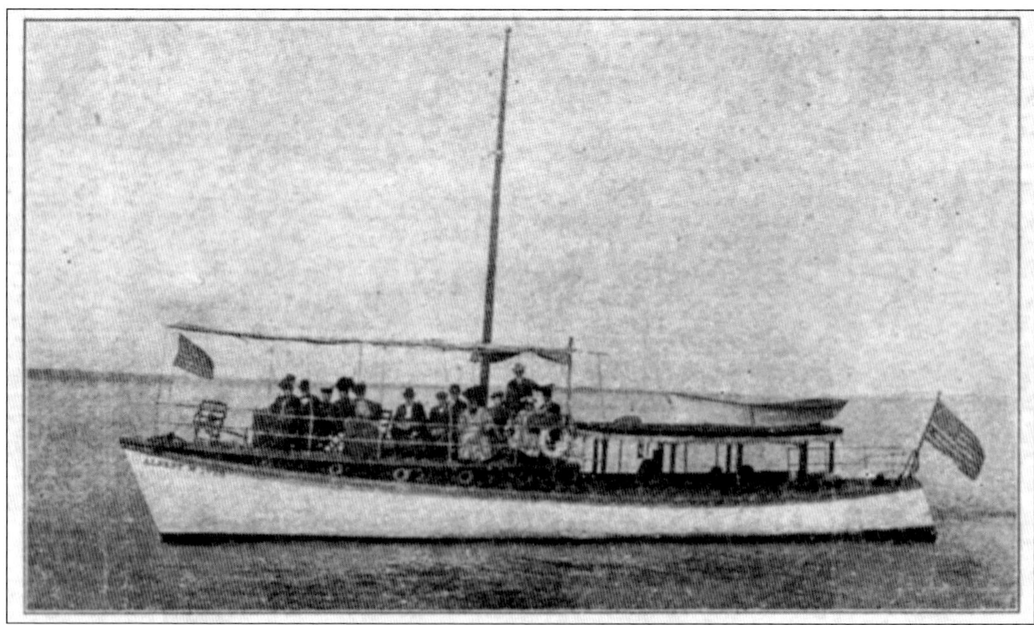

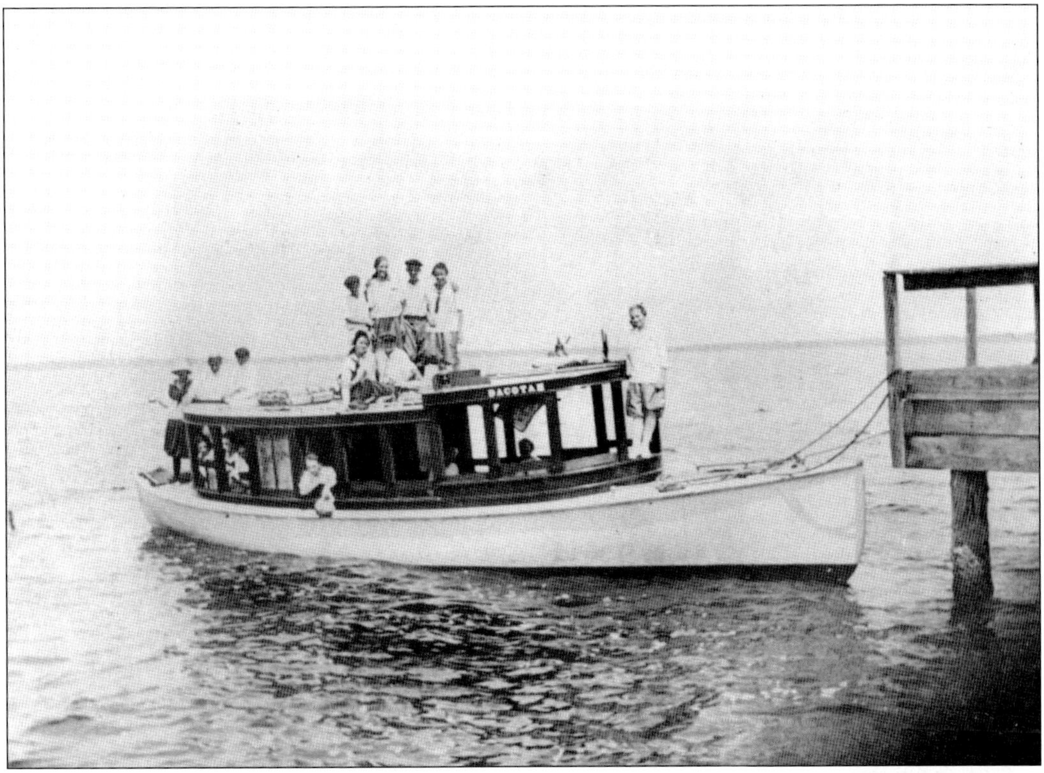

Pleasure boating of all kinds has always been popular with Mandarin residents. In the early days, it was especially so to those who lived on the river who would load up family and friends for a cruise to Julington Creek, Green Cove Springs, or to town. Today, the St. Johns is host to rowboats, sailboats, motorboats, canoes, kayaks, paddleboards, jet skis, and fishermen as residents continue to enjoy the beauty of the area's most important natural resource.

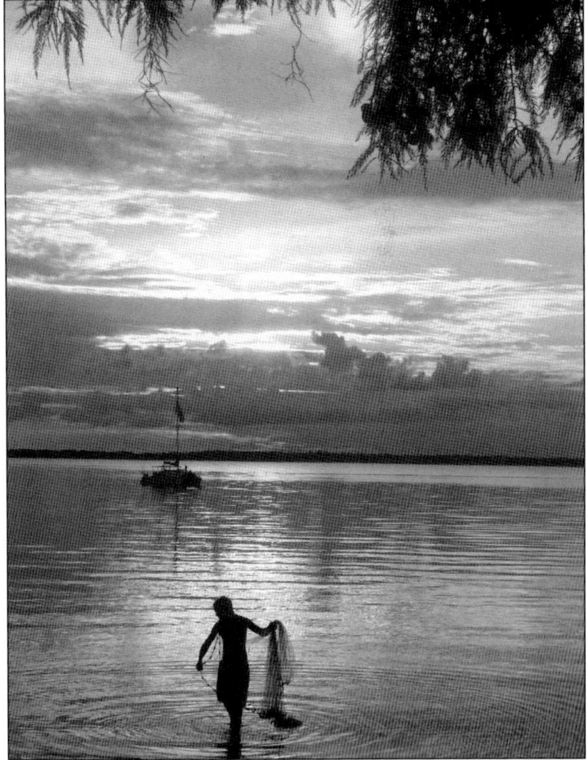

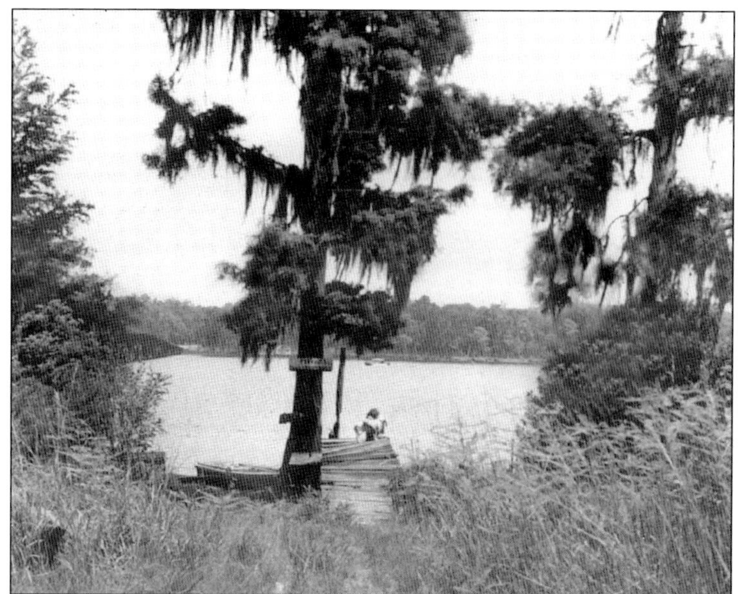

The river also brings peace and quiet and a place for meditating. This view is of Julington Creek (one side of Mandarin's peninsula) looking south into St. Johns County from the area that is Mandarin Park today. The young girl is believed to be Lovie Andreau, sitting with her dog and looking toward the old wooden Julington Creek bridge. For decades, the Andreau family has had a business to the east of this view that has included logging and a marina.

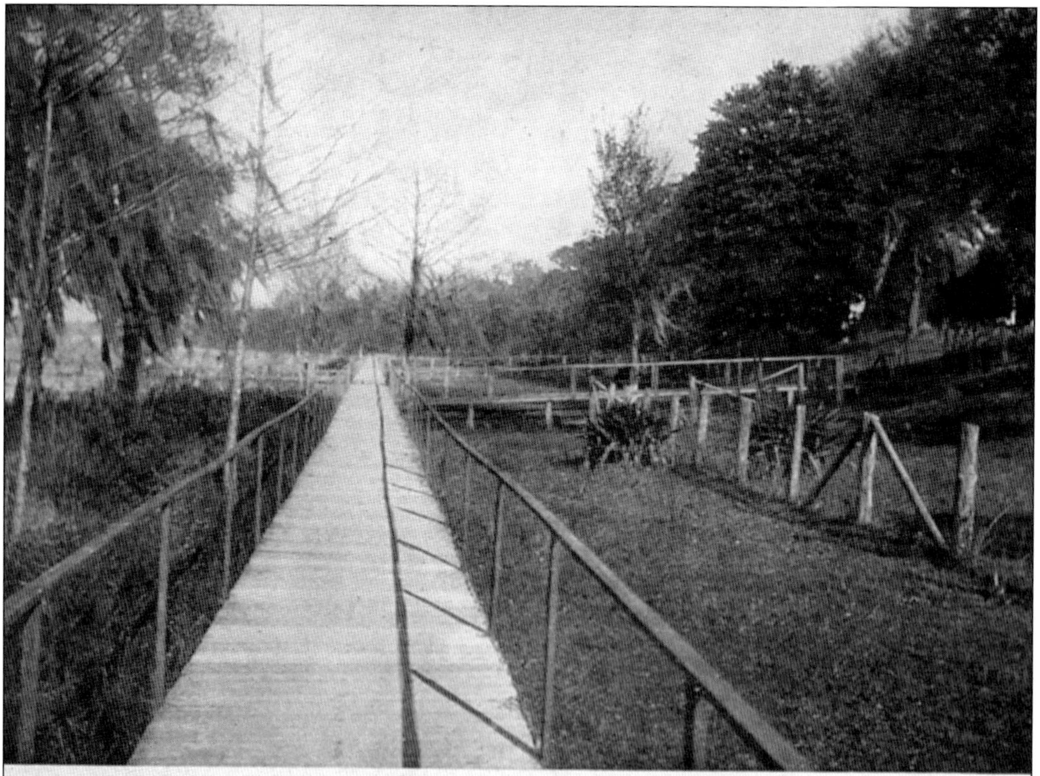

Board Walk by the St. John's River. Mandarin, Fla.

Mandarin historian Horace Glass tells us that the Mandarin Boardwalk along the river was built in 1855 by Calvin Read, at the same time the Mandarin Dock was built. It ran one nautical mile from the Waverly Dock to just beyond the Mandarin Dock. Every property owner was expected to care for their part, and there were gates to keep the cattle out.

It was a beautiful place to stroll anytime, as well as to get to the Church of Our Saviour, the Mandarin Dock, the store, the post office, and the Mandarin School. It was much better than the dirty and rutted road. In the early 1900s, it started to fall into disrepair as families moved away after the big freeze of 1899 and, by 1921, just remnants of it were left visible.

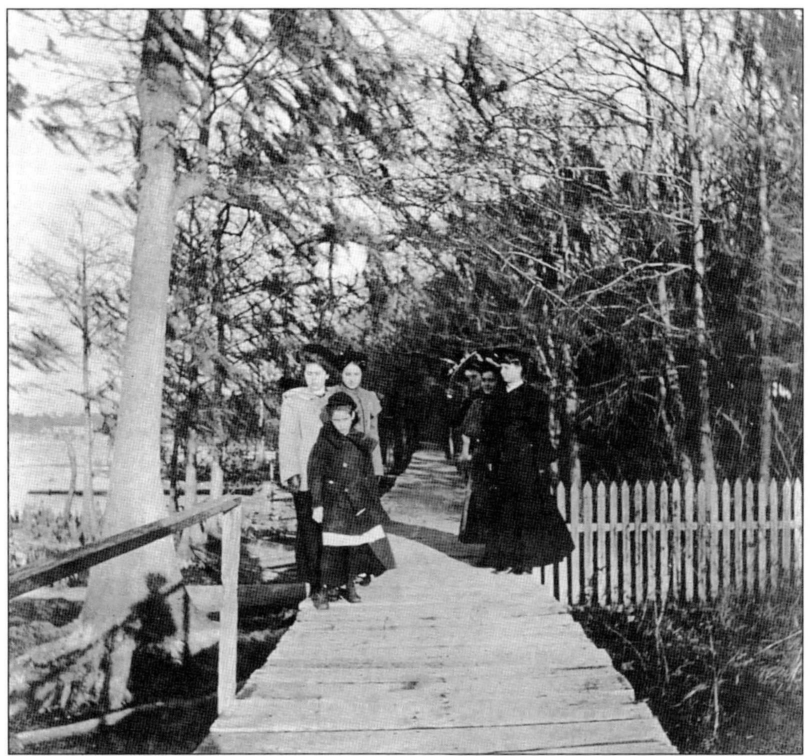

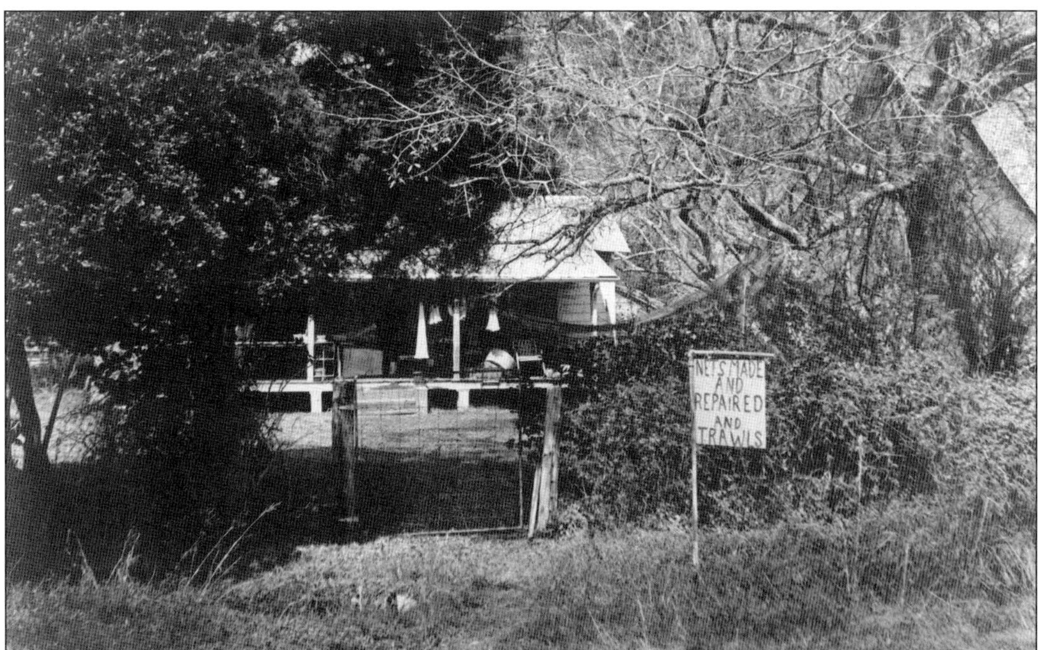

Fishing, shrimping, and crabbing in the St. Johns were very common, and catches were plentiful. Due to that, many people actually made hand-made nets that would be offered for sale. The owners of this house are unknown, but they probably had a good business.

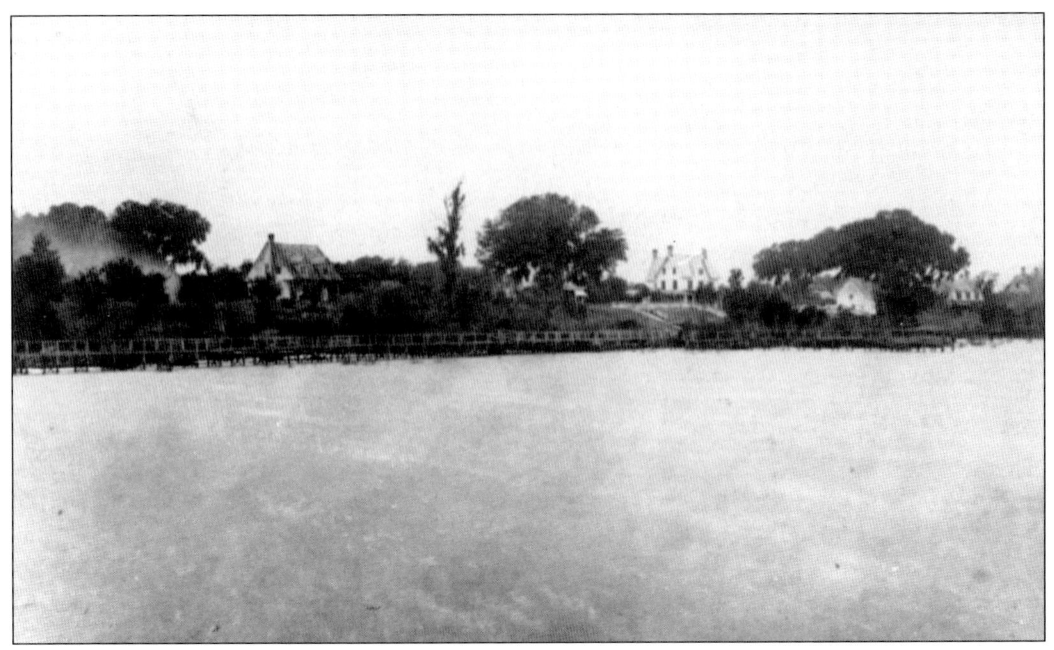

This view of the Mandarin boardwalk shows several houses that followed the banks of the St. Johns River in the 1870s. The Stowe home is second from the right. (Courtesy of the Morrow family.)

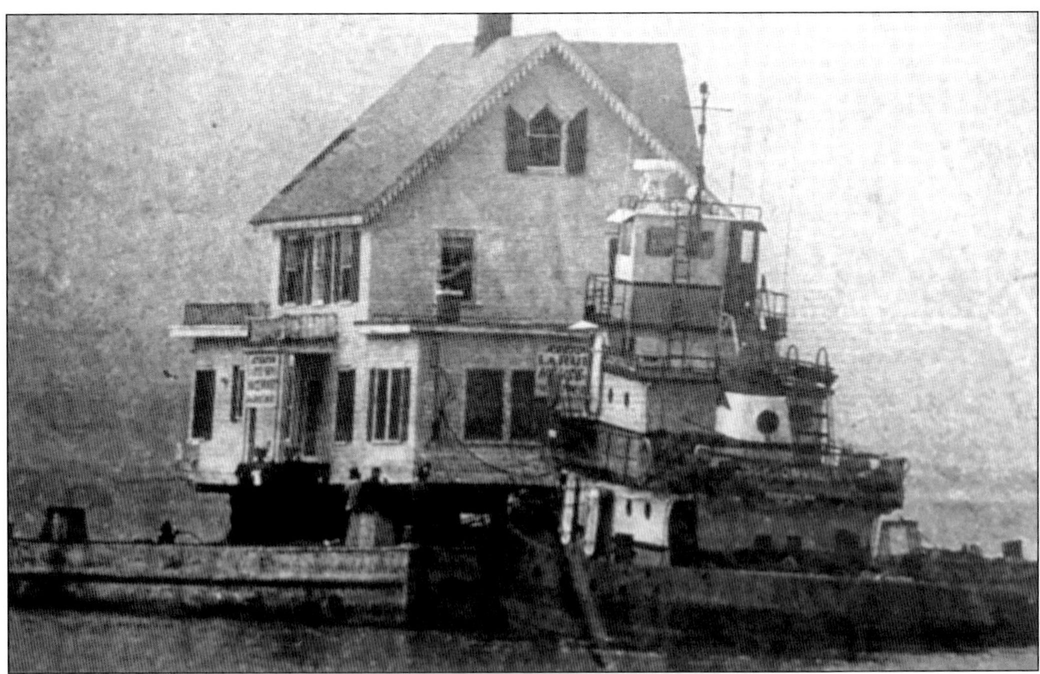

The river also served as a way to move houses from one place to another. This house was once the Elwin/Folds house. Lifetime resident Sam Folds believes it was built in the 1870s, and it once belonged to his maternal grandfather, Jack Elwin. It was sold out of the Folds family and then moved in the 1980s by river and Intracoastal Waterway to Palm Valley, where it remains today.

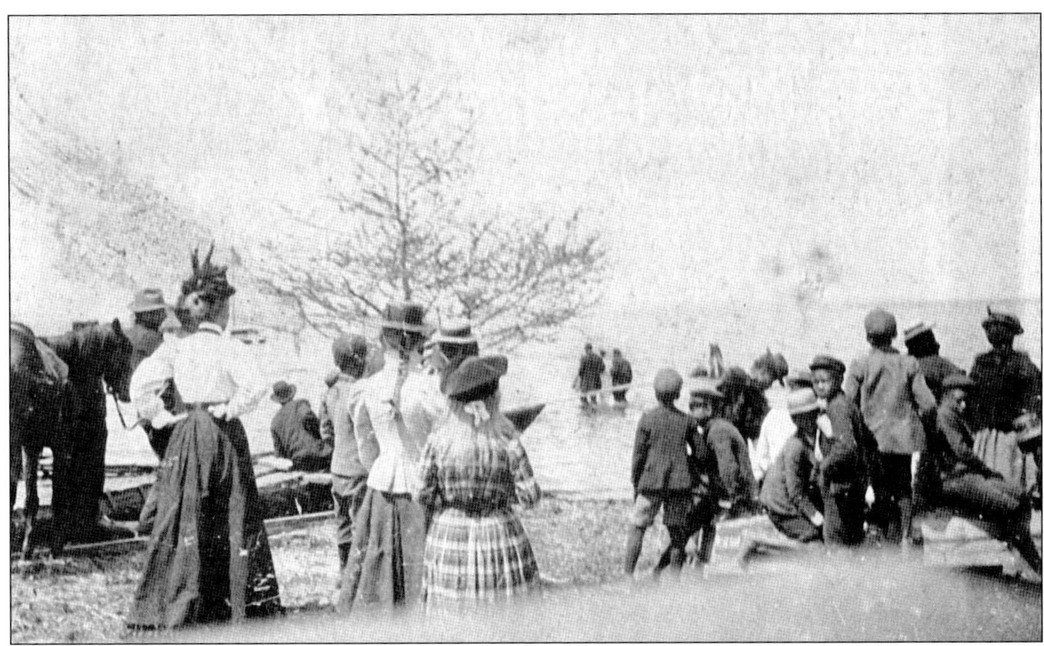

It was very common, especially in the early African American churches, to conduct the sacrament of baptism right in the waters of the St. Johns River. It appears to have been a community affair sometimes.

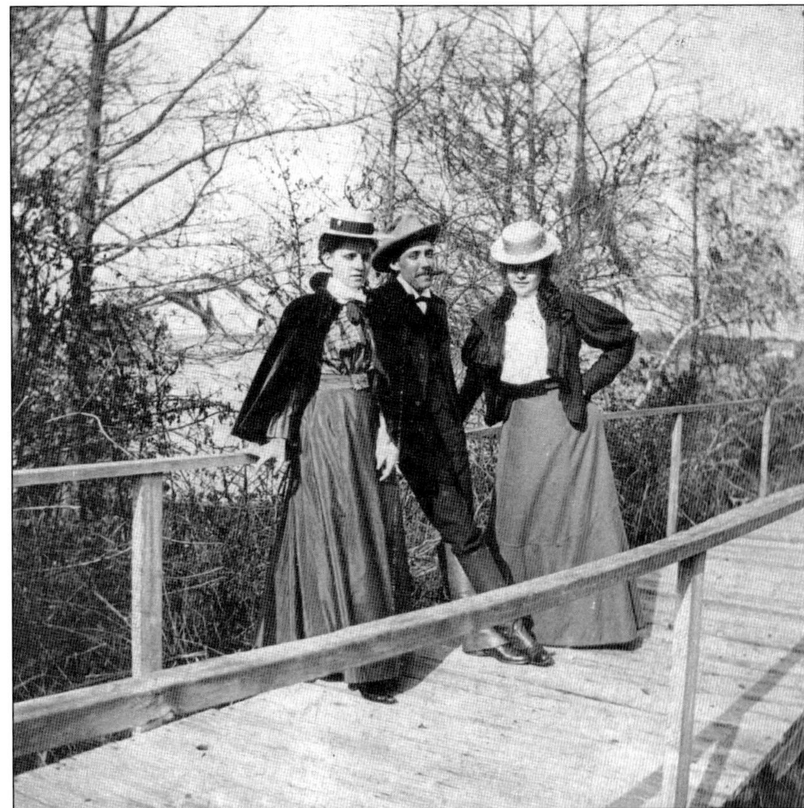

This is a typical scene from the early 1900s; the people are not identified, but they appear to be enjoying a beautiful day on the boardwalk. It was indeed a place for socializing and strolling. Today, the Walter Jones Historical Park offers a short stretch of boardwalk along the river that recreates these days gone by.

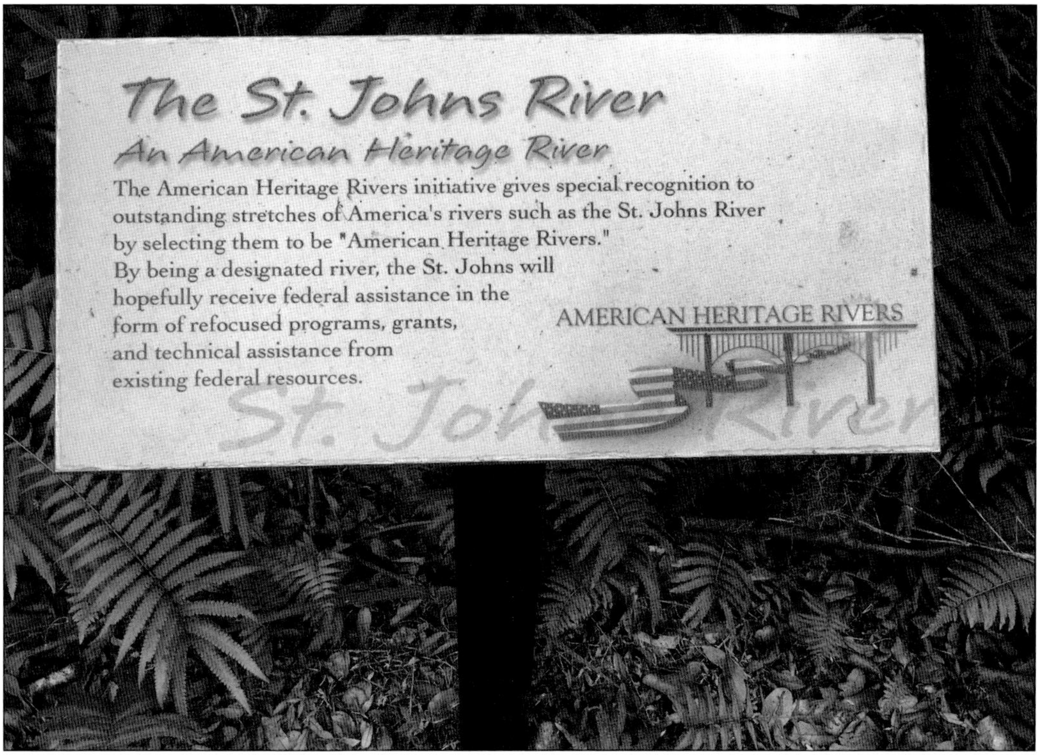

The St. Johns River

An American Heritage River

The American Heritage Rivers initiative gives special recognition to outstanding stretches of America's rivers such as the St. Johns River by selecting them to be "American Heritage Rivers." By being a designated river, the St. Johns will hopefully receive federal assistance in the form of refocused programs, grants, and technical assistance from existing federal resources.

AMERICAN HERITAGE RIVERS

St. Johns River

In 1998, the St. Johns was designated as one of only fourteen rivers in the United States to be an American Heritage River. The St. Johns starts in a swamp near Cape Canaveral and flows north 310 miles to go past Mandarin, through Jacksonville, and into the Atlantic Ocean. Because of this length and flow, it has been called the "laziest river in the United States."

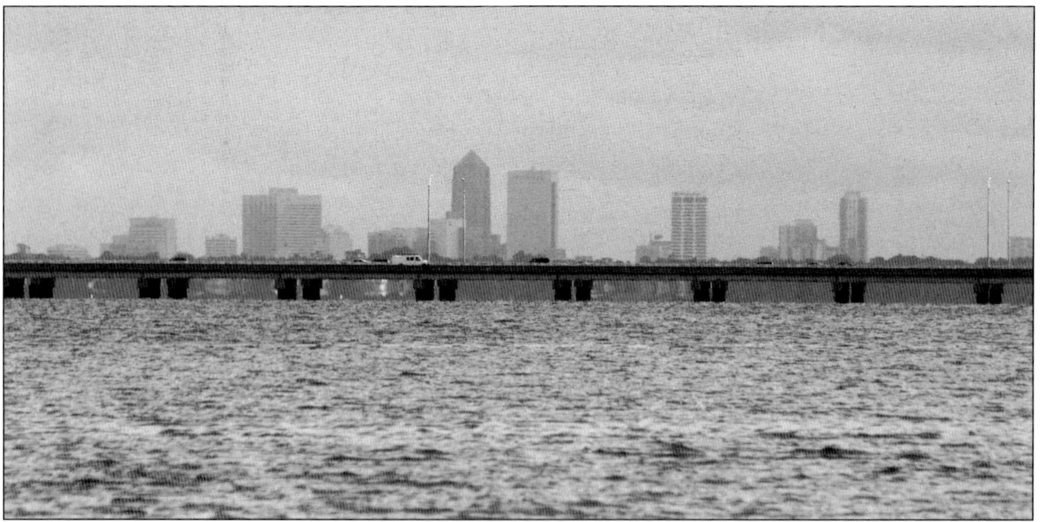

The view from County Dock looking north is much different now than when East Mandarin Wharf was present. The three-mile-wide Buckman Bridge (Interstate 295) has connected Mandarin with Orange Park since 1970, creating rapid growth and development in both places. The skyline of Jacksonville is no longer low brick and wooden buildings, but tall office complexes. Some say the bridge was "the end of paradise in Mandarin."

Two

HARRIET BEECHER STOWE

Harriet Beecher Stowe (1811–1896) was the most famous person to ever live in Mandarin and probably Jacksonville, too. She was an abolitionist and the author of the history-changing book *Uncle Tom's Cabin* (published 1851). There is no doubt that she was deeply disturbed by the conditions of slavery, and her novel about that inhumane institution influenced the country greatly prior to the American Civil War. Harriet Beecher Stowe came first to the state of Florida in support of her son Frederick, who was farming cotton at the former Laurel Grove Plantation, just across the St. Johns River from Mandarin. That venture did not prove to be profitable and Harriet and her husband, Prof. Calvin Stowe, chose to make a winter home in Mandarin. They bought a 30-acre tract in 1867 and "wintered" there until 1884, when Professor Stowe's poor health made the long journey to and from their home in Hartford, Connecticut, too difficult.

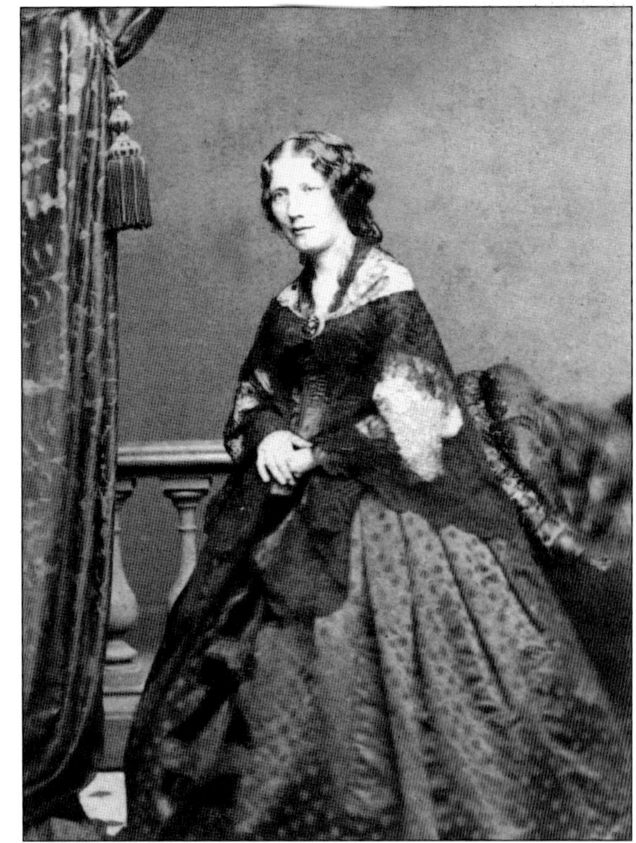

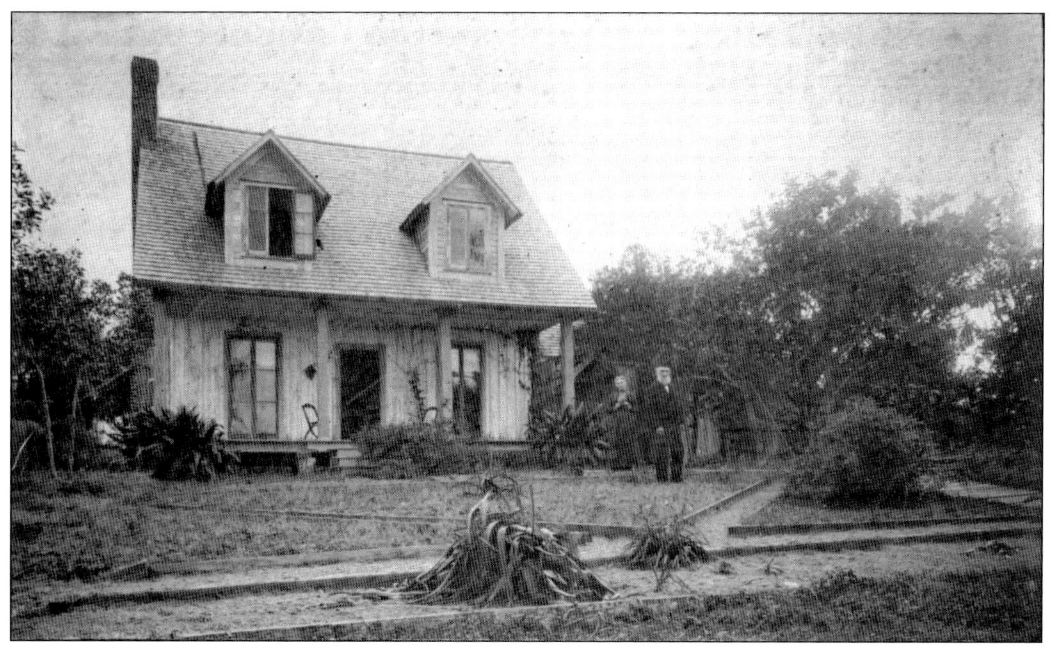

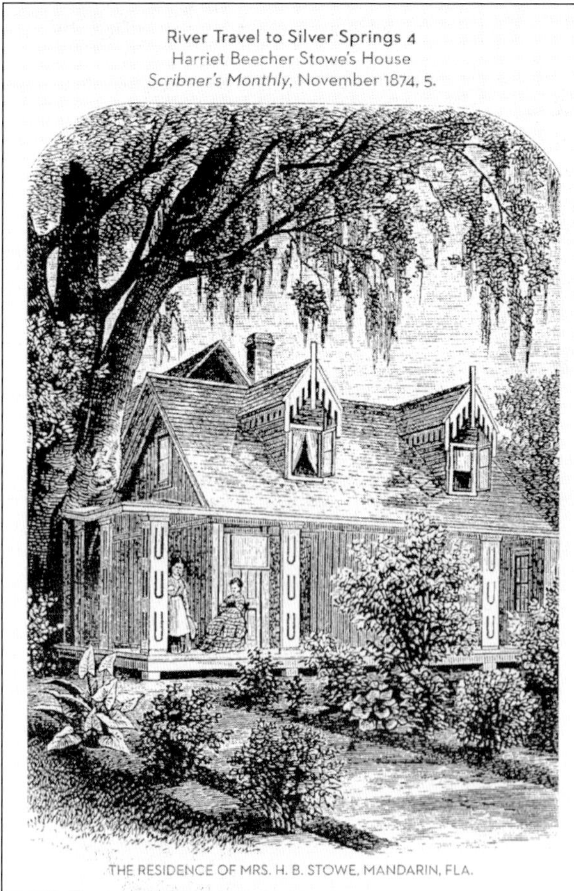
River Travel to Silver Springs 4
Harriet Beecher Stowe's House
Scribner's Monthly, November 1874, 5.

THE RESIDENCE OF MRS. H. B. STOWE, MANDARIN, FLA.

The Stowes are clearly identified here in front of this small house. It has been said to possibly be their house before the renovation, but that has not been confirmed. They remodeled the house that was on their property extensively, greatly increasing the size and building a large veranda around it.

The Stowe home was often featured in periodicals like *Scribner's Monthly*. It was a lively place with friends and relatives coming to visit all winter long. At this time, the roads in Mandarin were poor, and most travel was on the river, with steamboats coming in and out to deliver mail and goods and take citrus and produce to markets.

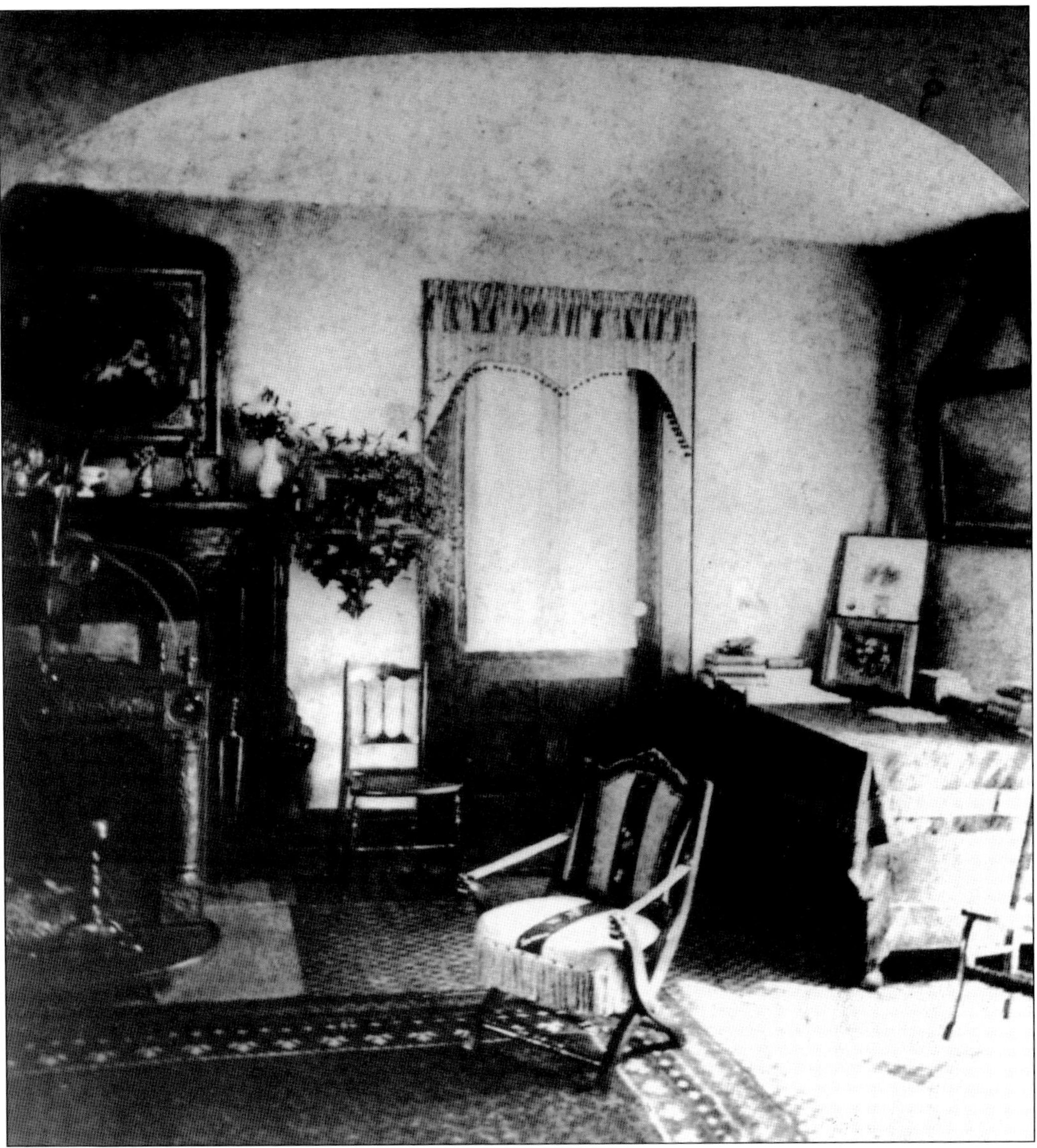

A glimpse inside the Stowe house gives an idea of how much furniture, art, and household goods they brought from Hartford to furnish their southern home. The small chair near the window was donated to the Mandarin Museum & Historical Society and is on display in the Harriet Beecher Stowe exhibit. (Courtesy of the State Archives of Florida.)

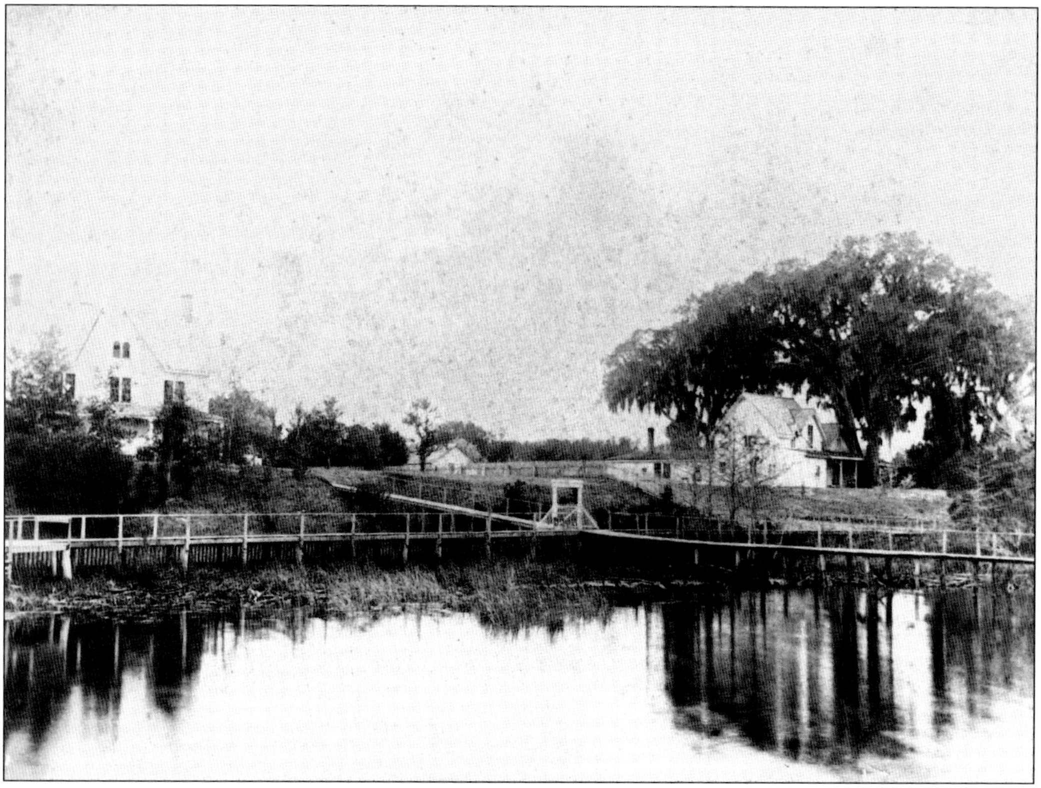

During the time the Stowes lived in Mandarin, a boardwalk stretched along the river for about one nautical mile. Starting at Waverly Dock on the east end, it reached just beyond the Mandarin Wharf. It allowed families to go to the store, post office, church, and school without having to walk on the rutty and dirty road. This view shows the William King house on the left and the Stowe house (with the large tree).

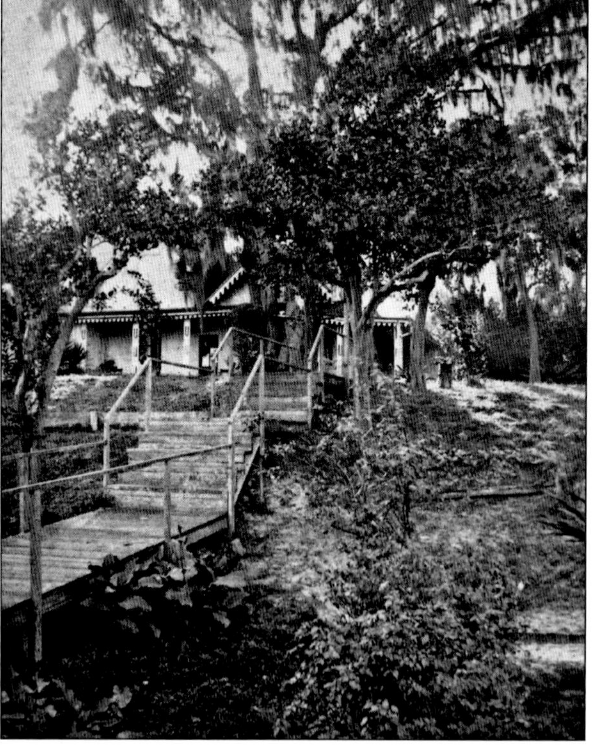

The Stowe house was on a bluff, so the stairs were necessary for access up from the boardwalk. Sometimes tourists from the steamboats would come right up to the yard and look for Harriet Beecher Stowe or snatch a souvenir orange from their grove. They would often catch a glimpse of Professor Stowe sitting in his chair reading, with a pile of books next to him.

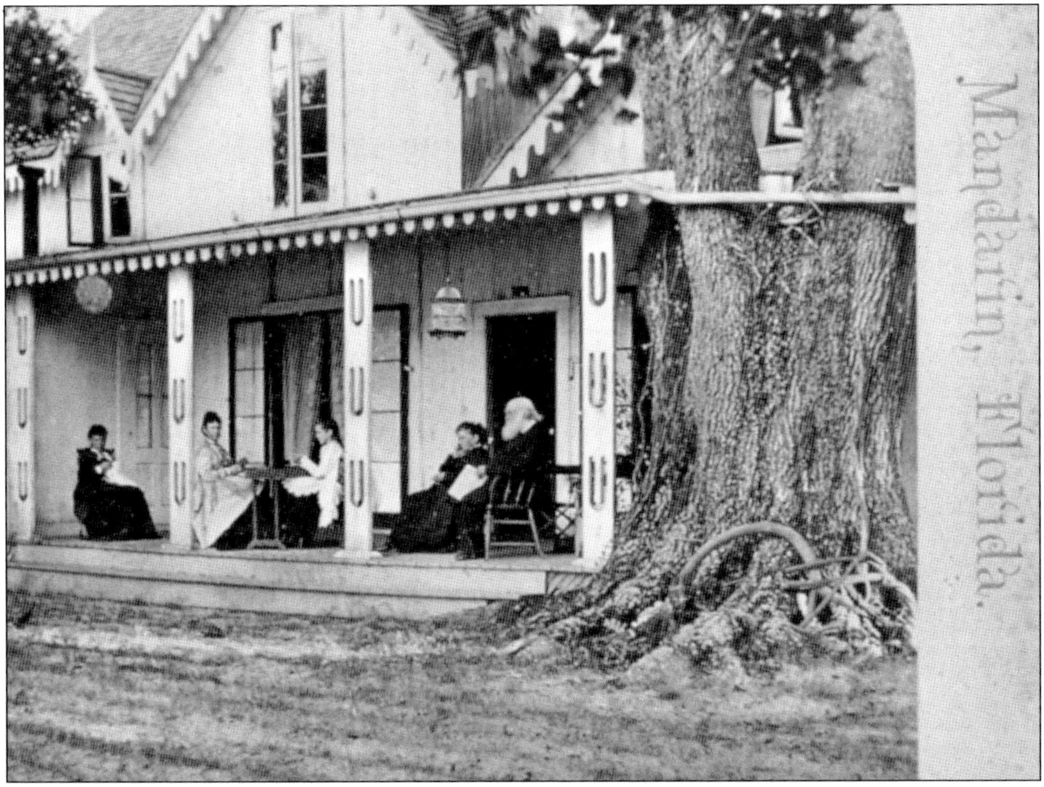

This may be the most publicized photograph of the Stowes in Mandarin. From left to right are their daughters Eliza and Hattie, friend Augusta Crane, and Harriet and Calvin. In a letter to George Elliot, Harriet describes the house: "We've added on parts and have thrown out gables and chambers, as a tree throws out new branches, until our cottage is like nobody else's, yet we settle into it with real enjoyment."

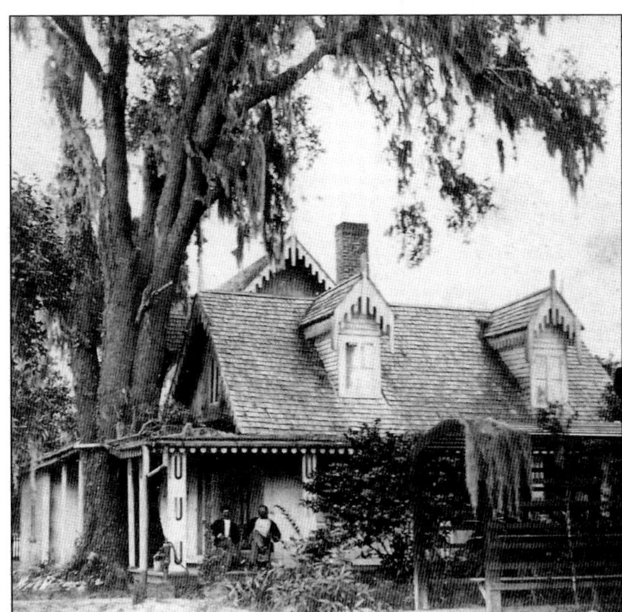

The Stowe home was always busy with friends and family, and the porch was the gathering place for visiting, reading, writing, Bible studies, and religious services led by Professor Stowe. They often called the porch their living room. The U-shapes in columns, gingerbread architecture style, and the huge live oak tree made their house distinctive and easily recognized. One of these columns is on display at the Mandarin Museum.

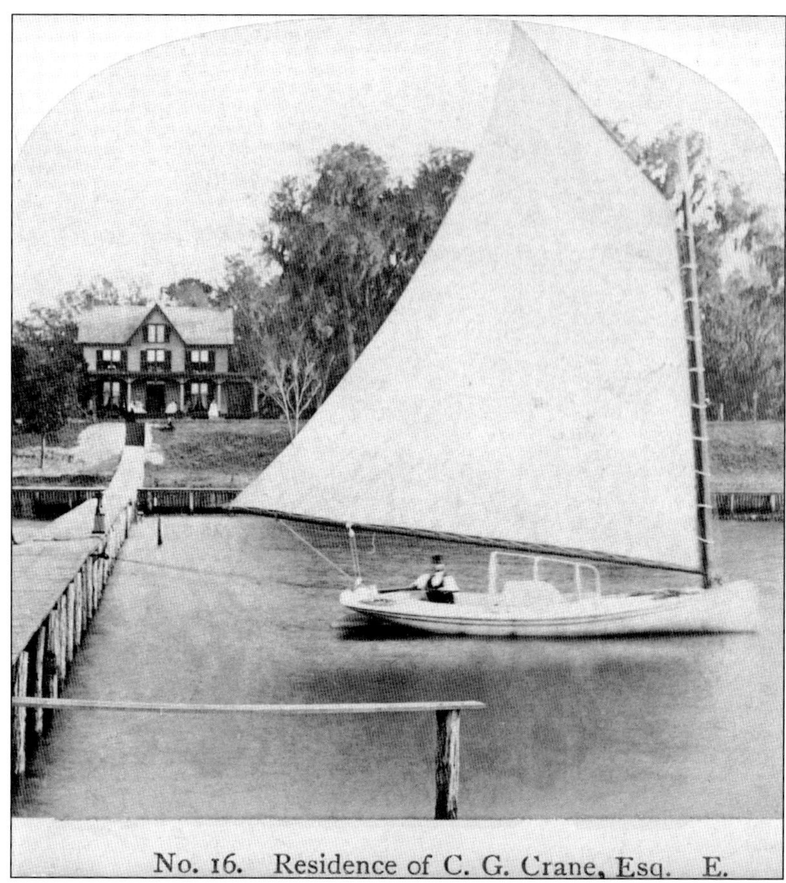

No. 16. Residence of C. G. Crane, Esq. E.

The large sailboat and home belonged to C.G. Crane, and the boat was called the *Nellie Thorn*. Harriet Beecher Stowe loved to go boating on the St. Johns with her friends, and she certainly would have sailed with the Cranes. However, Professor Stowe much preferred reading on their porch. In *Palmetto Leaves*, she describes going for a picnic at Julington Creek. (Courtesy of the Floyd and Marion Rinhart Collection and Wayne Wood.)

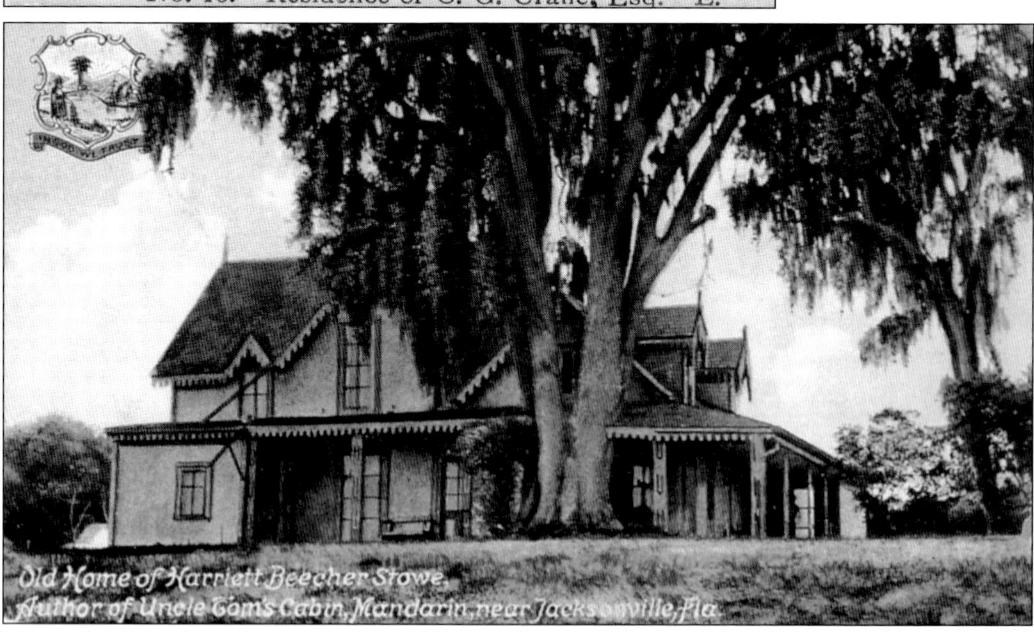

Postcards of the Stowe house, the live oaks, and the river were very popular. The oak tree that the porch was built around always stands out.

Harriet Beecher Stowe was driven to make the world a better place, and she created many legacies during her time here. Education was a priority and she quickly engaged with the Freedmen's Bureau to build a school across from her home. The first school burned down, but in 1872 it was rebuilt, though it was originally smaller than in this photograph. Both Black and White children were taught there.

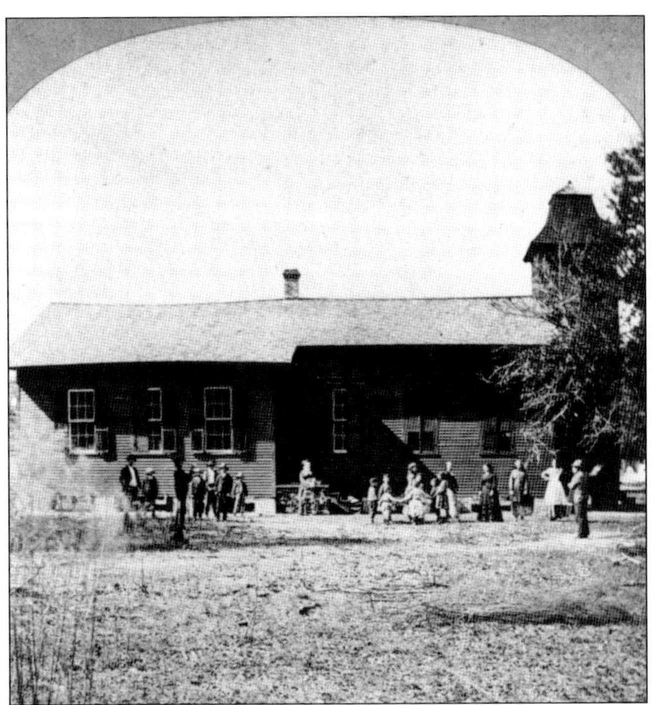

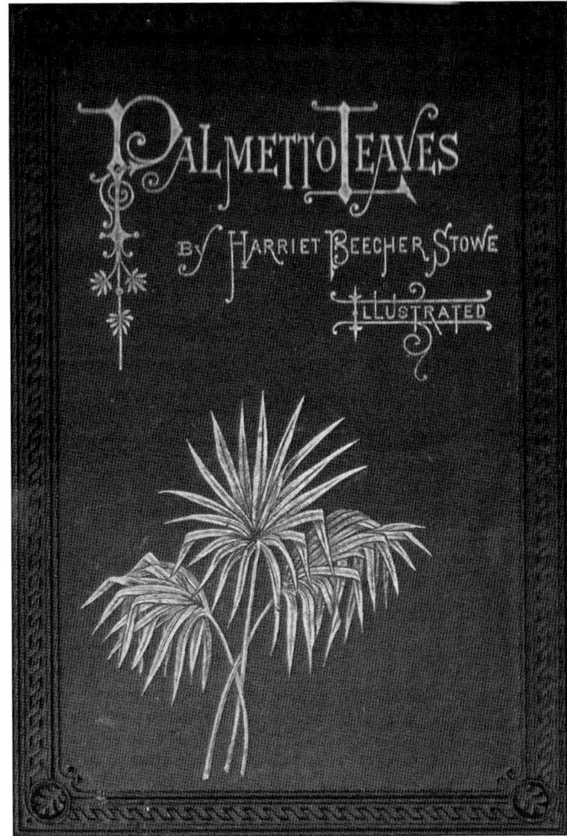

While wintering in Mandarin, Harriet Beecher Stowe wrote a series of articles about her life and observations in Mandarin and Florida. In 1873, they were published in a volume titled *Palmetto Leaves*. One of the impacts of this book was that it enticed people to come and visit Florida. The year after Stowe published *Palmetto Leaves*, 40,000 tourists visited Florida, up from 14,000 in 1872.

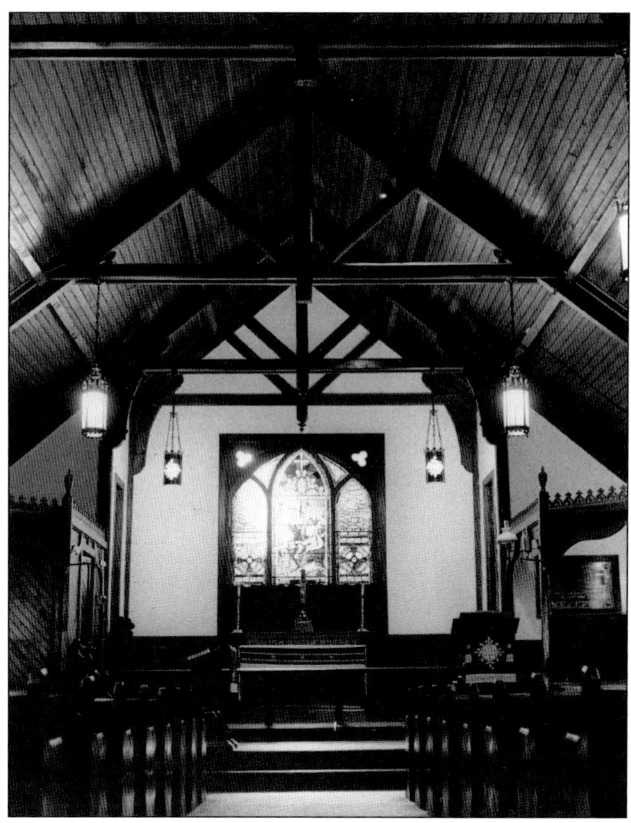

Deeply spiritual, Harriet Beecher Stowe hoped "to establish, along the St. Johns River, a nucleus of a Christian neighborhood whose influence shall be felt far beyond its own limits." The Bible readings of Calvin included a group of the Church of England, and a similar Episcopal service was adopted. The Church of our Saviour was built on the banks of the St. Johns River and opened in 1884.

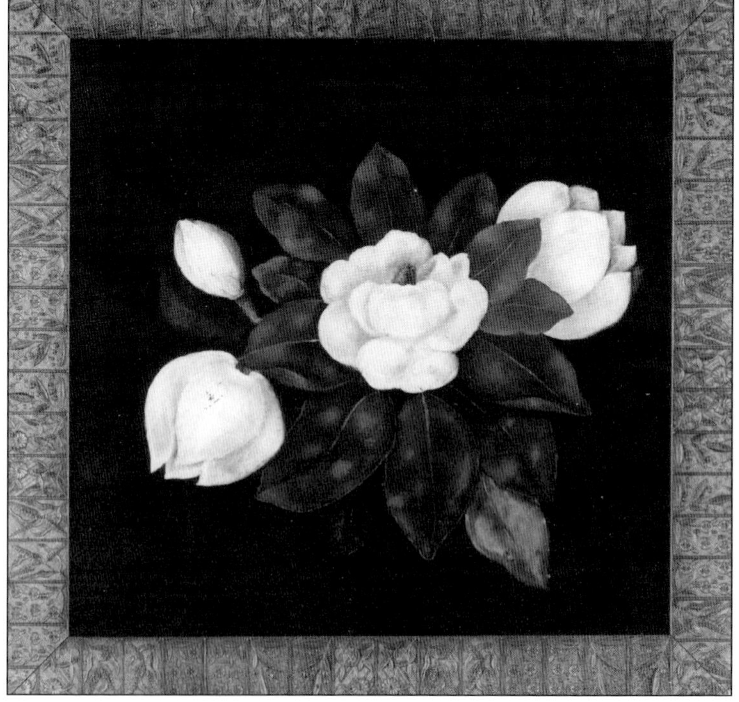

What many do not know is that Harriet Beecher Stowe painted prolifically while in Mandarin. Two of her favorite subjects were orange trees and magnolias. These beautiful magnolia blossoms were painted on cloth, to be part of a fundraising quilt for the Church of Our Saviour.

Three

THE MAPLE LEAF

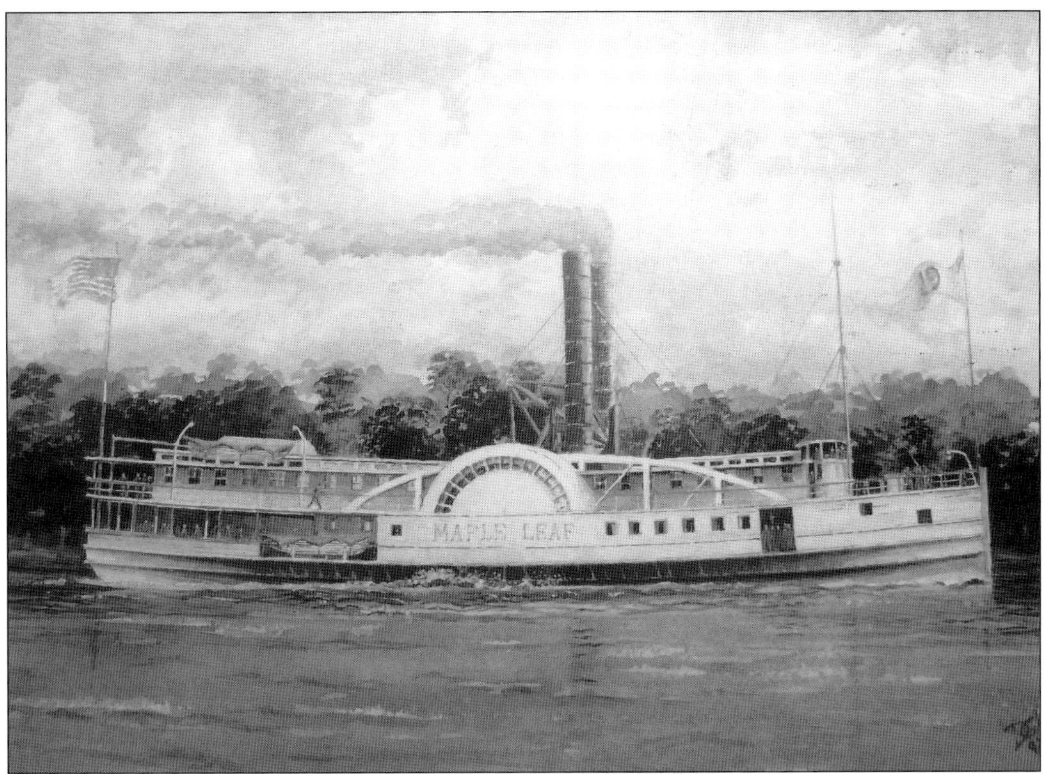

The *Maple Leaf* was built in 1851 in Toronto, Canada to sail Lake Ontario, carrying passengers, freight, and livestock. Ten years later, she was in Boston and chartered to the US Army Quartermaster Corps to transport soldiers and supplies along the East Coast during the American Civil War. On April 1, 1864, the *Maple Leaf* became an important part of Mandarin's history. (Art by Donald G. Ingram, courtesy of K.V. Holland.)

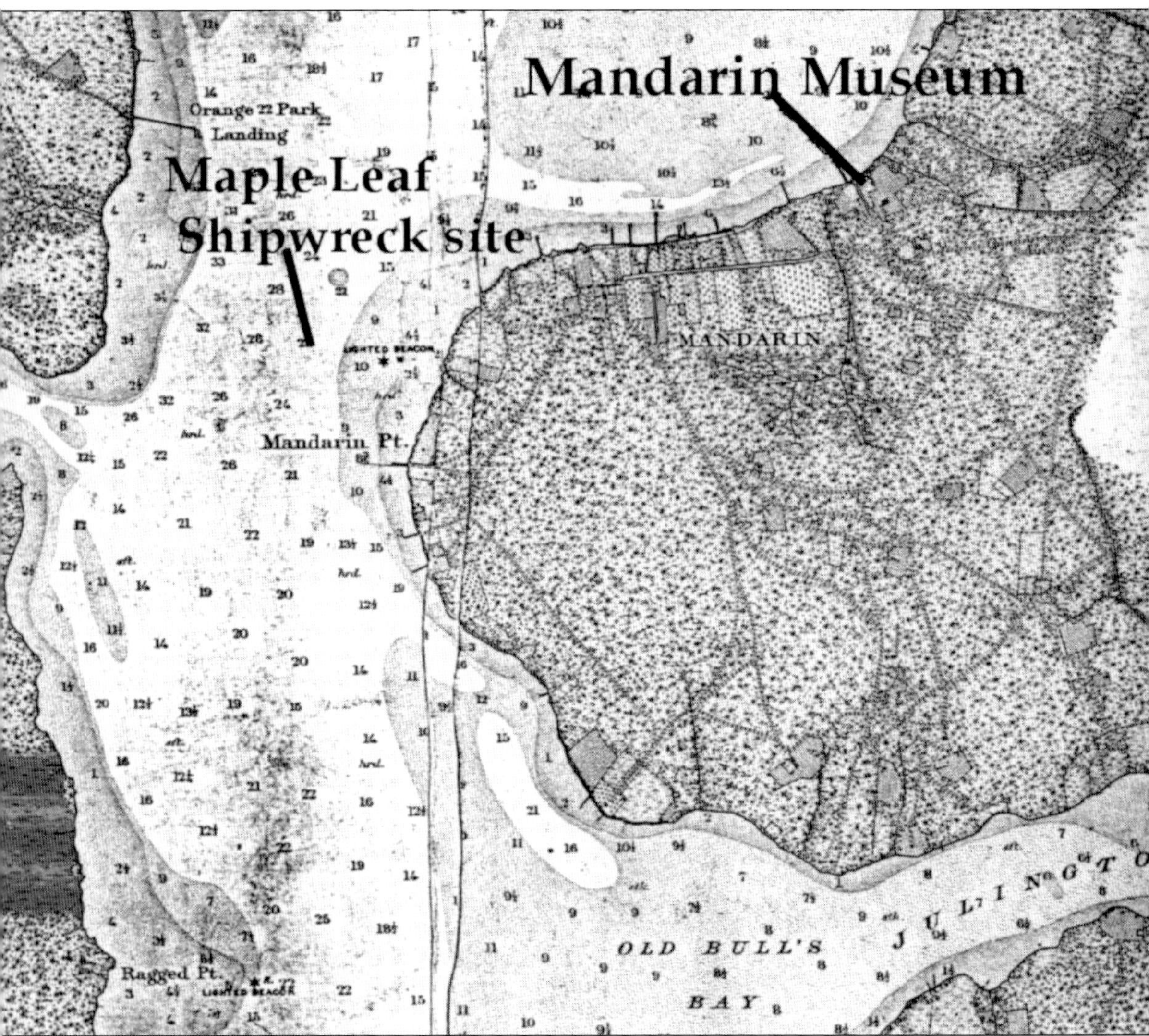

On March 31, 1864, the *Maple Leaf* arrived in Jacksonville with a full cargo of Union equipment. Jacksonville was occupied by the Union at the time. Upon arrival, the ship was ordered to take a cavalry unit and 87 horses south on the St. Johns River to reinforce troops in Palatka. Leaving Palatka in darkness, April 1 turned out to be the *Maple Leaf*'s last voyage. Confederate troops had placed 12 underwater torpedoes in the river between Mandarin and Clay County. Because they were unseen, it was inevitable that the *Maple Leaf* would strike one. She quickly sank into 25 feet of water with her whistle screaming at Mandarin Point. The St. Johns River narrows greatly between Clay County and Mandarin Point, a logical place for the placement of the underwater torpedoes, a new instrument of war. This map clearly illustrates Mandarin, a peninsula, and the location of the wreck. Most on board were able to get off the ship and row 12 miles back to Jacksonville. However, four African American crew were killed.

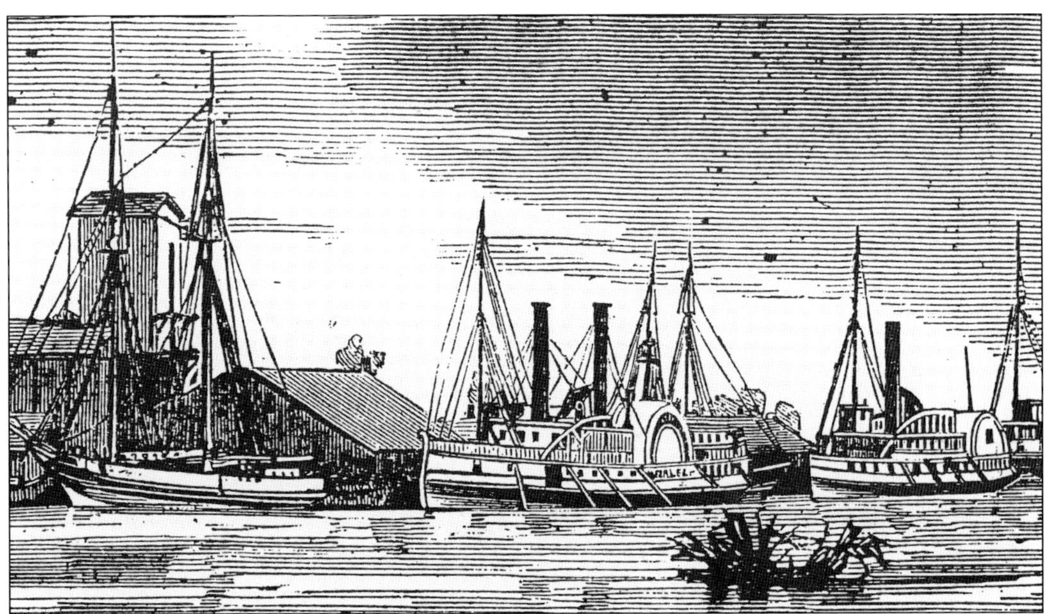

This illustration was published in *Frank Leslie's Illustrated Newspaper* in 1856. It shows the *Maple Leaf* (center) followed by the steamer *Highlander*.

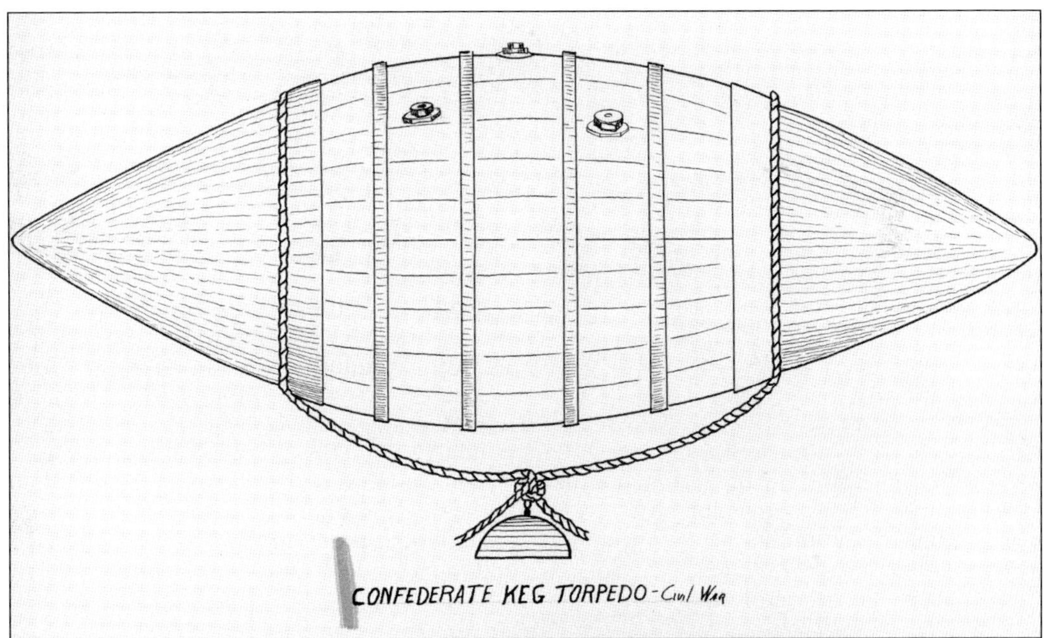

These torpedoes, called "mines" today, were filled with gunpowder and placed in the river by order of Confederate captain E. Pliny Bryan and five soldiers from the 2nd Florida Battalion. At 3:59 a.m., the *Maple Leaf* pilot, freedman Romeo Murray, could not see the mine. Murray lived in Mandarin after the war.

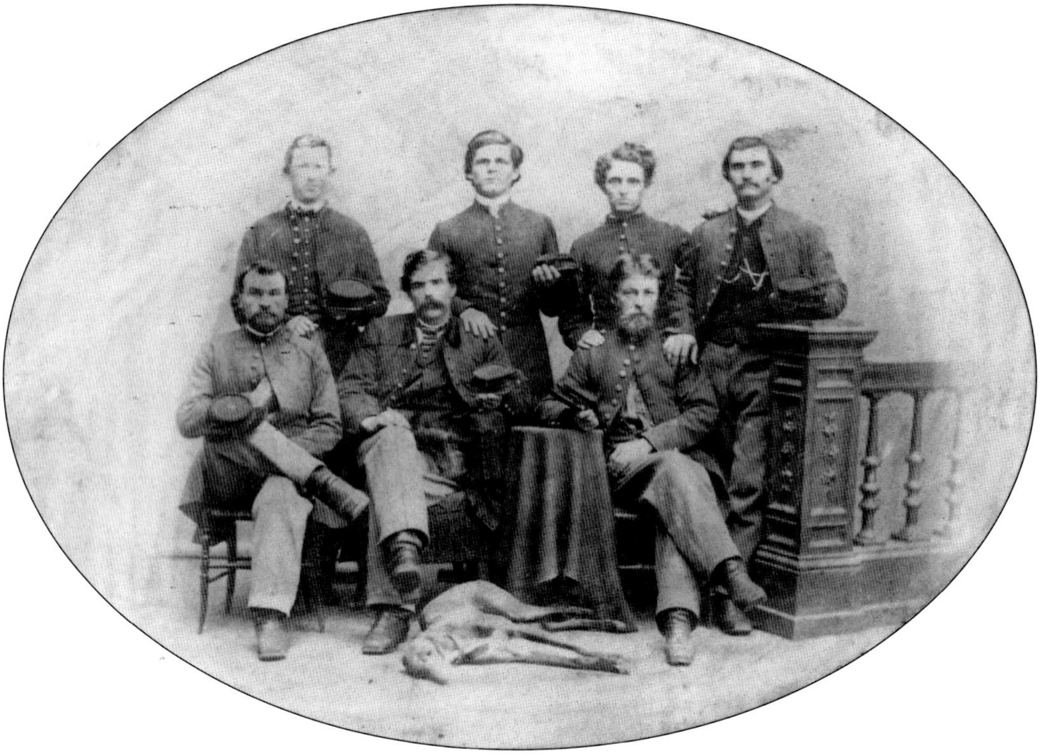

When the *Maple Leaf* arrived in Jacksonville from Johns Island, South Carolina, on March 31, she was carrying the equipment and supplies for three Union regiments: the 112th New York Volunteers, the 169th New York Volunteers, and the 13th Indiana. This group of 13th Indiana soldiers includes Barnabas C. Hitchcock (bottom right). Private Hitchcock and his unit had just moved to Jacksonville from Folly Island, South Carolina. (Courtesy of Rae Lahti Donnelly.)

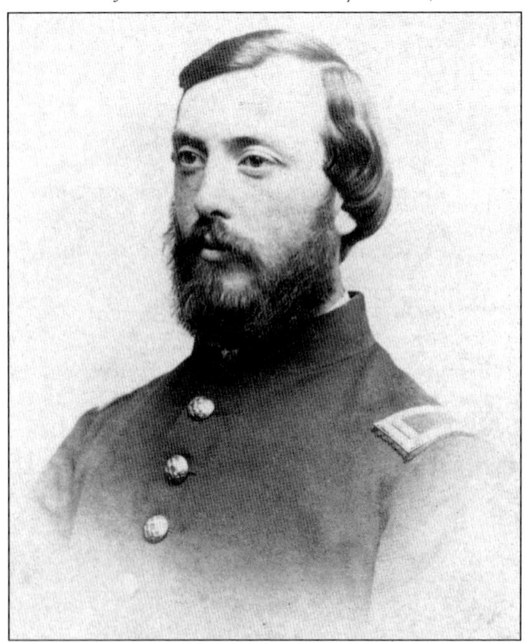

Onboard on April 1 was Lt. George Thompson Garrison, son of William Lloyd Garrison, editor of the Boston abolitionist newspaper the *Liberator*. Lieutenant Garrison, serving as an officer in the 55th Massachusetts Volunteer Infantry, a Black regiment, was coming to Jacksonville to procure tents for his regiment in Palatka. He wrote his mother a letter about the event the next day, describing the incident. (Courtesy of the Garrison family photographs, Massachusetts Historical Society.)

The *Maple Leaf* story remained forgotten in the St. Johns until 1984 when Dr. Keith Holland, made it his mission to find the shipwreck and recover Civil War material from it. He founded St. Johns Archaeological Expeditions Inc. (SJAEI), and for the next decade, he and his team of divers researched, dove, recovered, and preserved thousands of artifacts of cultural importance. Pictured here from left to right are Keith Holland, Lee Manley, and Larry Tipping.

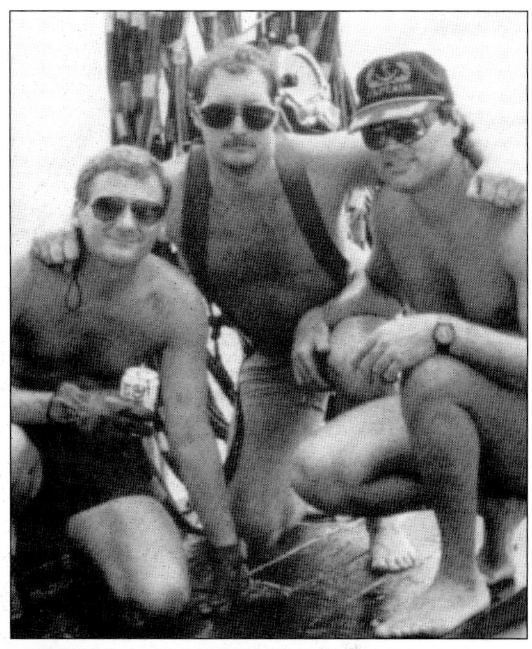

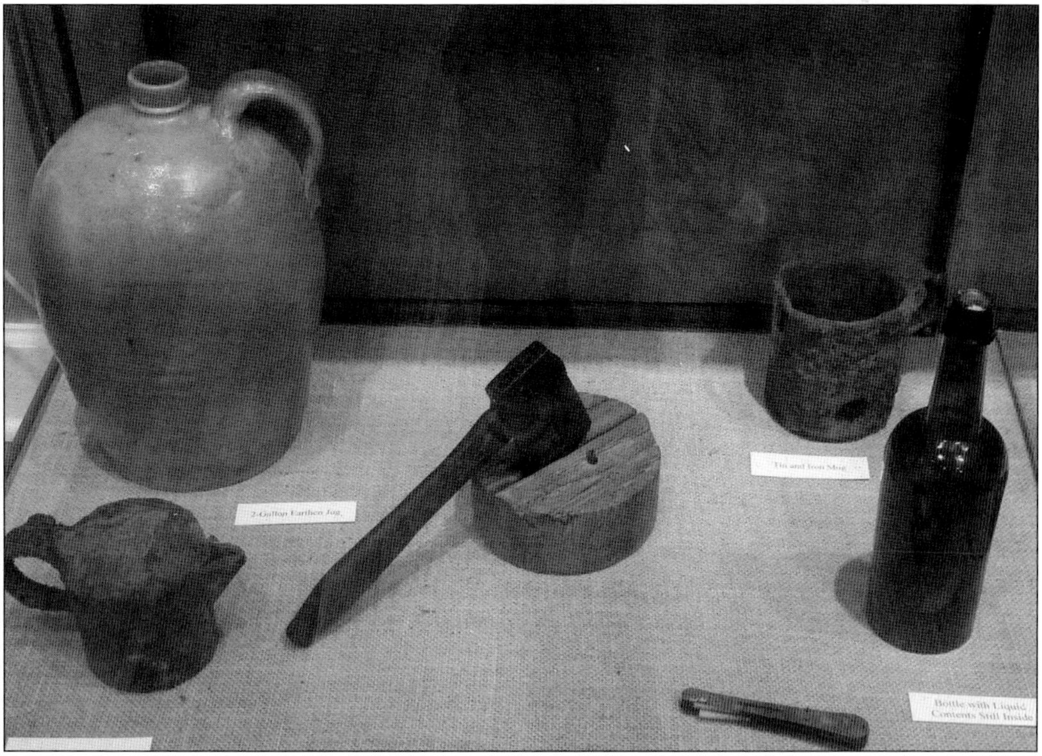

It was not easy. After finding the shipwreck, it took a long time of legal negotiating with the US government and the State of Florida about ownership and permission to salvage. The artifacts were given to the State of Florida in order to keep them all together. They are available for loan to museums in Florida through the Florida State Division of Historical Resources. Mandarin Museum has a vast collection on display.

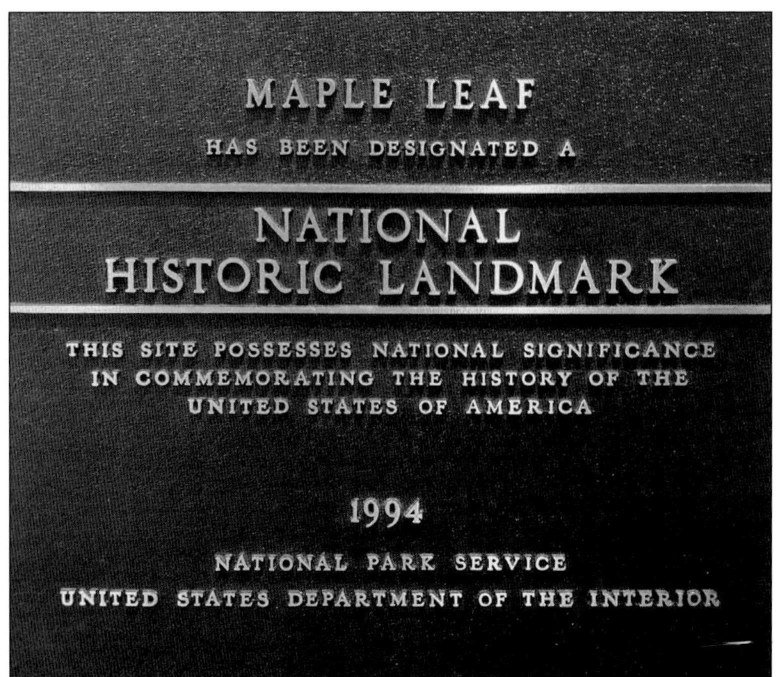

On October 12, 1994, the *Maple Leaf* shipwreck site was designated a National Historic Landmark by the Secretary of the Interior. It was the first such designation in Jacksonville and the fourth shipwreck to receive it. Plaques are located in Mandarin and Orange Park.

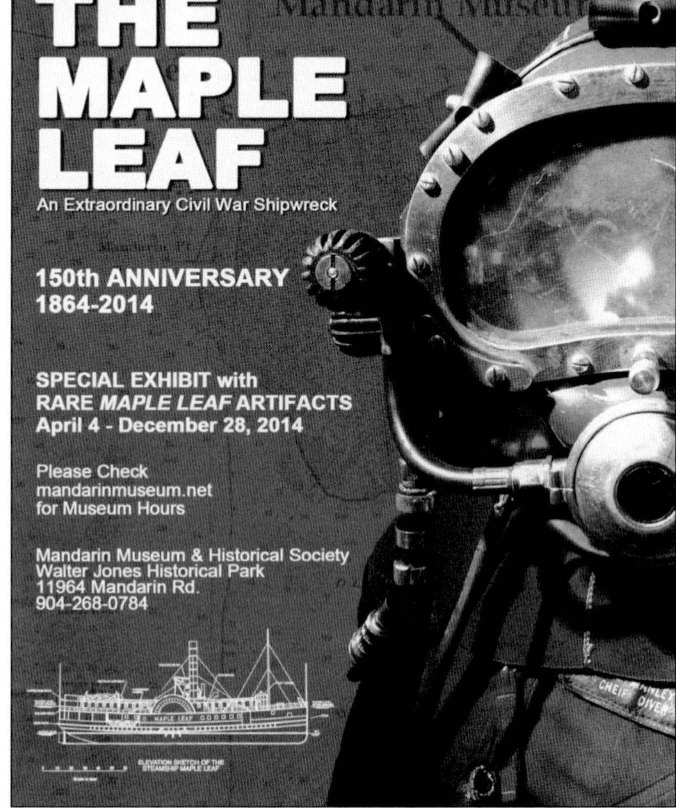

In 2014, Mandarin honored the 150th anniversary of the sinking of the *Maple Leaf*. In 2023, a brand-new exhibit hall will be dedicated to telling the *Maple Leaf* story at Mandarin Museum.

Four

Historic Houses

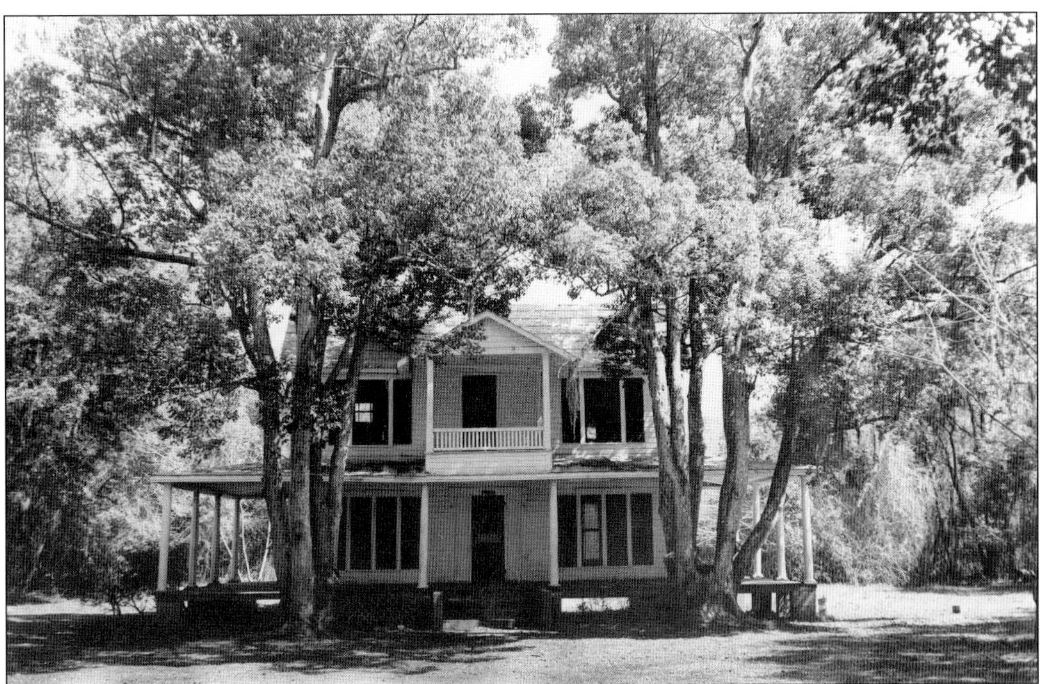

The Frederick Billard family came to Mandarin in the late 19th century and built this house on Brady Road with no professional help and using local materials. It was later owned by Agnes Jones, John Woolfe, and the Mandarin Community Club. It was demolished in 2005, but the Billard Commemorative Park, which honors veterans and hosts special events, was built on the property. (Courtesy of Virginia Barker.)

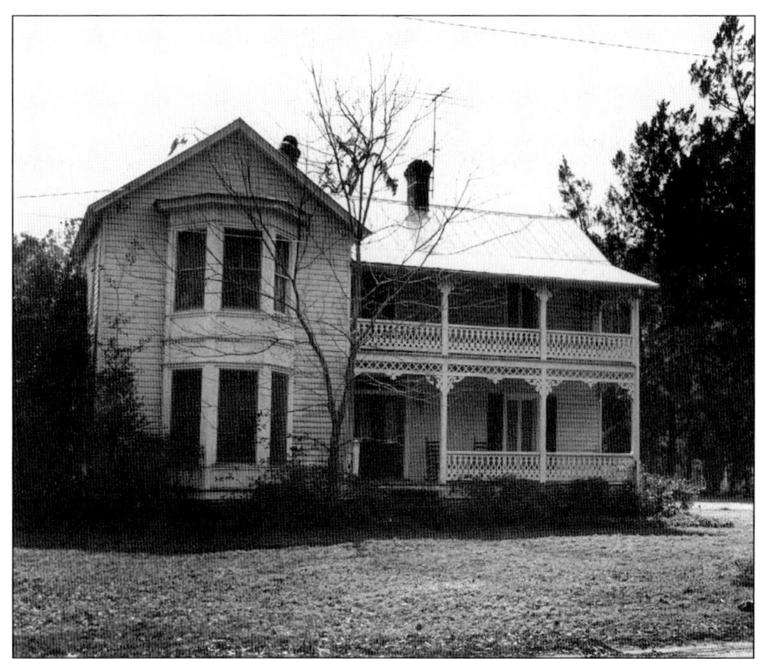

Dr. Henry Coleman was a doctor in Mandarin in the 1870s and 1880s. He was from South Carolina and had served the Confederate army as a surgeon. He brought his family to Florida and purchased this house with a small orange grove from W. Lockwood in 1878. As many did, he thought it would improve his family's health. The house has been renovated and still stands on Loretto Road. (Courtesy of Virginia Barker.)

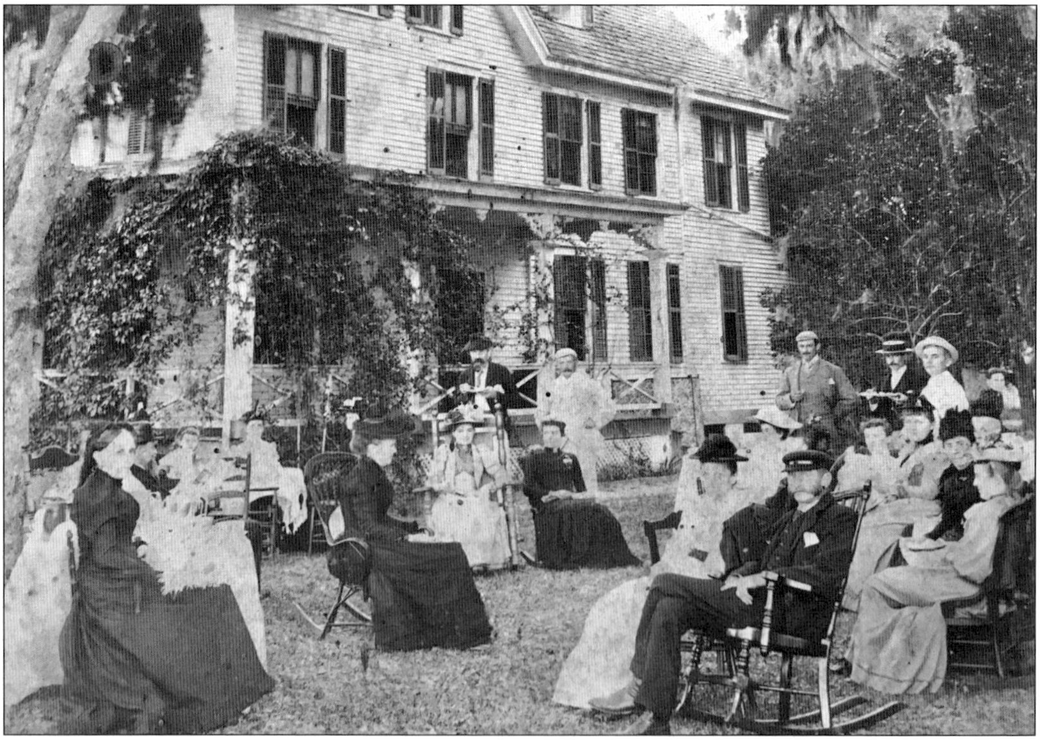

Englishman Walter Bertram Dismore made Mandarin his home in 1879 after purchasing 23 acres on the river. He was very involved with the community and helped raise money to build the Church of Our Saviour. He grew citrus and pineapples. This photograph shows a group of friends at his house for a lawn party. Dismore stands in the back row, center, with a dark mustache and cap. (Courtesy of the Dismore family.)

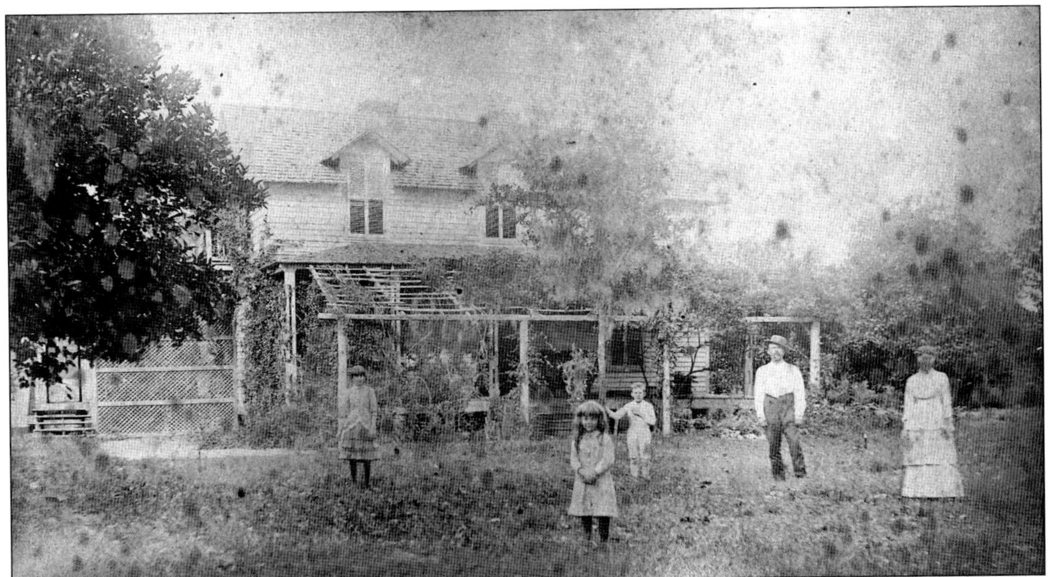

C.D. Duncan was the county overseer of schools. After the school for African Americans and White children burned down, Duncan completed making the winter arrangements for reopening the school. He built a home and moved to Mandarin in the early 1870s, while still a young man. He may have been influenced by his father's close friendship with Harriet Beecher Stowe's brother Henry Ward Beecher. (Courtesy of the Mary Graff Collection, Jacksonville Historical Society.)

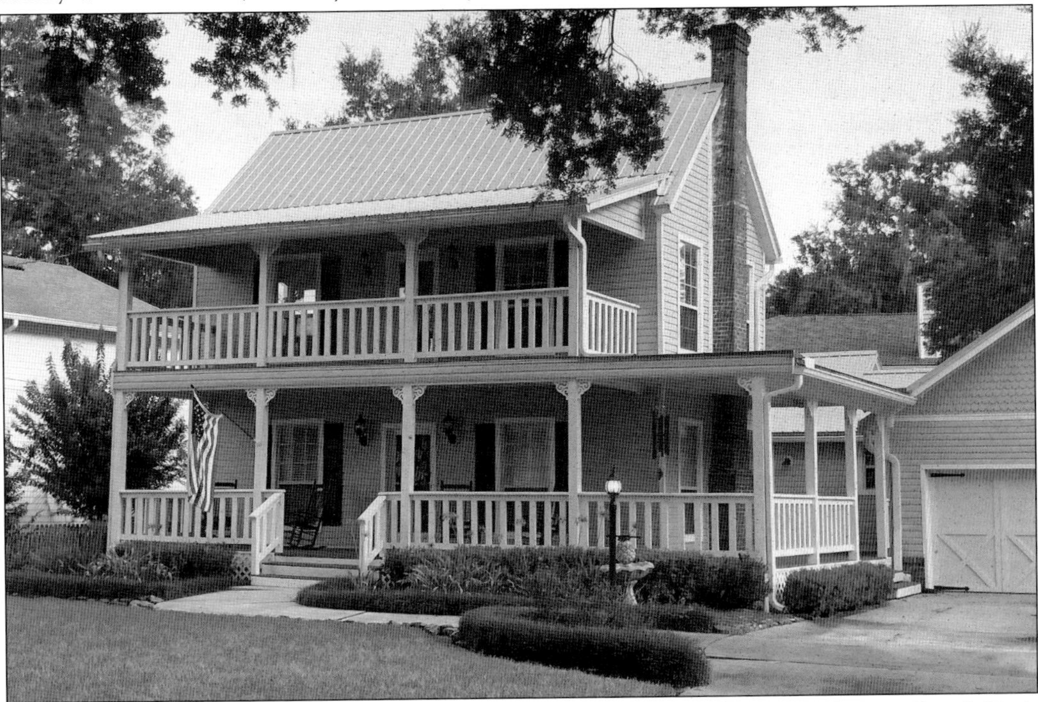

James Jefferson Flynn was a prosperous resident who owned a feed store on Loretto Road. He is also said to have been the first person in Mandarin to own an automobile and sell gasoline. This house was built in 1906 and still stands. The old feed store nearby has been converted to a private home. (Courtesy of Brett Nolan.)

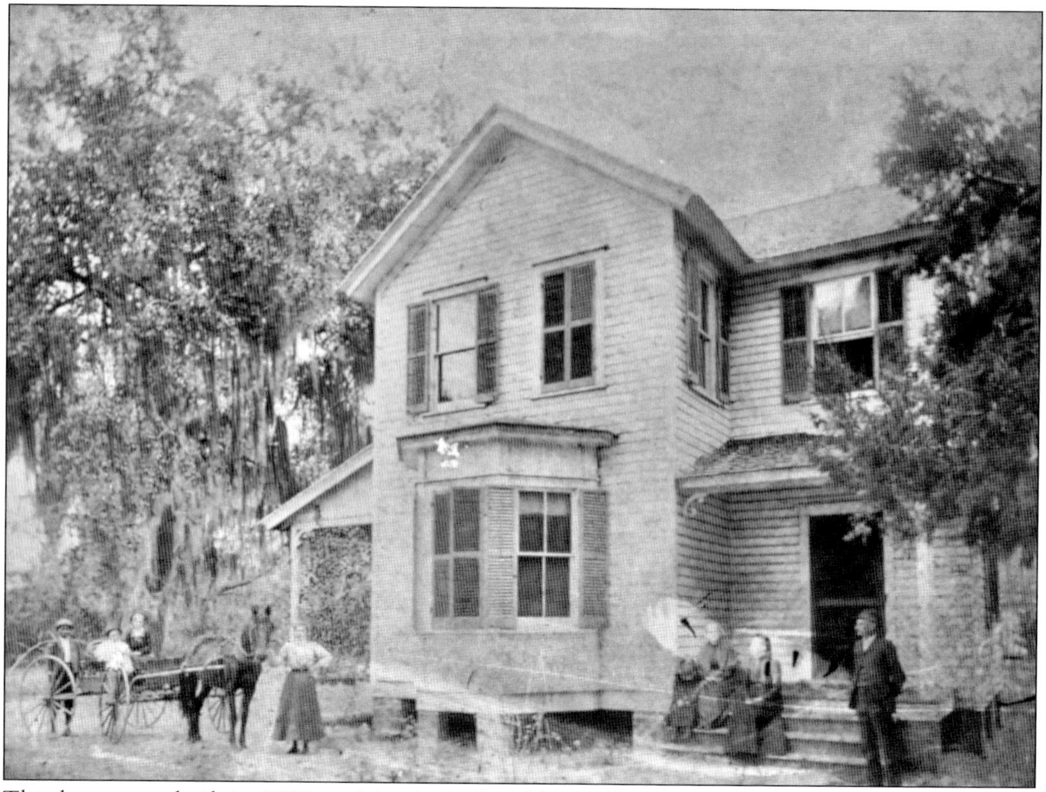

This house was built in 1887 on Mandarin Road by William Monson for the John Henry Jacks family. John Henry Jacks is seen on the far right. Monson was a popular builder in Mandarin at the time. Jacks was well known for growing celery, which was a new crop to Mandarin. He was a farmer, and his wife was a teacher. The house was renovated in 2021. (Courtesy of Bill Morrow.)

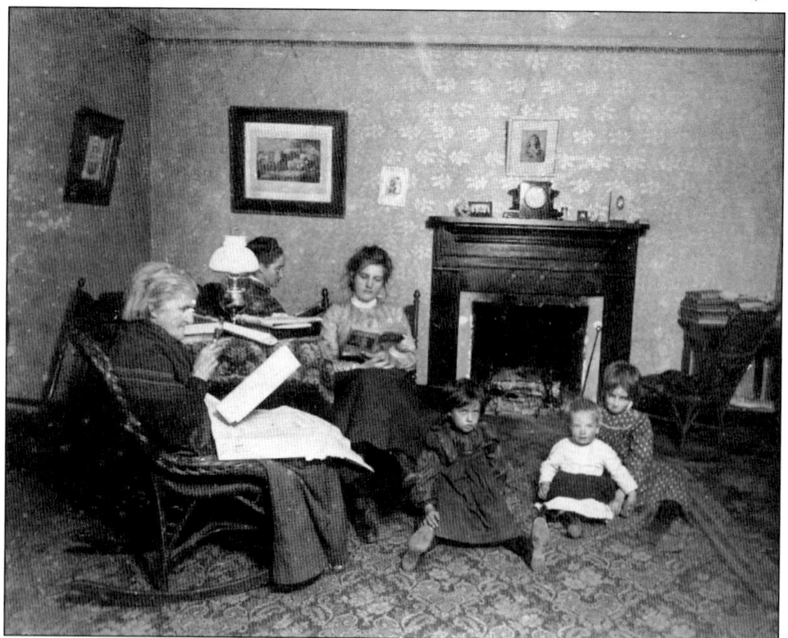

This is a rare view into the Jacks' parlor in 1902. Pictured from left to right are Mary Jane Schofield Eaton, Ella Evelyn Eaton Jacks, Letitia Frances Jacks, Helen Kearsing Jacks, Robert Henry Jacks, and Mary Eaton (Polly) Jacks. (Courtesy of Bill Morrow.)

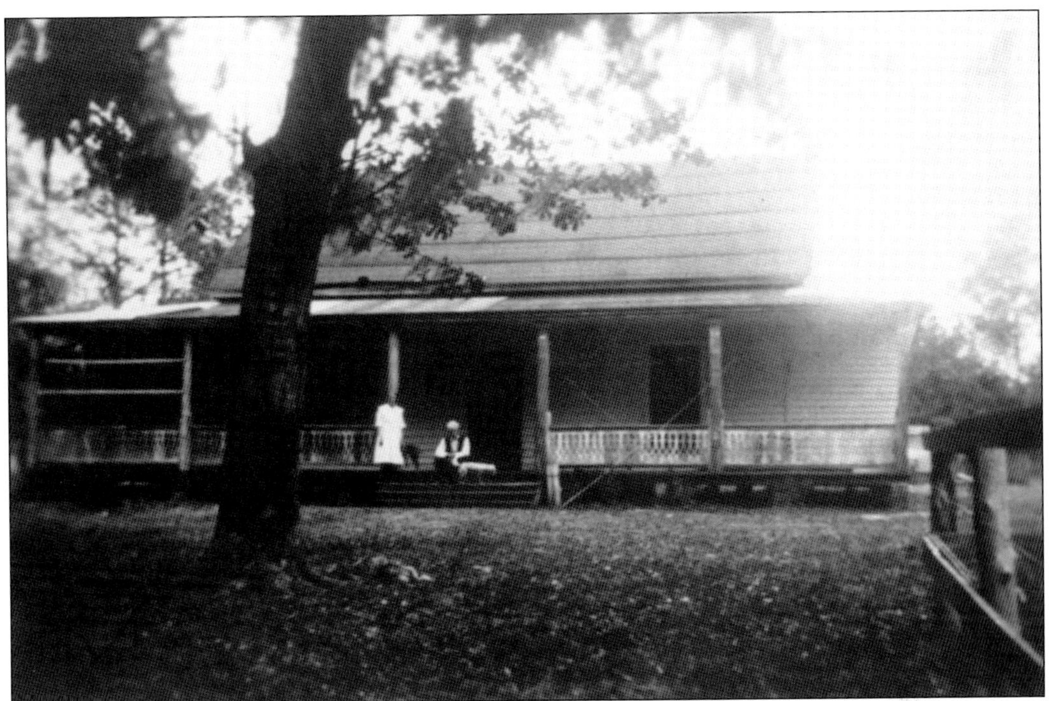

Walter Jones came from England in 1888 after hearing about the orange groves in Mandarin. He worked at the first general store on the river where he met Edith Mary Dawson, also from England. They married and raised their four boys and three girls in what is now known as the Webb/Jones farmhouse in Walter Jones Historical Park. Maj. William W. Webb built the house in 1875, but the Jones family lived in it the longest. Walter had become the postmaster, and in 1911, a new store and post office on Mandarin and Brady Roads was built by William Monson. After Walter's death in 1928, his daughter Agnes became the postmistress and operated the store until 1963. The store is now in the National Register of Historic Places. Agnes, or "Miss Aggie," lived in the house until 1992, and the property, including the house, was purchased by the City of Jacksonville after her death.

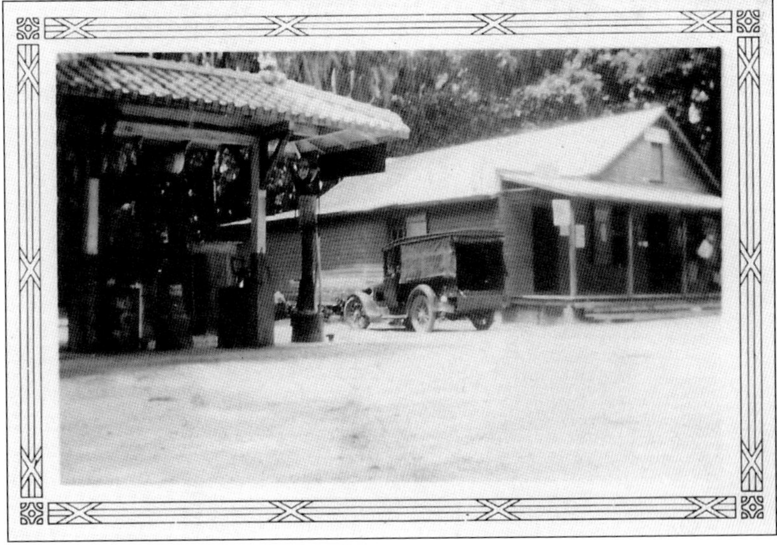

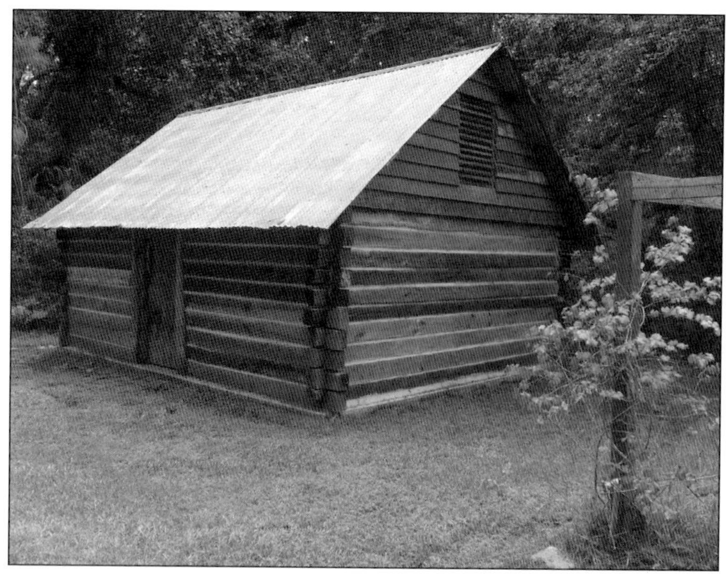

Francisco Losco and Dometilla Danese Losco operated a 160-acre truck farm and winery while raising nine children on Losco Road. They had seven acres of scuppernong grapes and produced about forty barrels of wine per year in this little log cabin winery. The log cabin was saved and moved to Walter Jones Historical Park in 2005. Their son Marion was the only man from Mandarin killed in World War I, and he is buried in France.

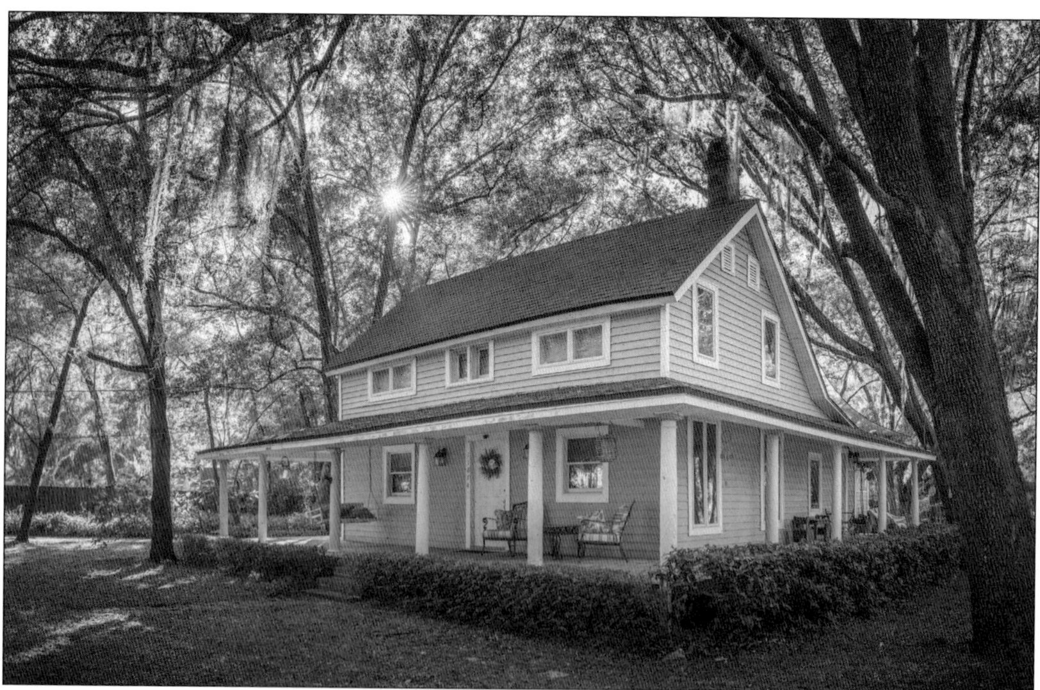

The Hartley House, built in the 1880s on Hood Landing Road, is said to be located on the site of what was called the "Mandarin Massacre." On December 31, 1841, a group of Seminoles attacked and burned the house of William Hartley. He was not at home, but his wife, her infant, and Domingo Acosta were sitting by the fire when they were attacked. Another neighbor, a Mr. Malphus, was shot but ran outside where he was found dead. (Courtesy of Olis Garber.)

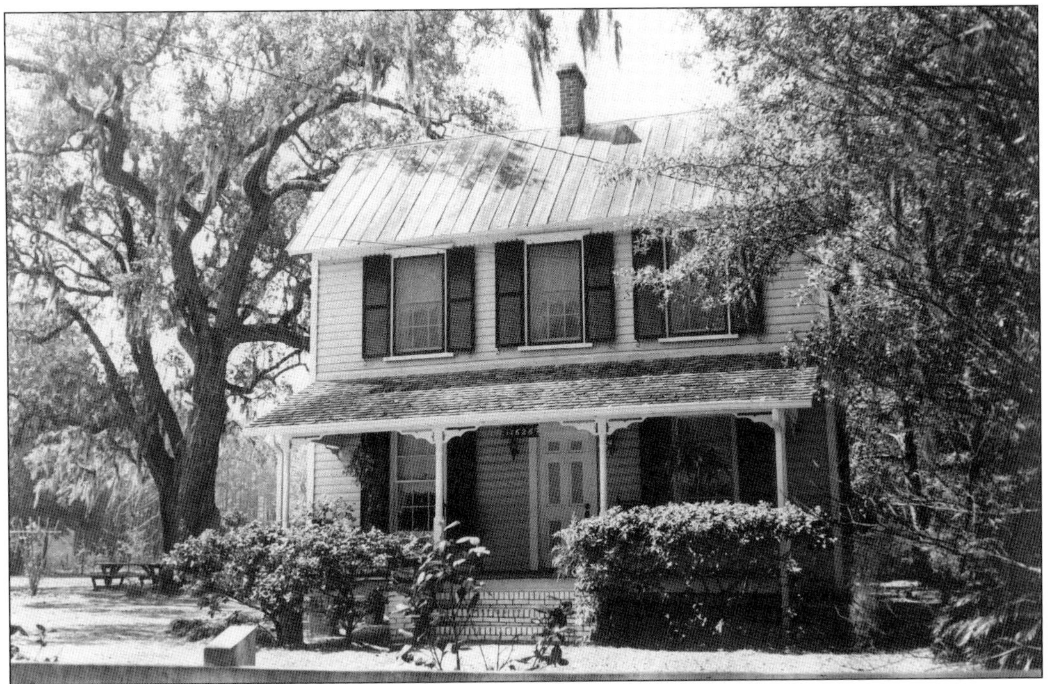

This home on Brady Road was built in the late 1800s for Calvin Read, the grandson of Calvin Read (1798–1878) who came from Vermont to Florida after 1819 and became postmaster in 1836. The senior Calvin owned a large tract of property on the river where the Mandarin Wharf, the post office, and stores were located. He is credited with naming the community Mandarin in 1830. (Courtesy of Virginia Barker.)

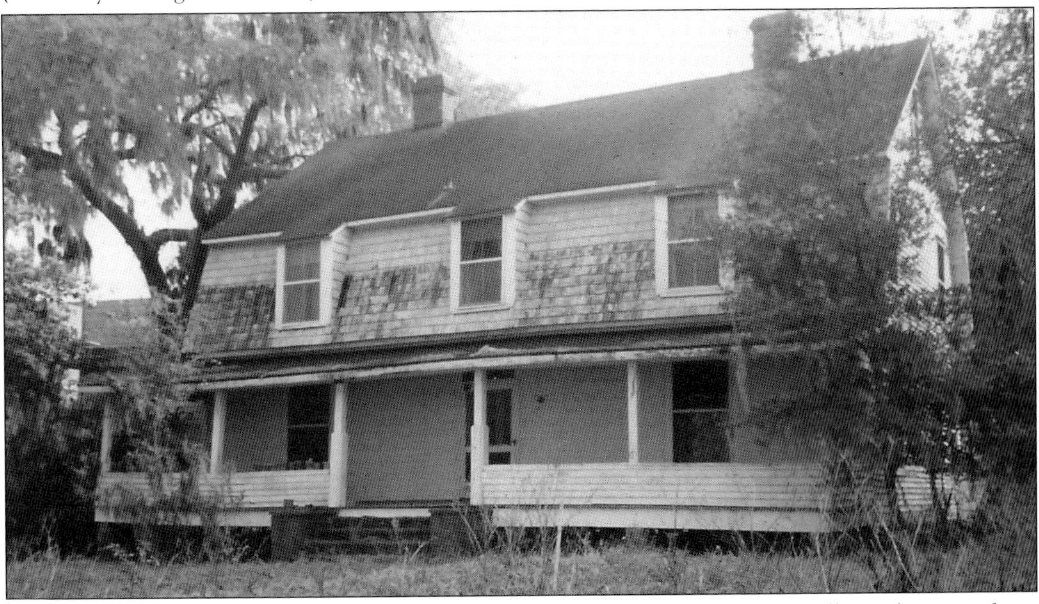

The Tweedle House was built by William Monson in the 1870s for Dr. Tweedle, a physician from Pennsylvania. The house, next to the Stowes, was later the Palms Boarding House. But it may be best known as the home of renowned artist and potter Charles "Charlie" Moses Brown Jr. and his sisters Eleanor, Mary, Adalyn "Deenda," and Fannie. The home was destroyed in the 1980s.

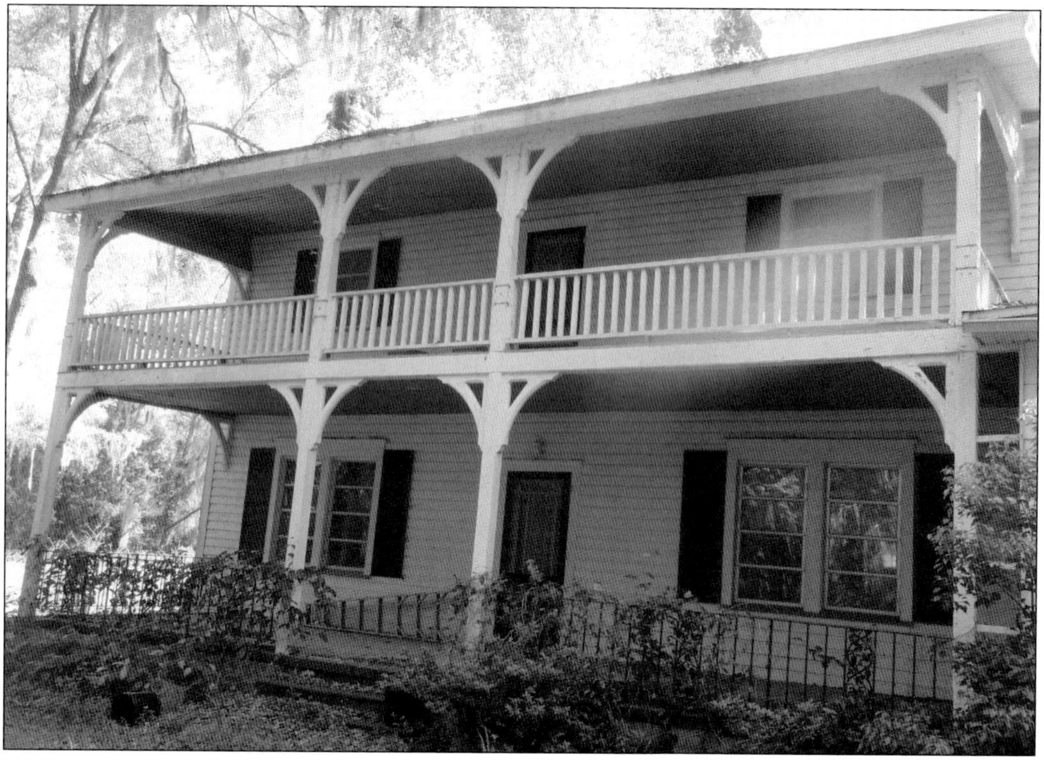

Englishman Charles F. Winton's home, between Loretto and Mandarin Roads, was known as "Jubilee Hall." It was built by William Monson in 1887 for the family. Winton served as a representative of Lloyd's of London and was responsible for overseeing the export of produce shipments. The home was demolished in 2014.

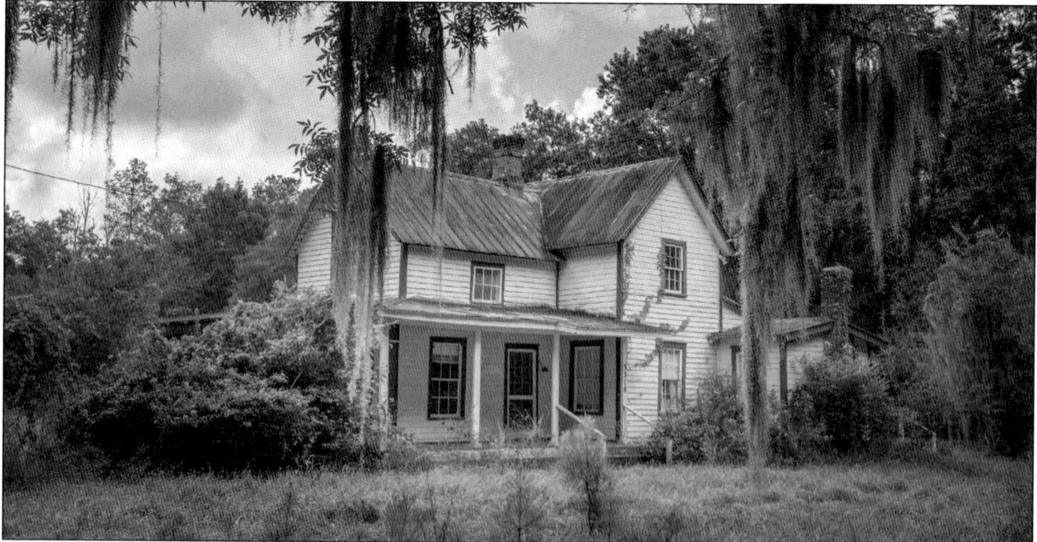

This home is the only residential building in Mandarin to have the status of being in the National Register of Historic Places. It was built by Henry C. Arpen, a citrus grower, but it was not along the river. Rather it was in an area off of what is now Marbon Road. The materials for the home were said to be from a sunken barge in the river. (Courtesy Olis Gaber.)

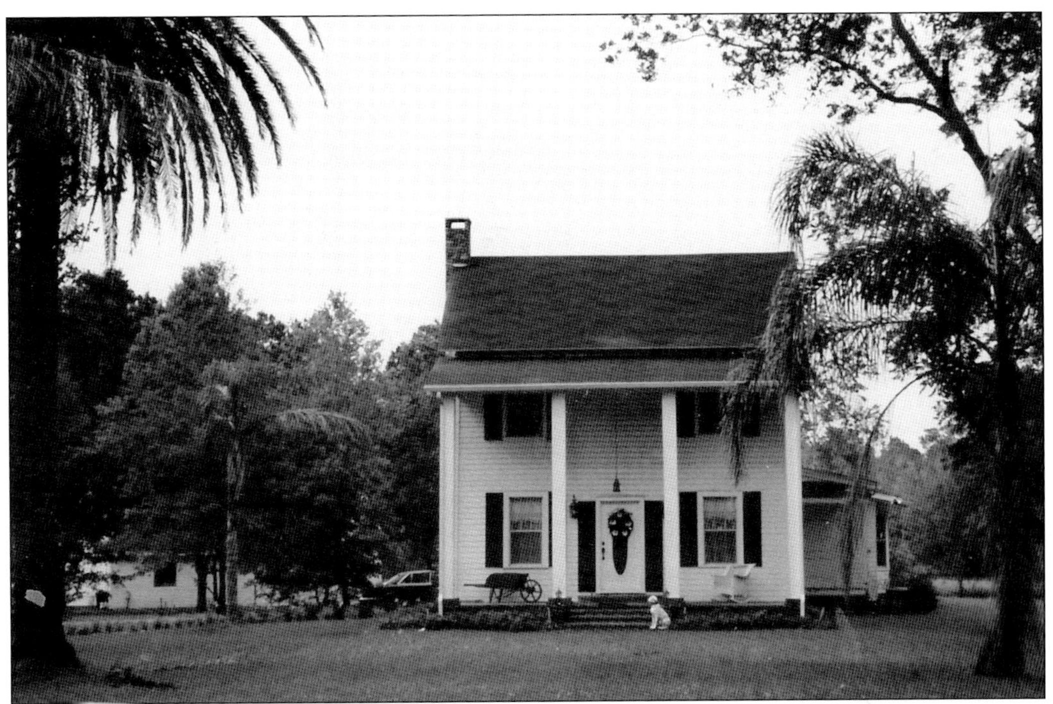

Fleming H. and Nettie Ponce Bowden raised their family in this house on 25 acres on Loretto Road, built in 1906. Fleming was born in Mandarin and was a blacksmith for much of his young years. He also gathered locally grown fruits and vegetables and hauled them to Jacksonville to resell. Later, he served for 21 years as Duval County's supervisor of elections until his death in 1964. The house was later owned by the Cissell family for many years.

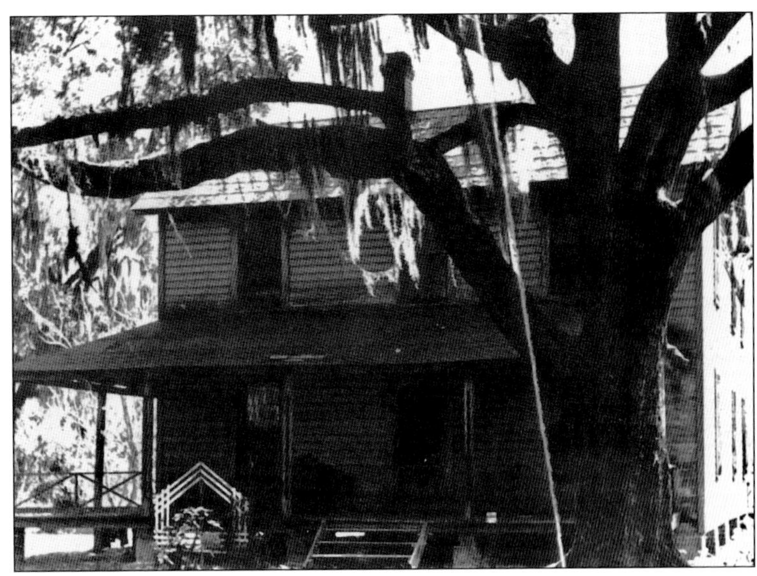

This 1889 farmhouse was once owned by the Robert J. Stormes family. It was on Old Mandarin Road, now called Mandarin Terrace Road. In 1981, it was purchased by Rex and Carmen Rowe. It was torn down in 2022. (Courtesy of the Rex L. and Carmen D. Rowe family estate.)

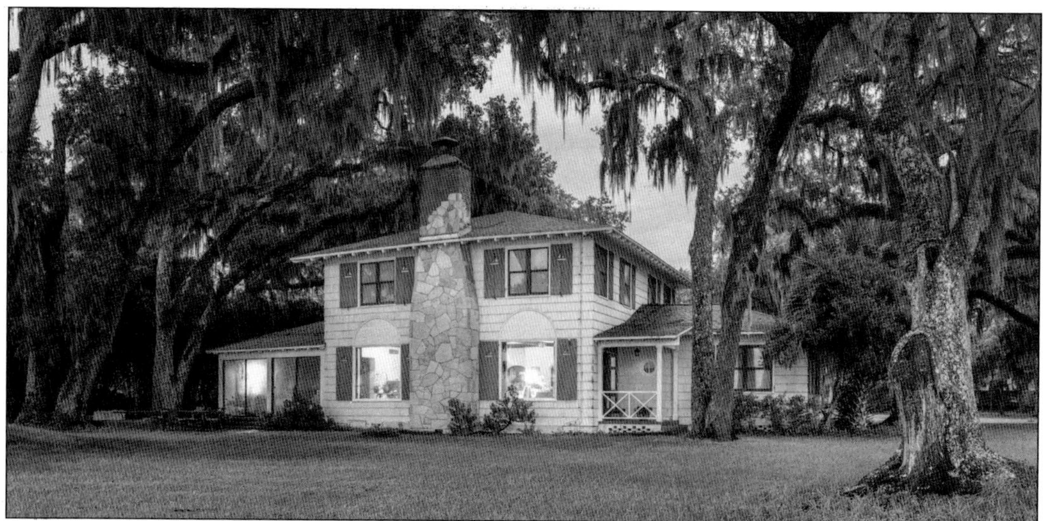

This County Dock home was built in 1937 after electricity came to Mandarin. At that time, the address was Mandarin Road because the property was seven acres and extended all the way to Mandarin Road. The original owners were Mr. and Mrs. W.H. Dernell, who lived there fairly briefly. Most of the house is original to this period, including oak and heart pine flooring. (Courtesy of Olis Garber.)

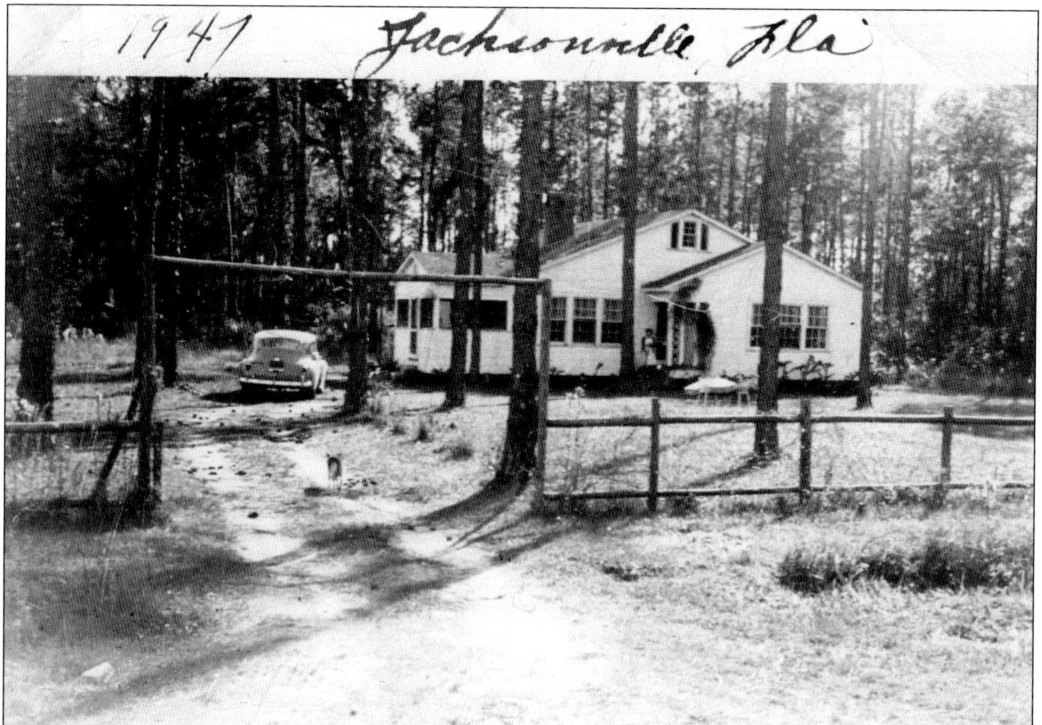

This home, still on Mandarin Road, is illustrative of typical middle-class houses that were built in the mid-20th century. It is clearly less spacious and ornate than most of the homes along the river, but it represents a very common and affordable style that was very popular. (Courtesy of Claire Fleming King.)

Five

Untold Stories of Black Mandarin

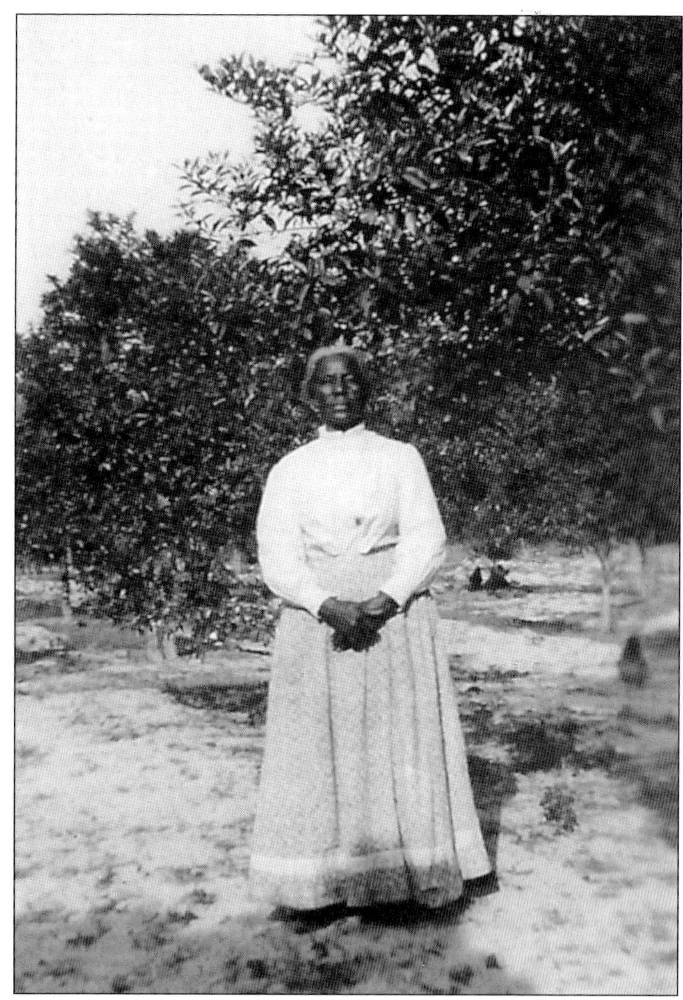

The intent of this chapter is to honor Mandarin's rich Black history somewhat chronologically and cohesively. For 250 years, Black residents have been a vital part of, and have made major contributions to, this community. Mandarin's overall history was built on their shoulders as well as those of their White neighbors, but their stories have been relatively untold in a public way. We want to share at least part of that story. This woman's full name is unknown, but on the back of the photograph, it identifies her as "Matilda" or "Ma Tilda," and she stands tall in one of Mandarin's orange groves.

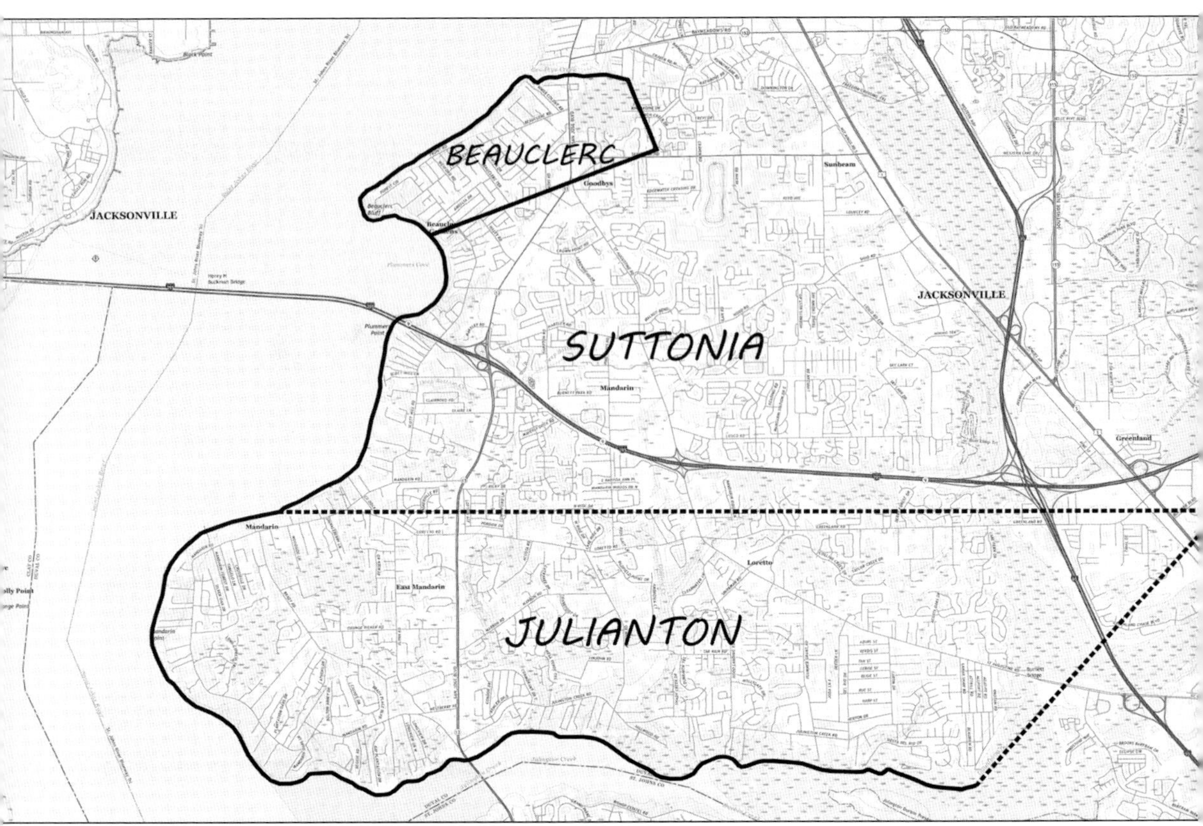

The story begins in 1763 as enslaved people were brought to work on the English plantations in the territory known as East Florida. This map illustrates what was then called St. Anthony. There were three sizable plantations: Beauclerc Bluff (33 enslaved people); Suttonia (unknown number) and Julianton (over 80). The work performed by those enslaved people helped the area's economy grow. Later, after freedom, they developed places of worship, owned land and businesses, served the community in many ways, and served the government as soldiers and elected leaders.

In the early 19th century, a prominent but short-term resident was Anna Kingsley. Anna had been purchased in 1806 by Zephaniah Kingsley and brought to the area across the river from Mandarin, owned by Kingsley. She bore children with Kingsley, who freed Anna and the children from slavery, which allowed Anna to move to San Antonio (now Mandarin) in 1811, where she owned property. (Courtesy of Dr. Daniel L. Schafer.)

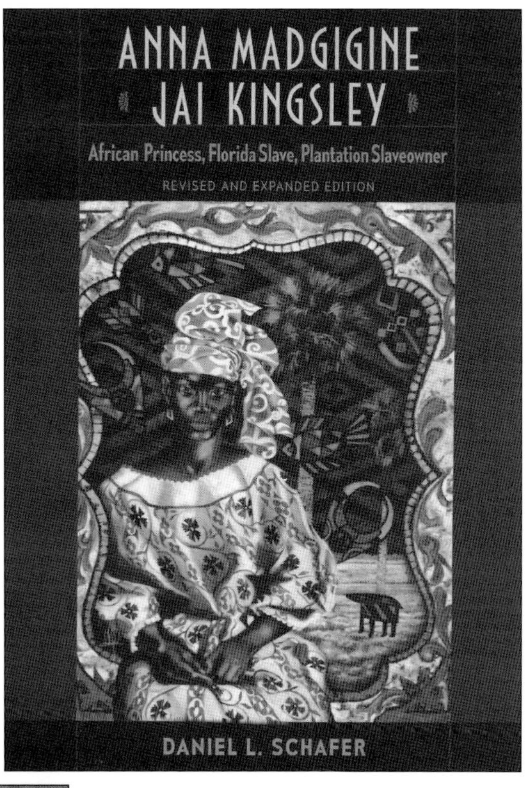

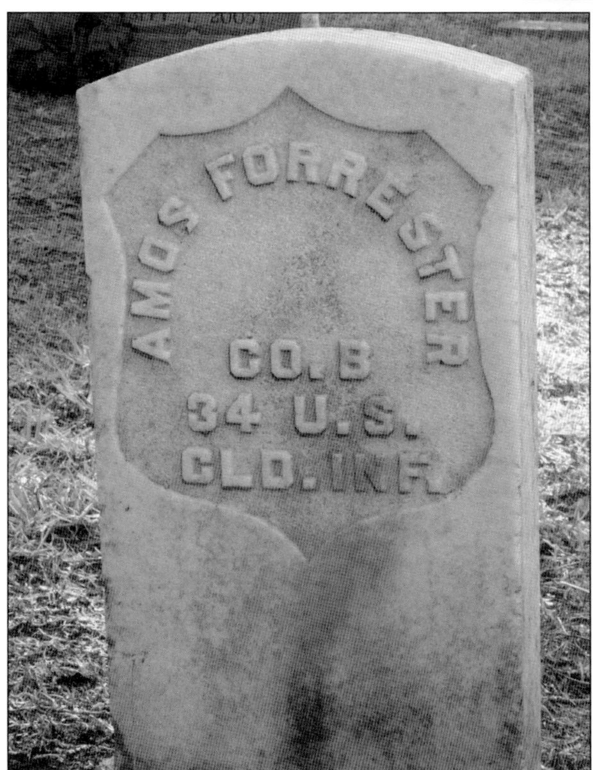

During the Civil War, many Mandarin men who were previously enslaved enlisted in the Union army in Jacksonville during the 1863 Union occupation, after the Emancipation Proclamation. Most served in the 33rd or 34th Infantry of the US Colored Troops (USCT). Names of those who served had family names still known in Mandarin today, including Forrester, Cody, Robinson, and Wanton. Amos Forrester is buried at St. Joseph's Catholic Church Cemetery.

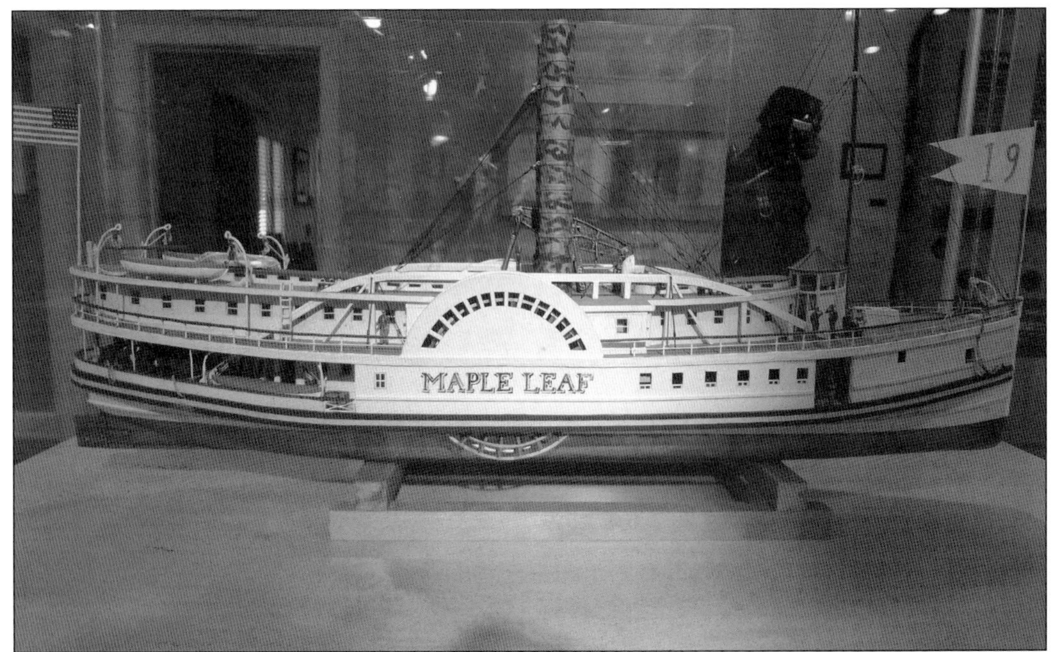

Romeo Murray, the pilot of the *Maple Leaf*, was born into slavery around 1820 at the Kingsley Plantation. By the time of the Civil War, he was a free person and was navigating steamboats. He was hired to navigate for the Union army and was serving as the pilot the night *Maple Leaf* hit a Confederate torpedo at Mandarin Point. Murray and his family settled in Mandarin after the war.

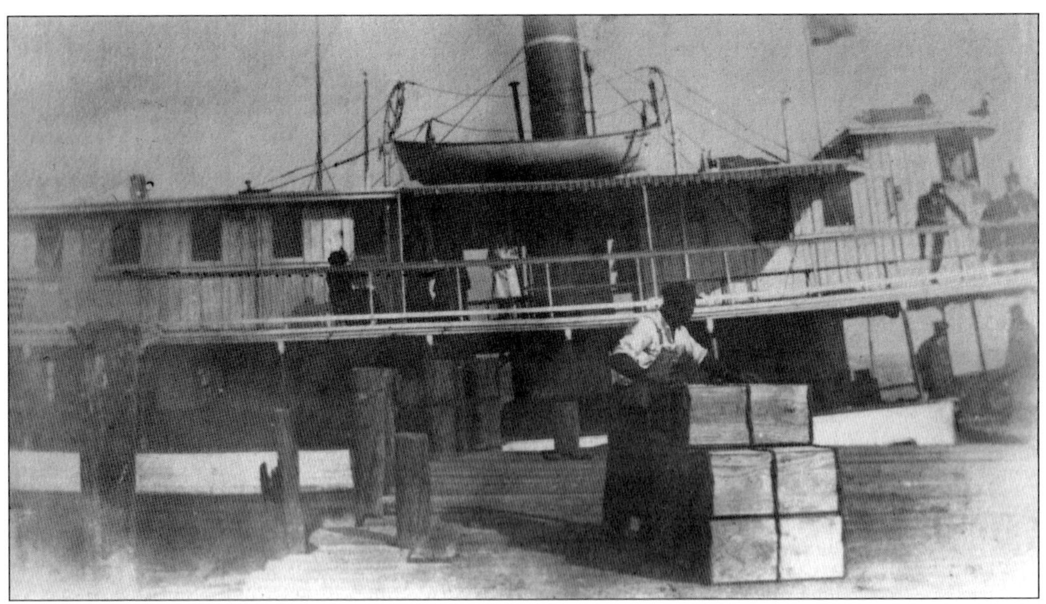

After the war, the community became active again. Many of Mandarin's Black families stayed. Some Union army veterans came here after service, and others migrated from South Carolina and Georgia. There were opportunities for land and work in the area. Many steamboats that came into Mandarin went out with boxes full of citrus. There were large gardens growing everything from pineapples and strawberries to celery. All of this required labor to be successful.

Jobs for Black residents were plentiful but limited in scope and poor in pay. The 1870 census lists the following occupations: farm laborer, keeping house, gardener, domestic servant, farmer, carpenter, retail grocer, fisherman, lumber mill, saw operator, and seamstress. Growing and grinding sugar cane into cane syrup was also a common occupation in the area, one that was seen into the late 1960s.

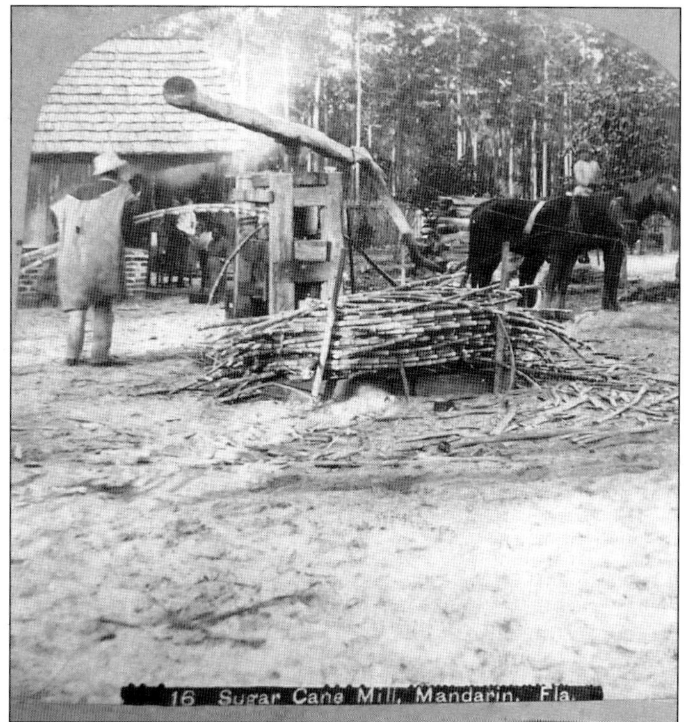

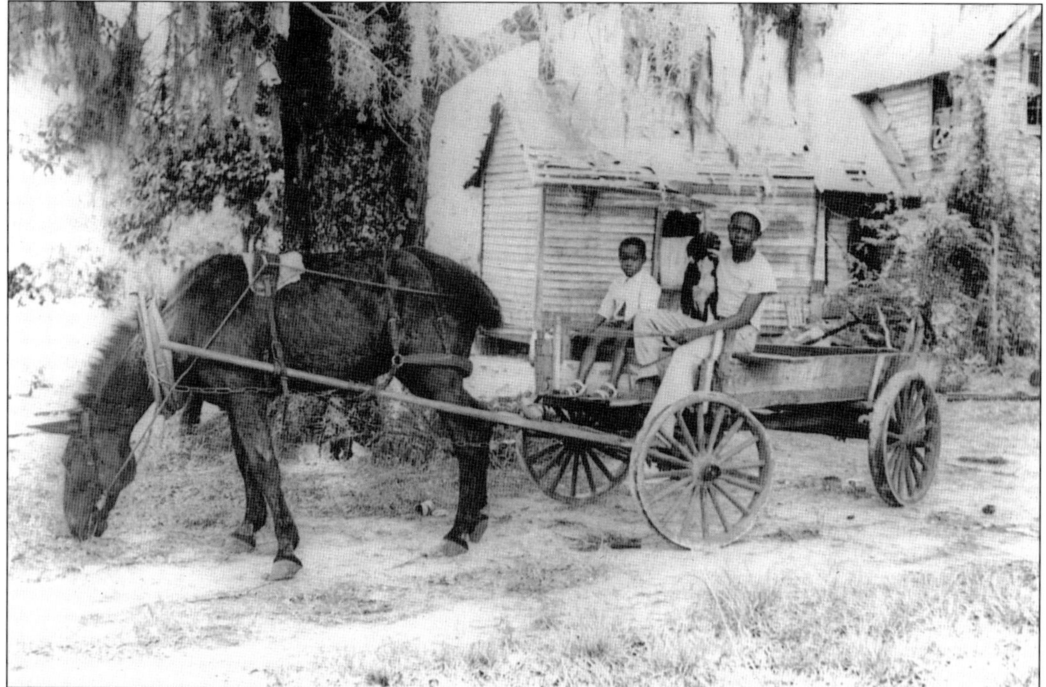

The young man in the cap seems to be in charge. He has been identified as possibly being Ike Robinson, though it has not been confirmed. This was the main mode of transportation on the sandy roads in Mandarin which eventually were paved with oyster shells. Wagons were seen around even into the 1960s.

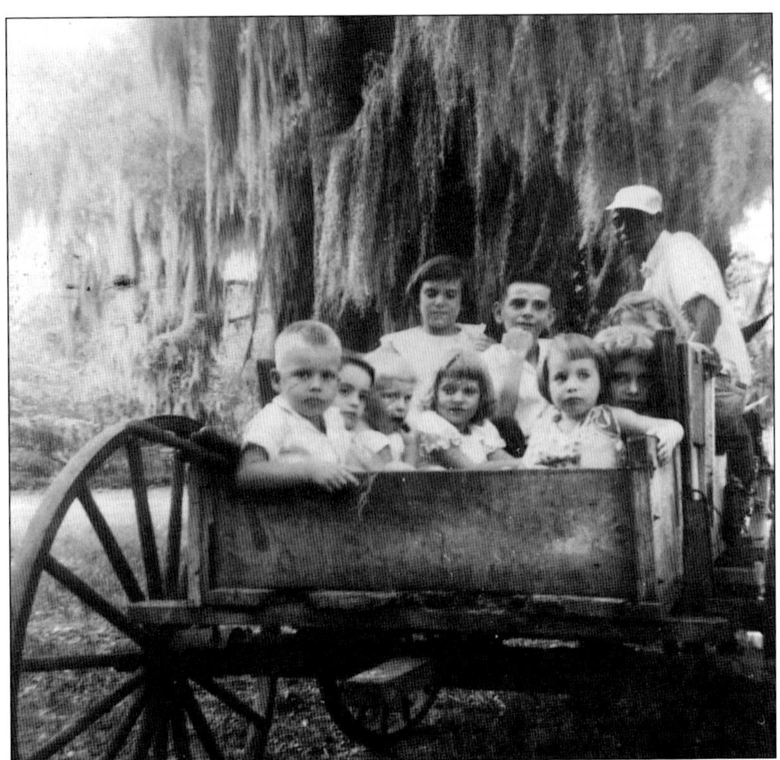

Leo "Mossa" Anderson was well known to all in Mandarin, as he owned a large piece of property at Loretto Road and State Road 13. He had a large and productive garden and was hired by many to plow gardens throughout Mandarin. Many in Mandarin, Black and White, speak of Anderson giving them a ride in his wagon. In this case, he was taking a group of children to Miss Aggie's store for a party in the 1950s.

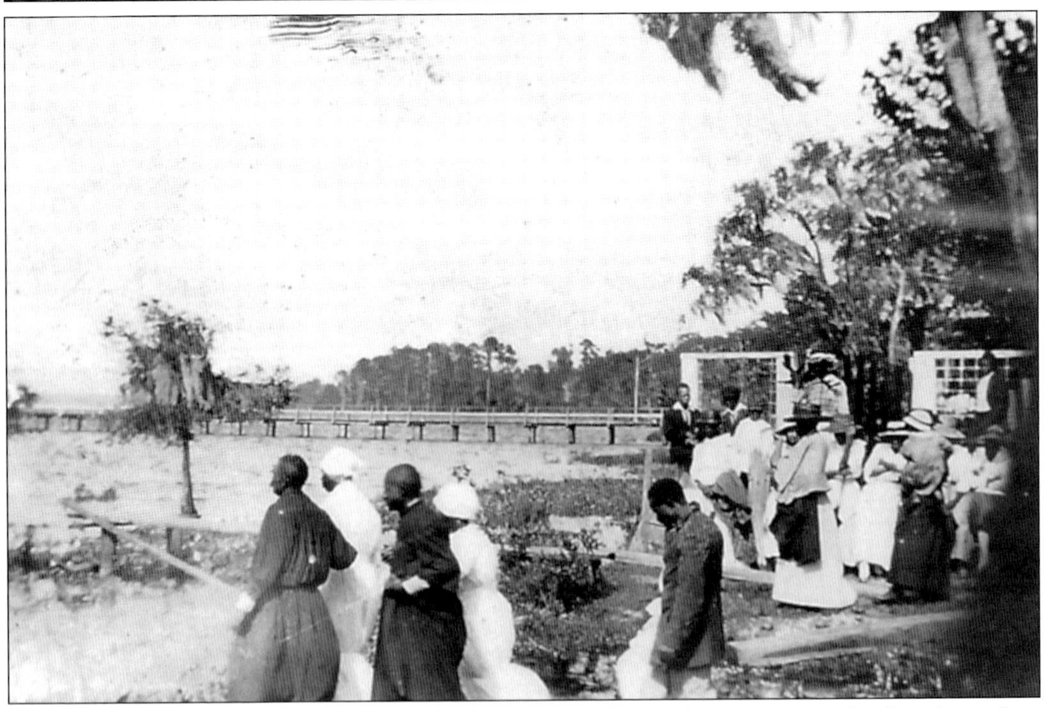

Outdoor baptisms were once very common among African Americans in the South, and in Mandarin, they would take place along the St. Johns River. Eventually, churches would be built, but even then, occasional outdoor baptisms might still occur.

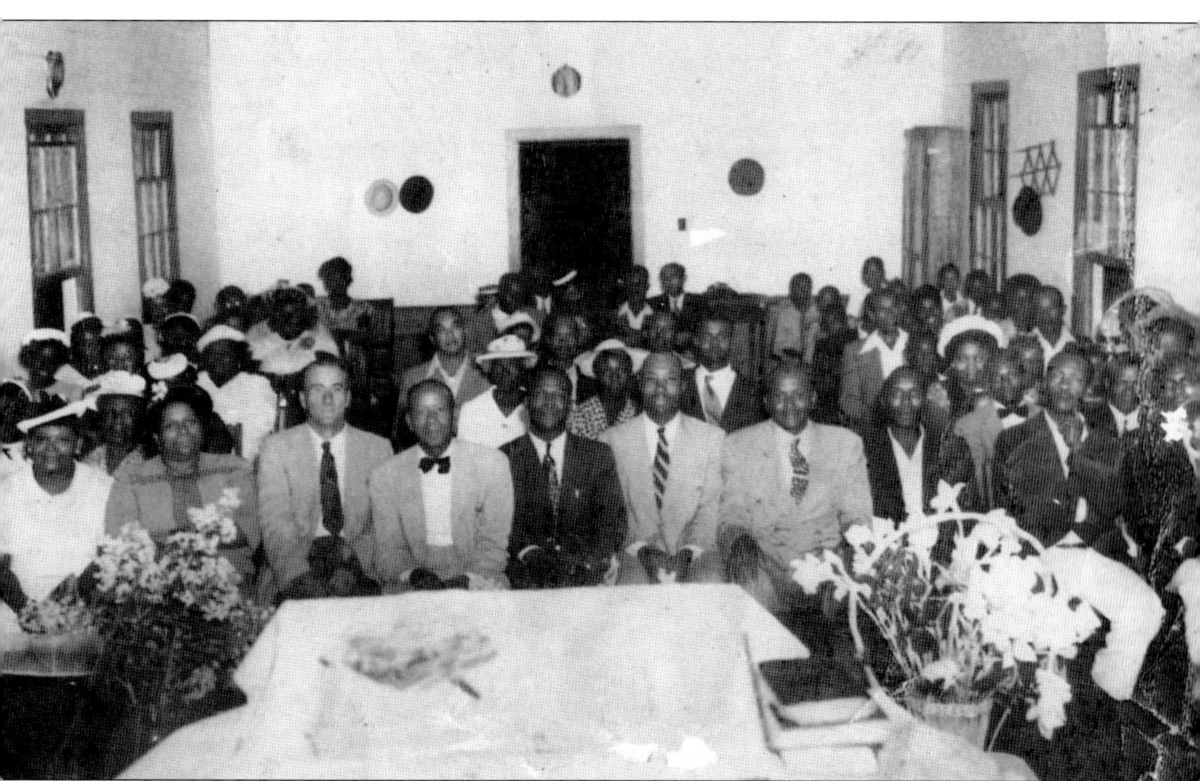

In the late 1800s, congregations began to spring up across the landscape. Three of those first churches are still active today, including the First Baptist Church of Mandarin. It began by meeting in the woods under a lean-to. The photograph is inside their early sanctuary located on State Road 13. Today, this large congregation is named Hopewell and has been led by Rev. Gary Williams for over 30 years. (Courtesy of Yvonne Monroe.)

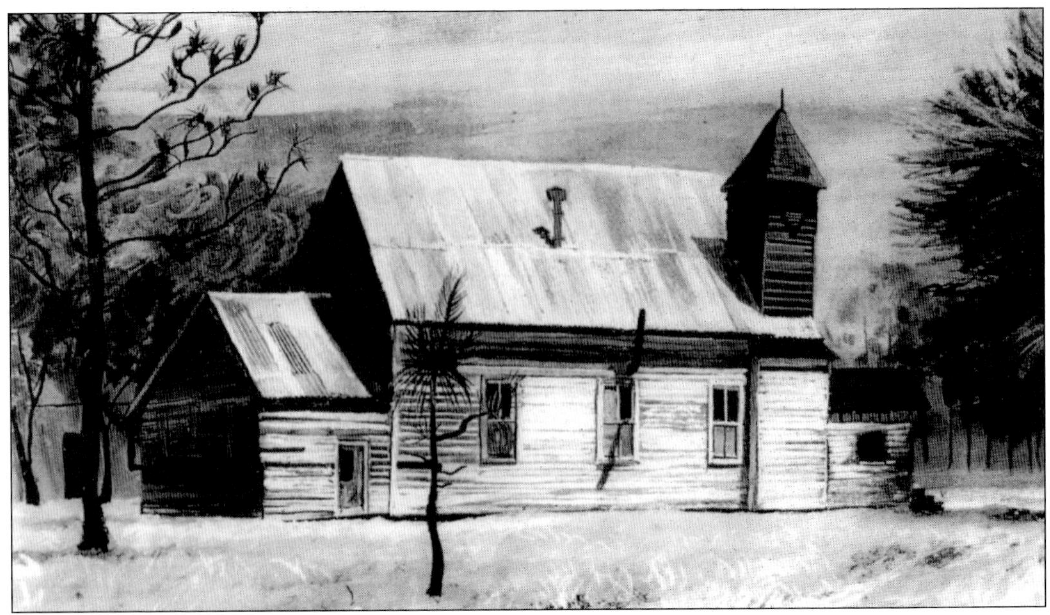

Mount Zion American Methodist Episcopal (AME) Church began in the 1870s on property that is now on Orange Pickers Road. In 1990, Mt. Zion merged with Julington Creek's Mount Pleasant AME to become Philip R. Cousin AME Church. Rev. Eugene Mosely, a Mandarin native, was the pastor of this congregation for over 25 years. This church continues to serve the community in the same place of its founding.

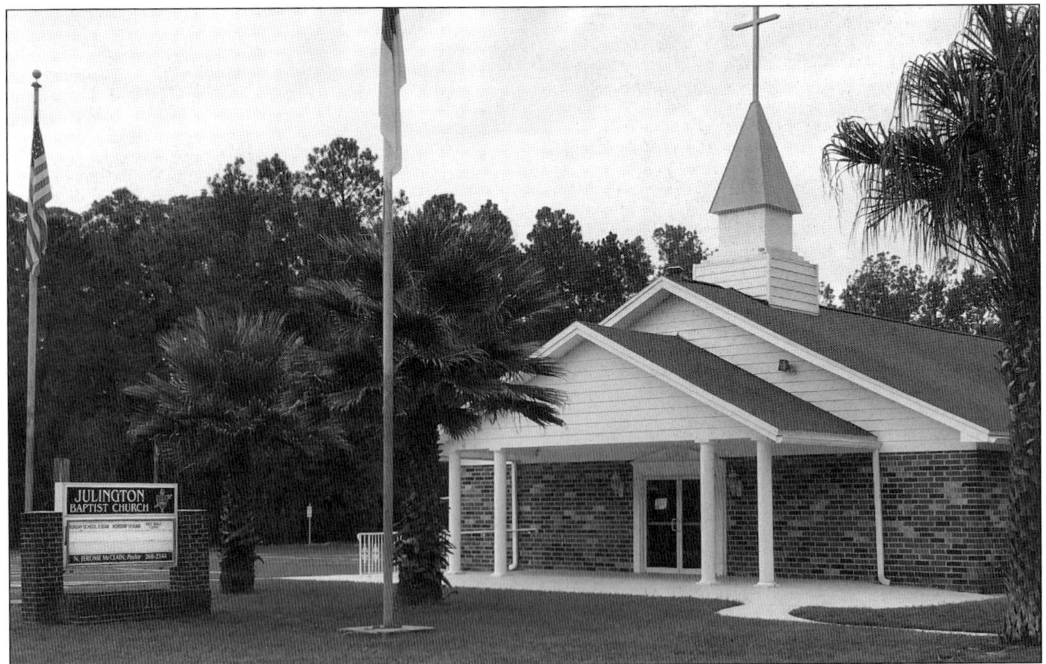

Julington Baptist Church was founded in 1872 by Rev. John B. Green and newly freed people who migrated from Edisto Island, South Carolina, to the Loretto area. The community that was formed on St. Augustine Road was also called Edisto, and it brought Gullah Geechee culture to the area. In 1986, the church was relocated to Bayard (as seen here), where it remains very active.

Education was extremely important. The Freedmen's Bureau and Harriet Beecher Stowe started a school on the peninsula and the Sisters of St. Joseph also opened a school for Black children in Loretto. Public schools began to be built in the area, including in Mandarin, Edisto, Bayard, Greenland, and Sunbeam. Rufus Payne, a resident of the Greenland area, was the first supervisor of Negro Schools in Duval County in 1928. An elementary school is named for him.

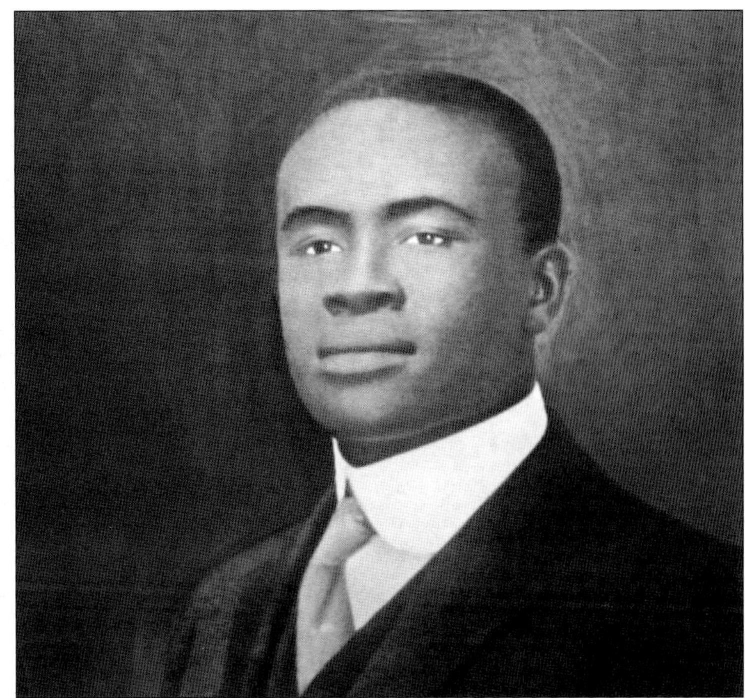

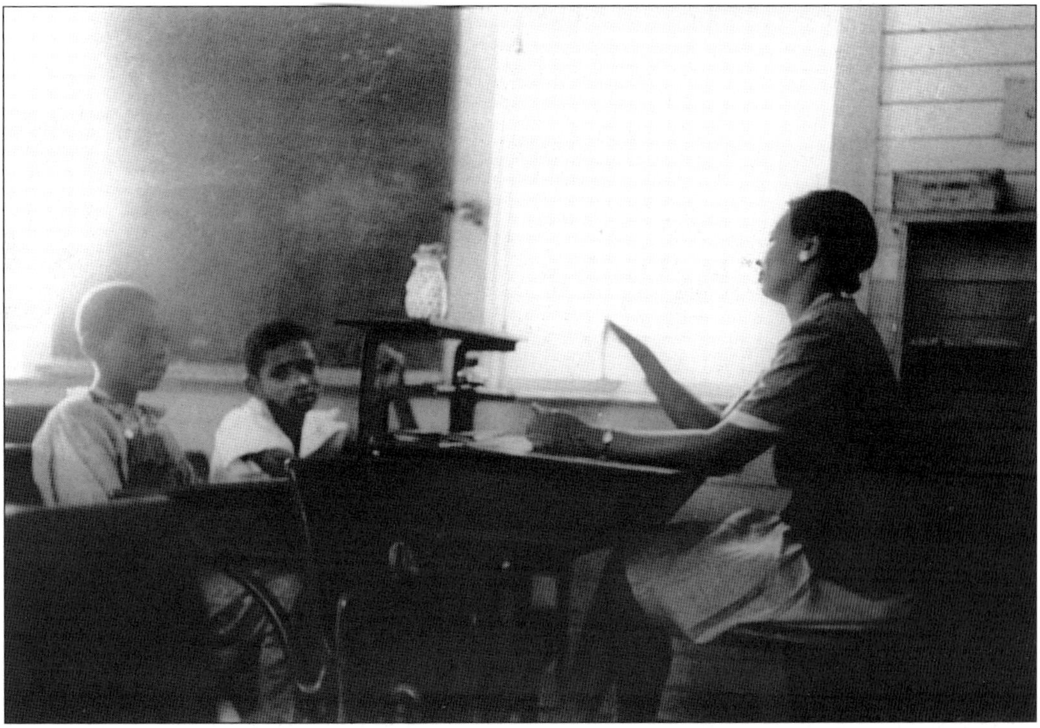

Florida Holmes Cook was a Loretto area native who attended the Mandarin Graded School on Orange Pickers Road as a child. She went on to become a teacher, taught at this same school (seen here) from 1937–1952 and later at several other schools within the Duval County school systems until she retired in 1975. Other teachers at this school were Mabel Johnson and a Mrs. Foster.

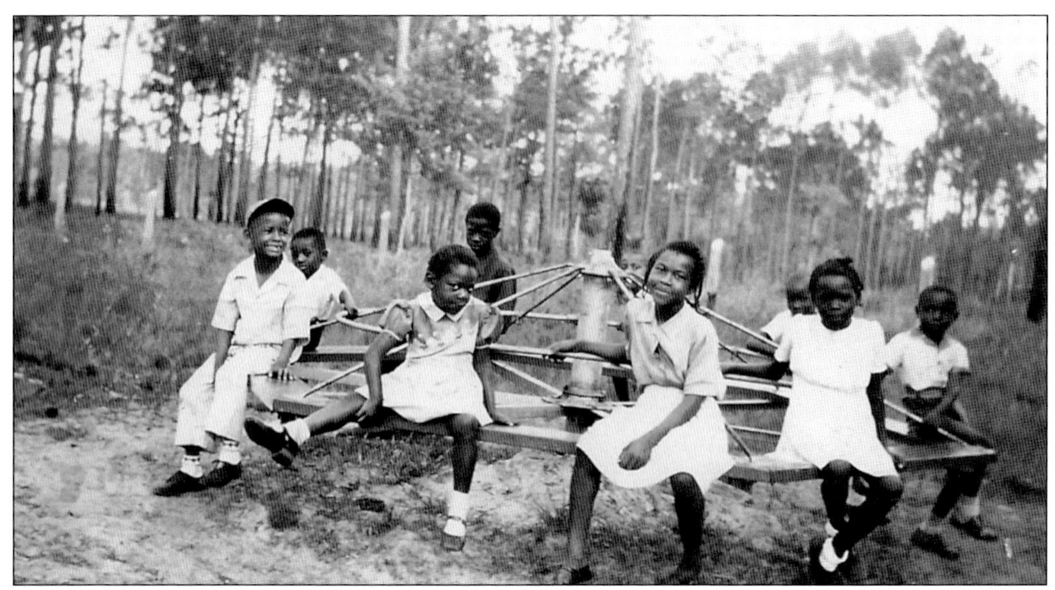

These unidentified children enjoyed the very popular merry-go-round at the Mandarin Graded School, which was located next to the Mt. Zion AME Church on Orange Pickers Road. (Courtesy of Ridgely Cook.)

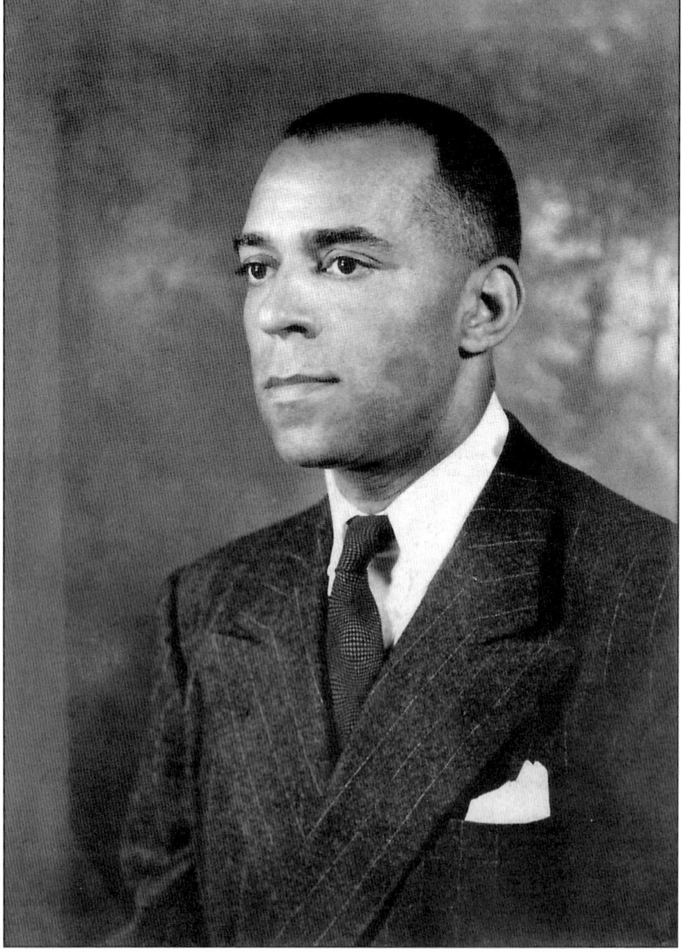

Richard H. Cook II was from Massachusetts but came to Jacksonville to teach history at Edward Waters University. It was there that he met Florida Holmes, whom he married in 1939. He was also assigned to Mandarin Graded School as the assistant principal. He served a long career as a principal within the Duval County systems. (Courtesy of Ridgely Cook.)

Schools in Duval County were segregated until 1967. At some point, the community schools closed and all the Black children in the Mandarin attended the Douglas Anderson School from first grade to ninth and eventually through high school. Herbert Burney attended the Mandarin Graded School in 1941 and reached graduation from the eighth grade.

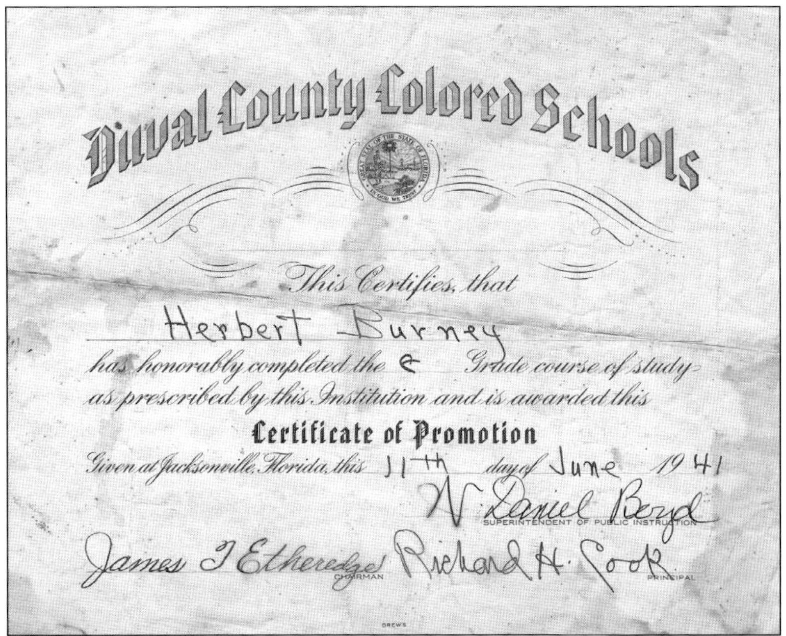

Duval County Colored Schools

This Certifies, that

Herbert Burney

has honorably completed the 8 Grade course of study as prescribed by this Institution and is awarded this

Certificate of Promotion

Given at Jacksonville, Florida, this 11th day of June 1941

N. Daniel Boyd
SUPERINTENDENT OF PUBLIC INSTRUCTION

James T. Etheredge
CHAIRMAN

Richard H. Cook
PRINCIPAL

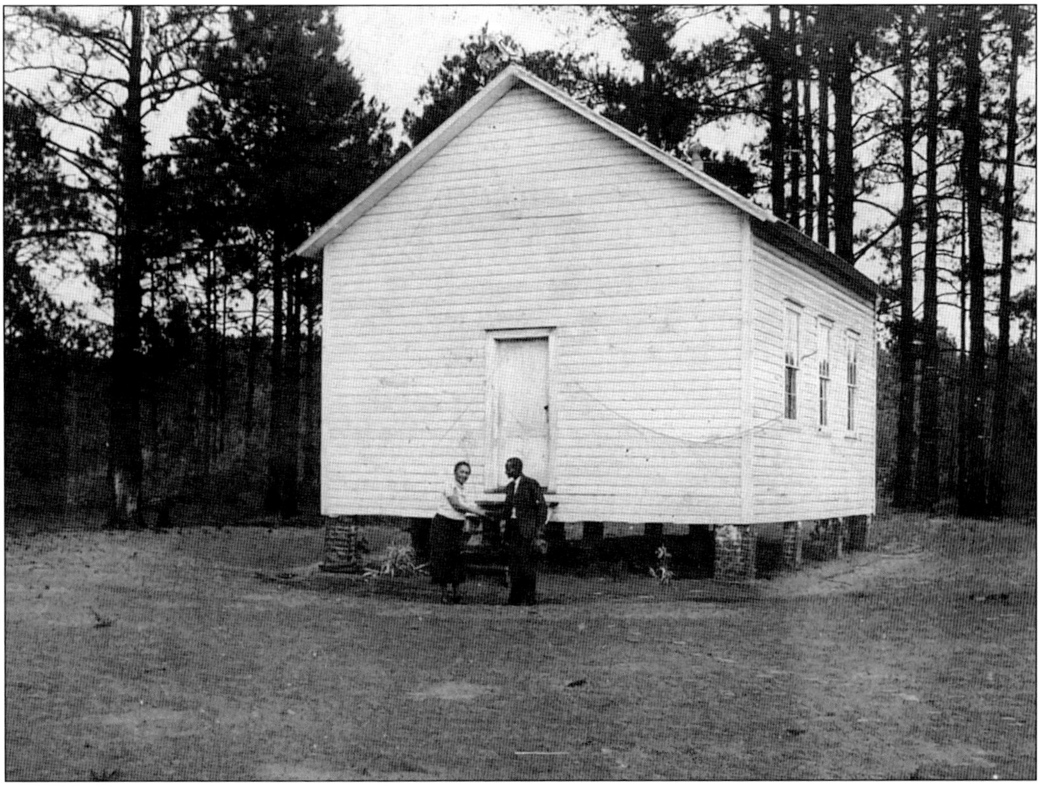

The Bayard School–Public School 126 was established in 1899 under the direction of Eartha White. She gathered the donations of land and supplies necessary to build the school and taught there for 16 years. It was demolished in 2010. White, a philanthropist and humanitarian, later founded the Eartha White Nursing Home and Clara White Mission.

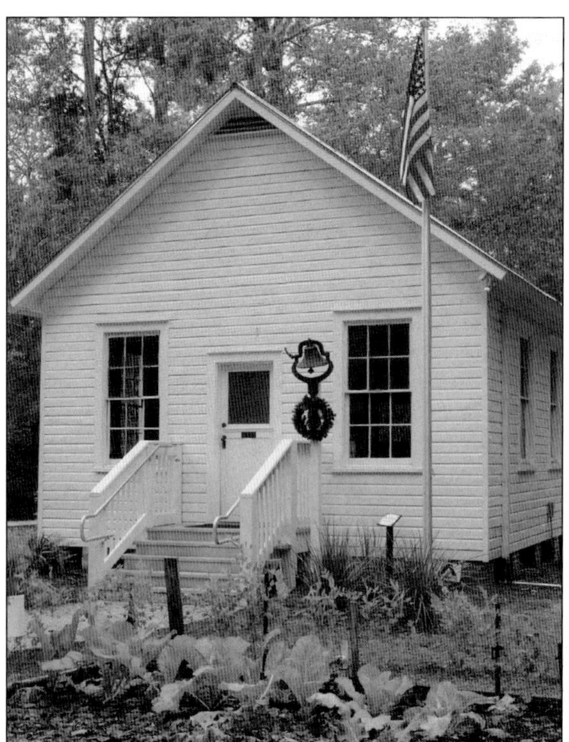

The Sisters of St. Joseph came from France in 1866 specifically to teach children who were formerly enslaved. Their first school was in St. Augustine, and their second school opened in 1868 in Mandarin. This one-room schoolhouse was built for them in 1898. In 2015, the Mandarin Museum & Historical Society, with much community support, relocated it to Walter Jones Historical Park, where it now serves as an interpretive museum.

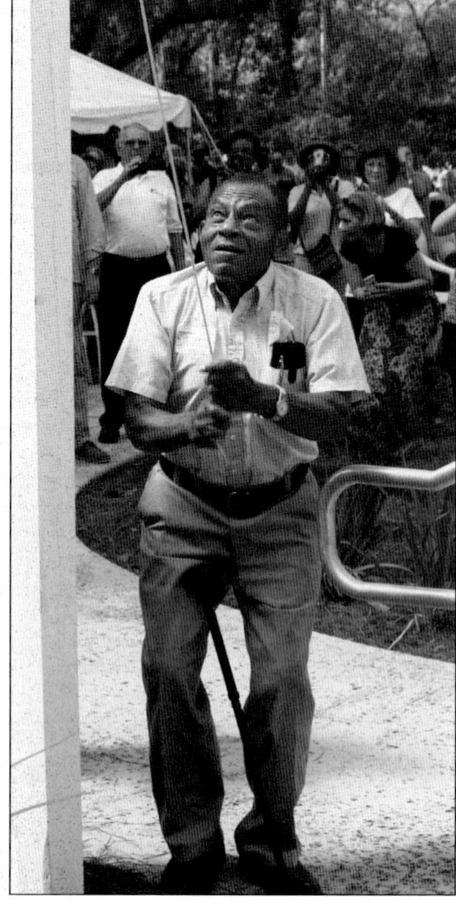

Samuel Burney rings the bell of the restored St. Joseph's Mission Schoolhouse for African American Children at the grand-opening event in 2016. He was a wonderful historian and a great friend to Mandarin Museum. Both of his parents, Julia Forrester and Richard Burney, were educated in this very schoolhouse, and he rang the bell in honor of them and all the other students who attended.

Just a few years after Samuel W. Wolfson High School was integrated, Willy L. Cody, of Mandarin, was the senior class president, a member of the Key Club, on the Bi-racial Committee and the student senate, and was listed as "Who's Who Among High School Students" in 1974. This photograph is from the Wolfson yearbook, *Rhombus*.

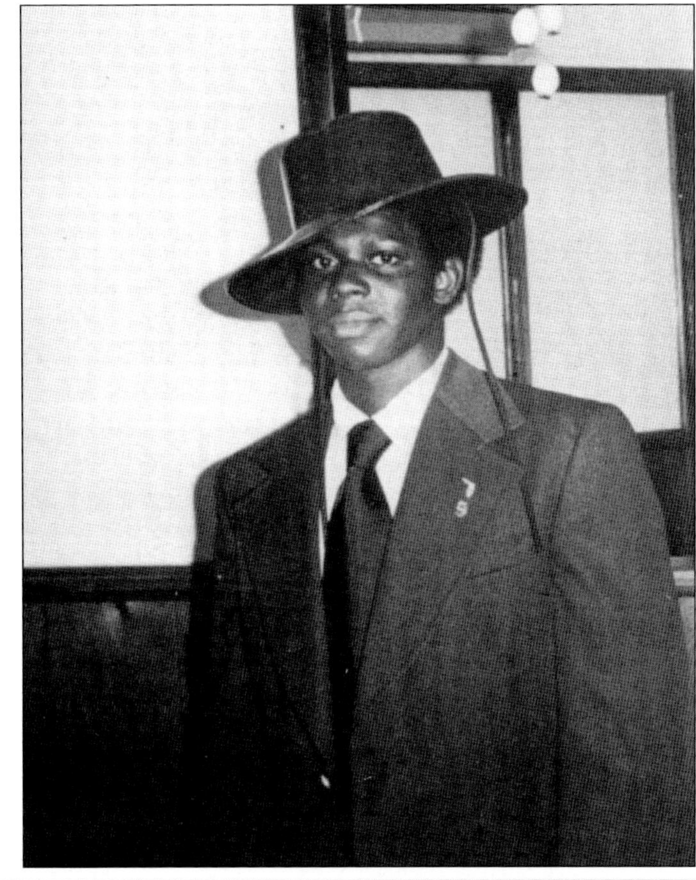

The land for the original Harriet Beecher Stowe Community Center, at the corner of State Road 13 and Orange Pickers Road, was given by philanthropist Eartha White to the Black community of Mandarin in 1938. Seen here is Mandarin native Eugene Moseley in front of the original coquina building. Moseley led the effort to build a new building in 1975, which is still in use today.

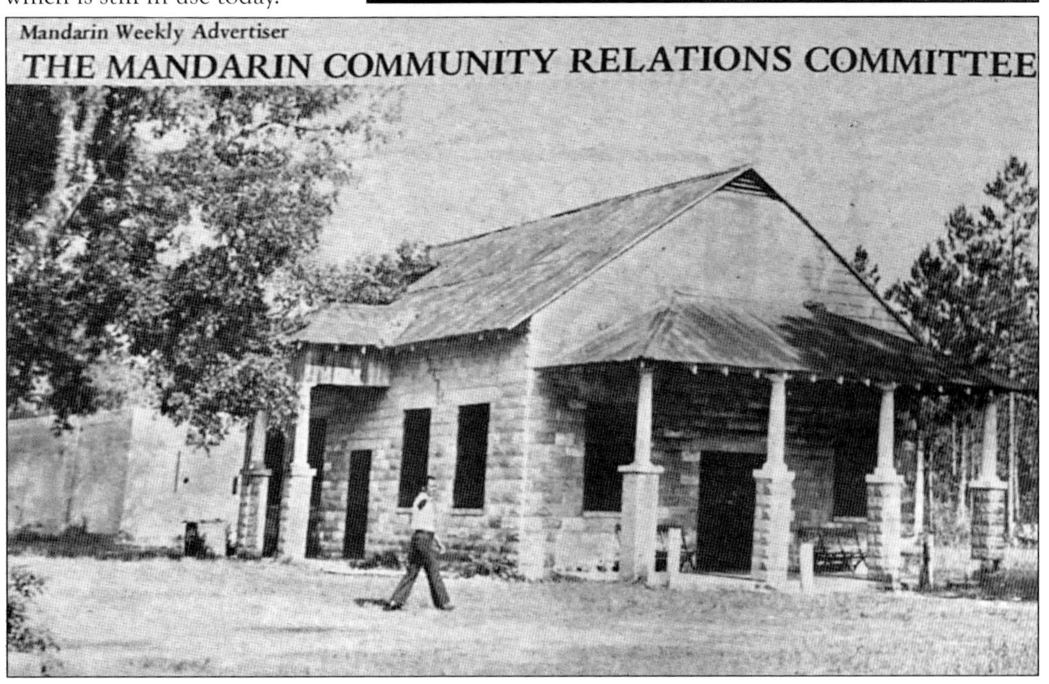

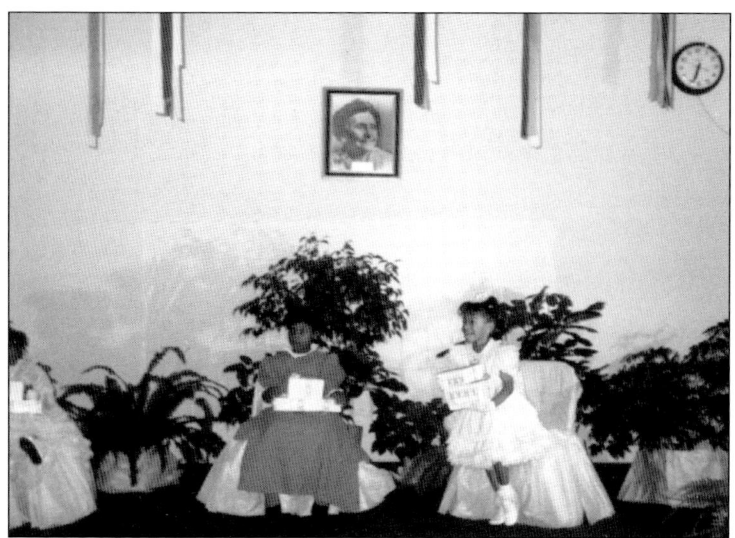

Inside the community center, a portrait of Eartha White hangs above the girls attending a special event there. The center hosted BBQs, parties, dances, contests, special events, a well baby clinic, and music lessons. At one time, it was the center of community life along with the churches. Miss White was known to come to the center herself for Christmas parties, bringing goodies to the children. (Courtesy of Yvonne Monroe.)

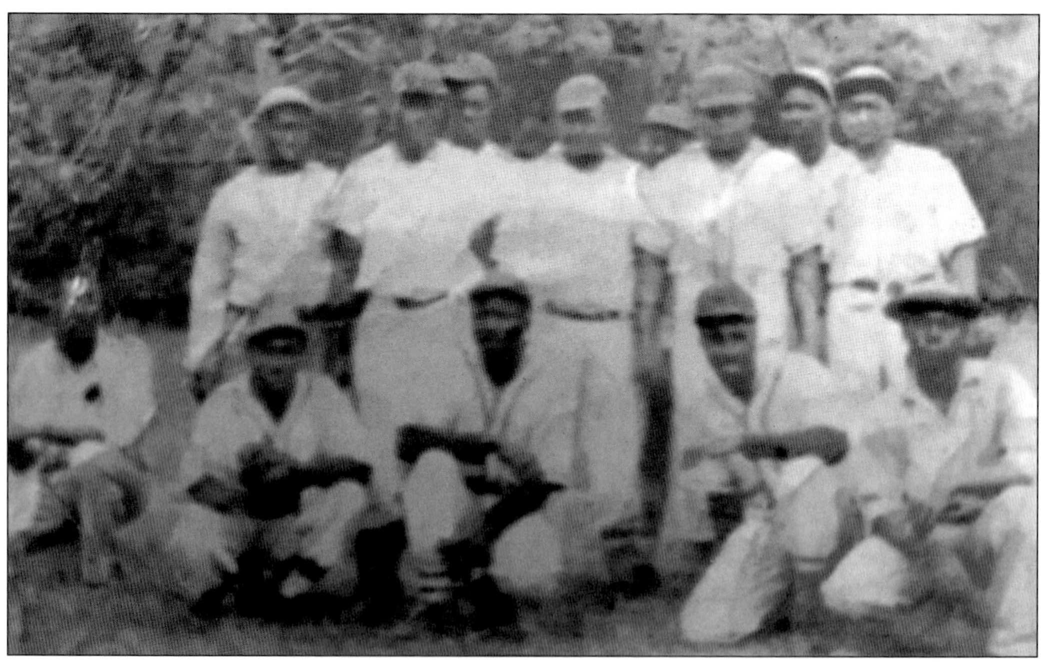

Baseball was another important activity. This team was called "the Ball Team" and is from the late 1940s. Due to segregation, Black teams played Black teams. Their field was off Brady Road. Pictured from left to right are (first row) two unidentified players, Clyde Hartley, unidentified, and Walter Forrester; (second row) Freddie Jackson, Chester Forrester, Emory Howard, Joe Davis, and Alphonso Burney; (third row) unidentified players. (Courtesy of Helen Forrester Walker.)

The Mandarin Raiders in the early 1970s was coached by David Monroe. Their field on Orange Pickers Road was just called "the park" but is now Walter Anderson Memorial Park. From left to right are (first row) Ervin Robinson Sr., Ervin Robinson Jr., and Purnell Robinson; (second row) Johnny Hartley, Chris Summerall, and Lester Hartley; (third row) Cleveland Hartley, Craig Mobley, Jeffrey Hartley, and Rodney Hartley. (Courtesy of LaTonnette Robinson.)

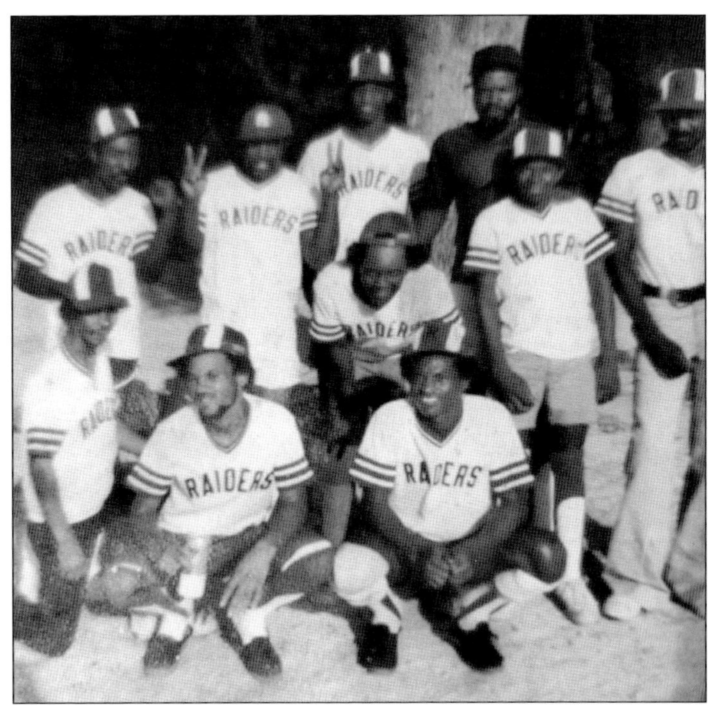

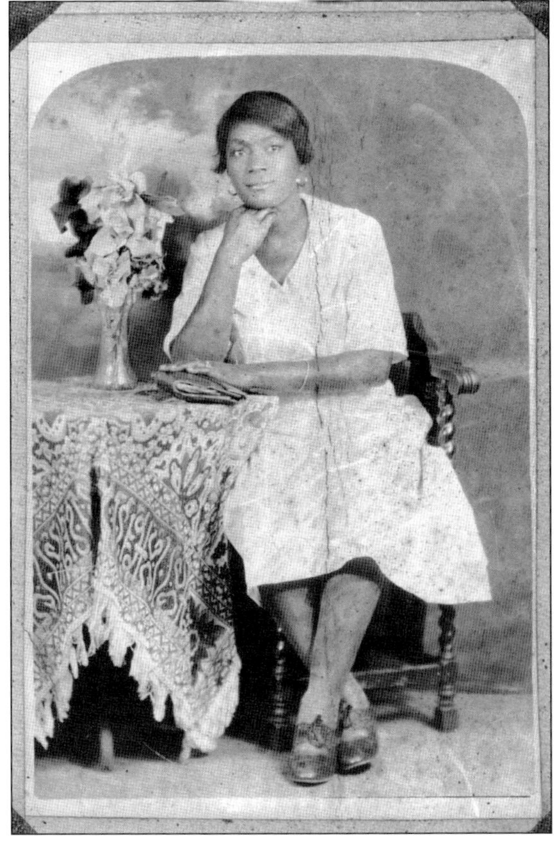

Lena Anderson (1895–1974) was married to Leo Anderson (1892–1974). She was very active at the First Baptist Church of Mandarin, running Anderson's Place, a confectionery and general store, and managing the Harriet Beecher Stowe Community Center for many years. (Courtesy of Yvonne Monroe.)

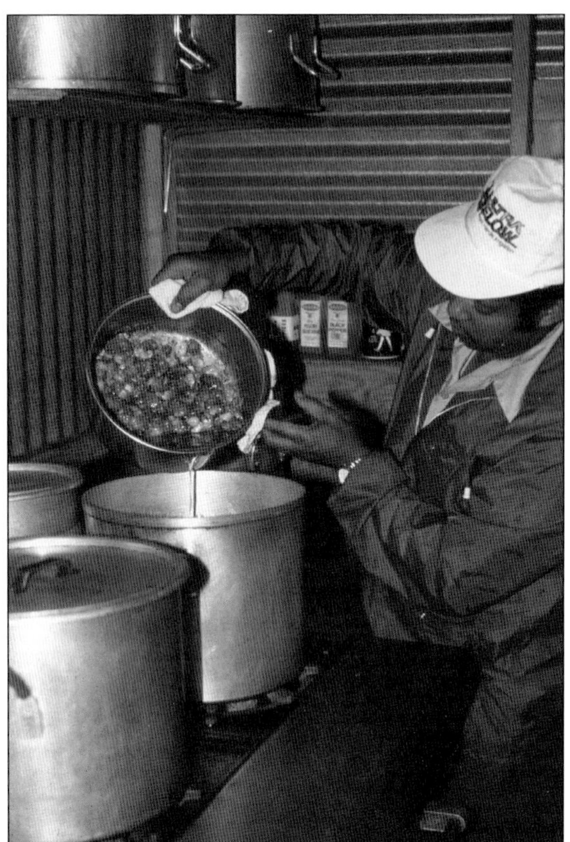

In this same area, on the west side of State Road 13, was Hiram's BBQ, run by Hiram Jenkins Sr. and Jr. Their specialties were all kinds of BBQ as well as greens and perlou. Jenkins Jr. was interviewed for the Duval County Folk Arts in Education Project in 1988. (Photograph by Gregory Hanson, courtesy of the State Archives of Florida.)

Located on Westberry Road, Lofton Cemetery has interred generations of Mandarin families. Two acres of land for the cemetery were deeded in 1899 to the trustees of African American churches in Mandarin: Mt. Zion African Methodist Episcopal (AME) Church, First Baptist Church of Mandarin, and Mount Pleasant AME Church. This included the adjoining lot known as "the Old Graveyard Lot," indicating the existence of a cemetery prior to 1899.

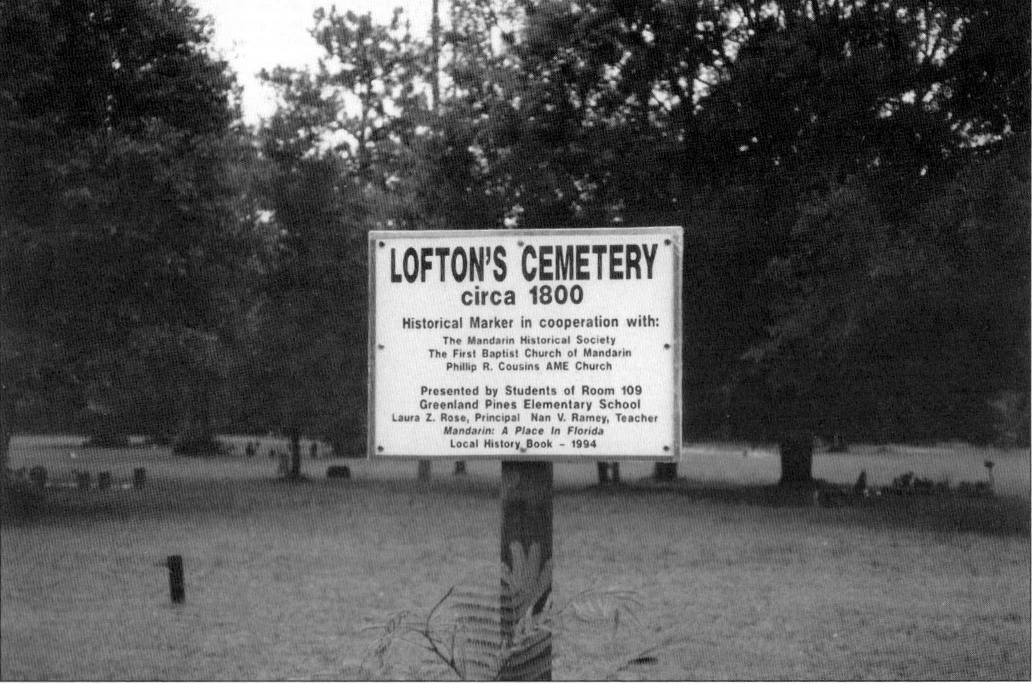

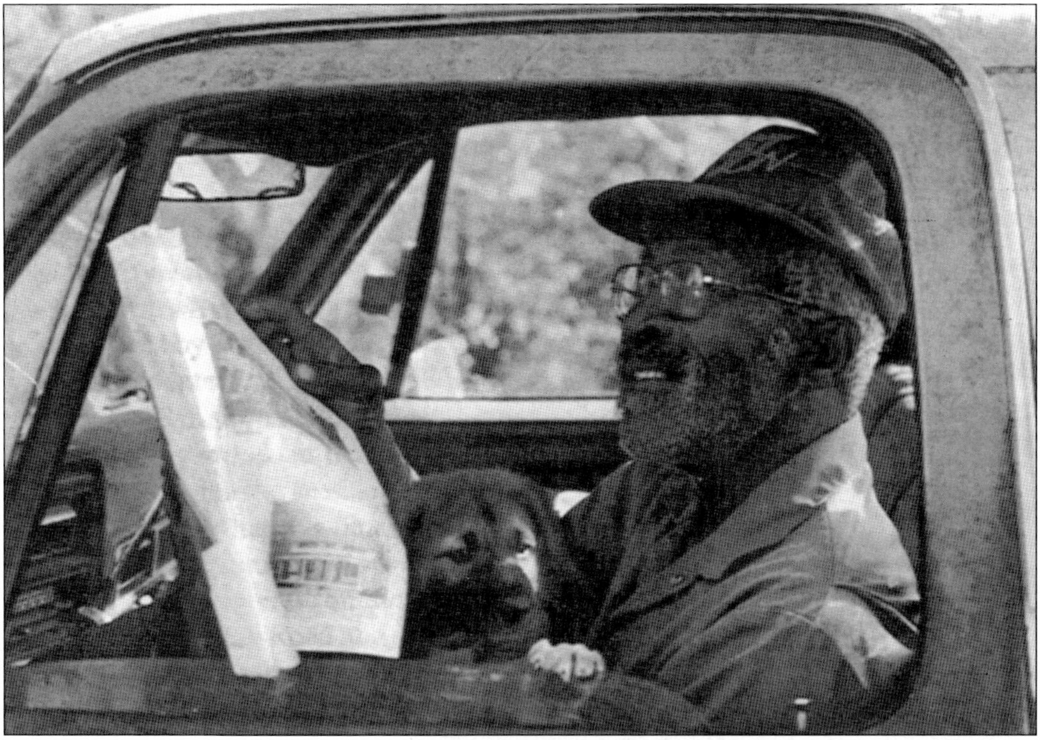

One of the most prominent citizens was Walter Anderson (1922–2009), son of Leo and Lena Anderson. He was a native of Mandarin, a veteran of World War II, a civil servant of the US Postal Service, an entrepreneur, and a large landowner. He was known for his generosity to members of the community, always lending a hand when someone needed it.

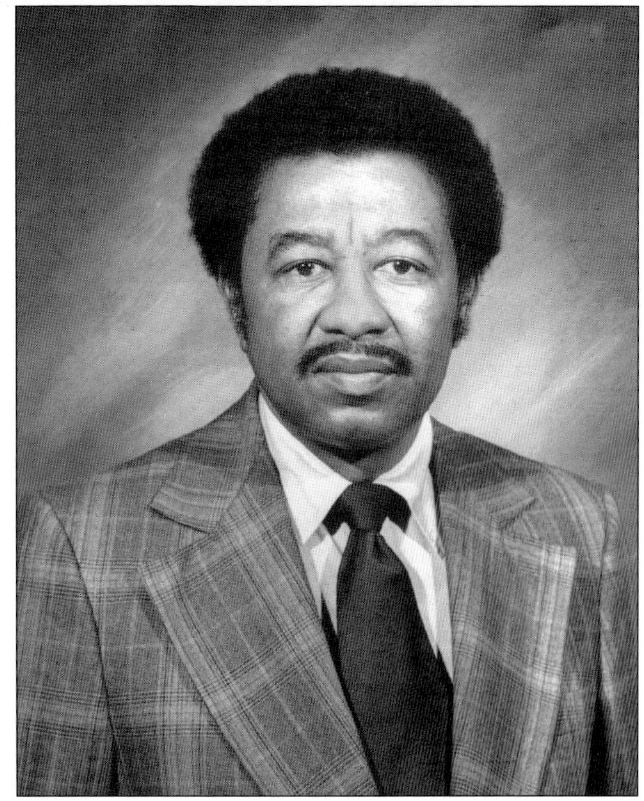

Earl M. Johnson lived on Scott Mill Road, where he hosted a meeting with Martin Luther King in 1964. He was an attorney and chief legal counsel for the Jacksonville, NAACP during the Civil Rights era. He was the first Black person to serve on the Consolidated City Council, serving for 15 years, and was elected in 2019 to the Florida Civil Rights Hall of Fame. (Courtesy of City of Jacksonville.)

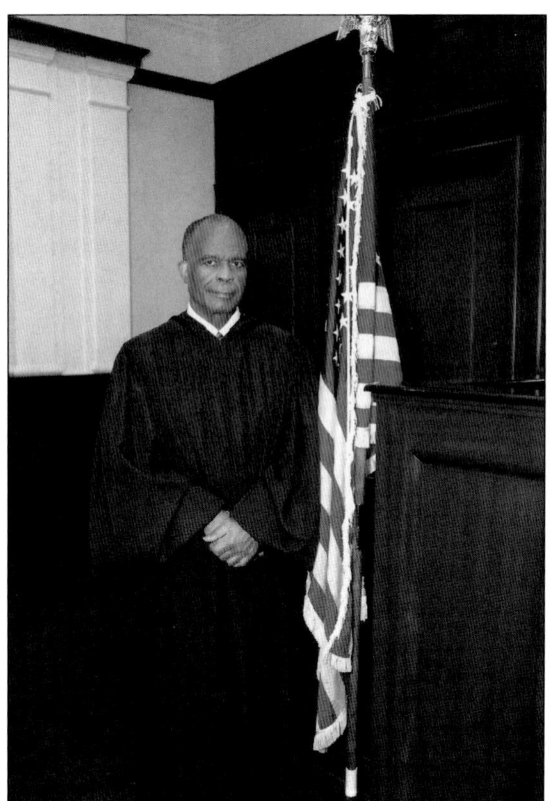

Henry E. Davis is a longtime resident of Mandarin. After serving as a naval officer, he graduated from Florida State University (FSU) Law School and was admitted to the bar in 1976. He then went on to work for the Department of Justice in Washington, DC, coming home after several years to work in private practice as an attorney. In 1992, Davis was appointed by Gov. Lawton Chiles to the office of circuit court judge, from which he is now retired. (Courtesy of Henry E. Davis.)

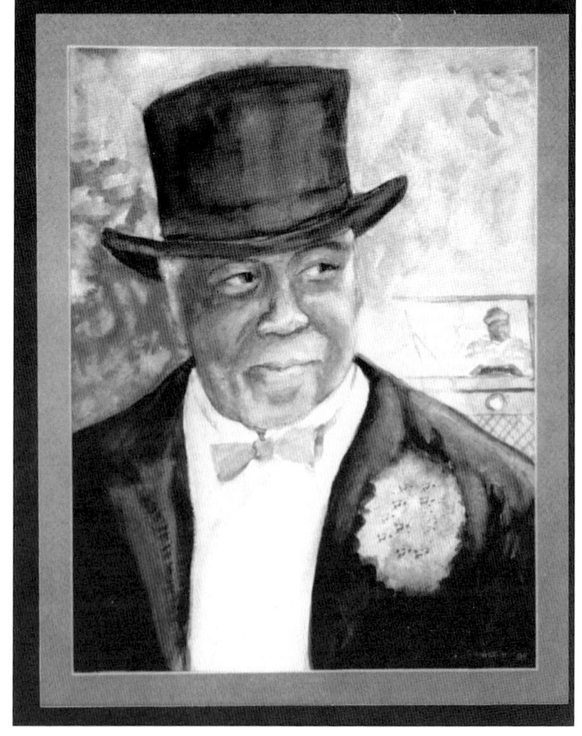

The family that produced the person (Black or White) from Mandarin who has reached the highest level of government service is the Butler/Woods family. James Butler was well known in Mandarin as a landscaper and "jack of all trades" and for working for 38 years at Wesley Manor, assisting and transporting residents around the property. This painting reflects his presence at the celebration of his faithful service to that community. (Courtesy of Gwen Butler.)

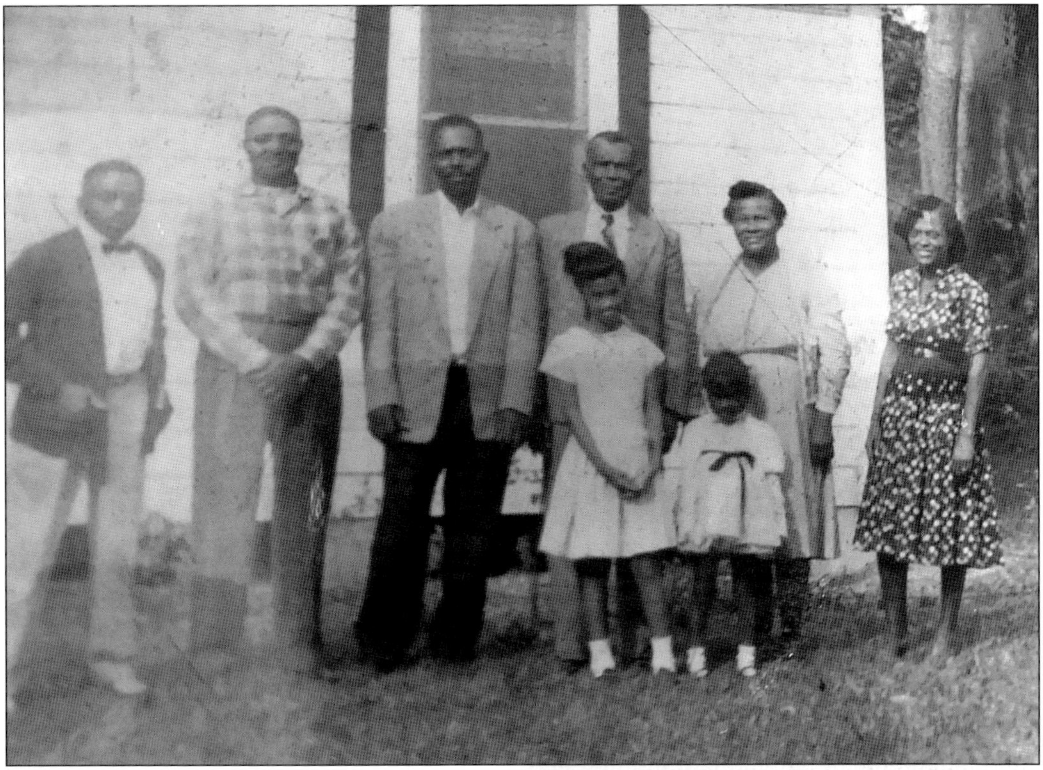

Many of the Woods family members are seen, from left to right (first row) Gwen Butler, Valdez Butler; (second row) Phillip Woods, Leroy Woods, Edgar Woods, Frank Woods, Pernella Woods, and Elouise Woods Butler. Elouise and James Butler worked hard and raised seven children in the country on Brady Road. One of their children grew up to serve in the US Congress. (Courtesy of Gwen Butler.)

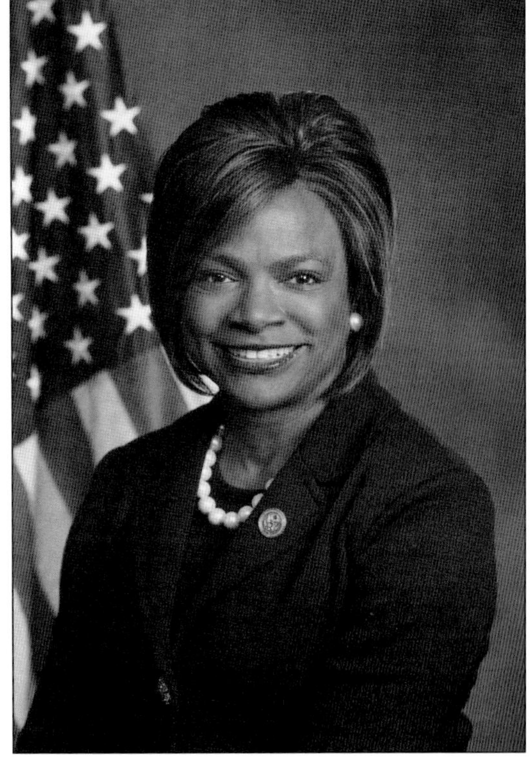

Valdez Butler Demings graduated from Wolfson High School in 1975 and Florida State University in 1979 with a criminology degree. She worked as a social worker and later got a master's degree in public administration and served the Orlando Police Department for 27 years as an officer and as chief of police. In 2017, Rep. Valdez Demings was sworn into the US House of Representatives representing Florida's 10th congressional district.

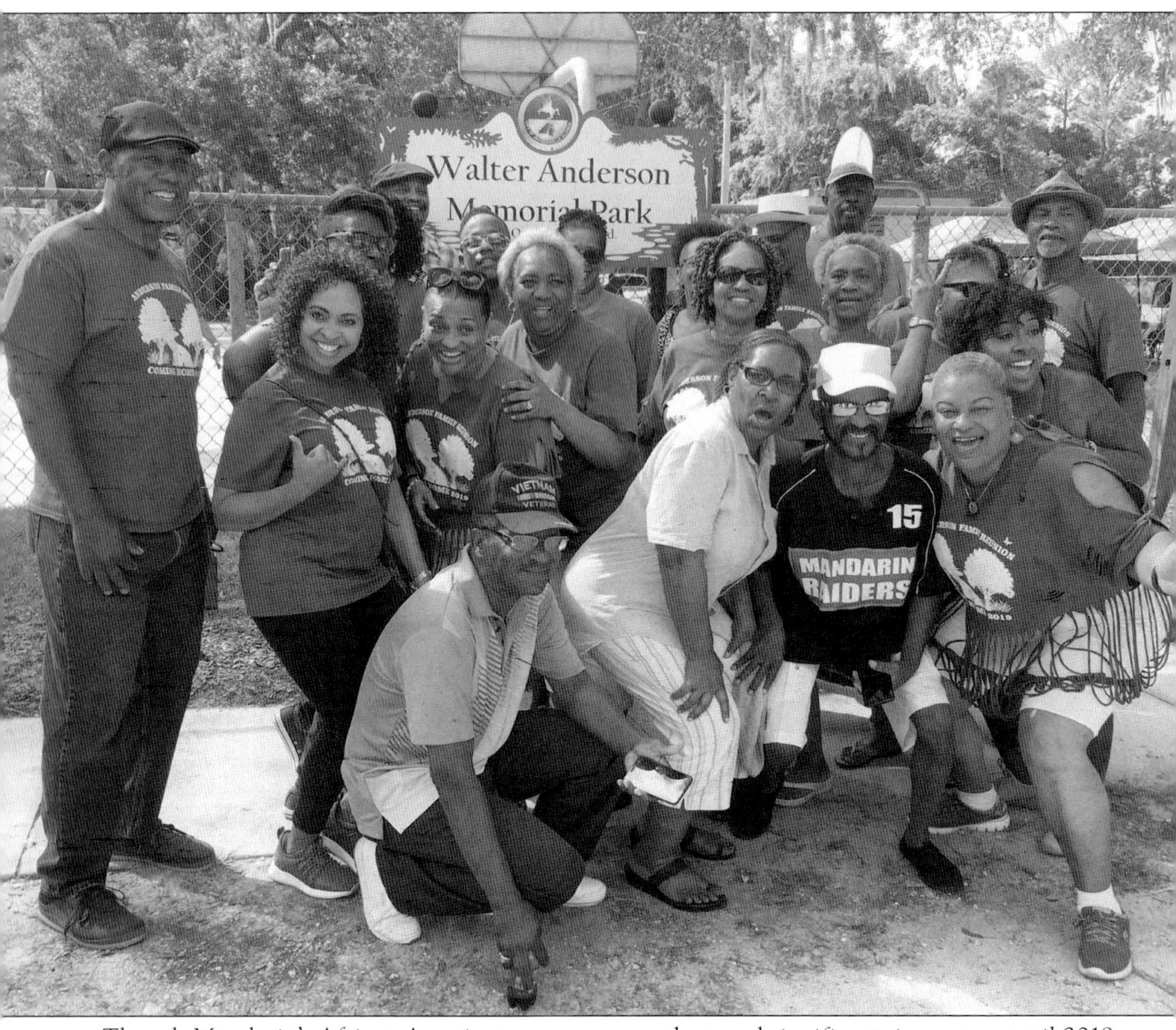

Though Mandarin's African American roots are very deep and significant, it was not until 2019 that a public space in Mandarin was finally named for a Black citizen. The City of Jacksonville owned a four-acre park on Orange Pickers Road that had been given to Duval County in 1955 by Walter Anderson for $1—with the stipulation that it be used as a park for Black citizens. Especially, it would be a place for Black athletes to play baseball. The park had various names over the years, and the Anderson family initiated a campaign to rename it after the man who made it possible. City councilman Michael Boylan made the renaming of the park his first piece of legislation and the entire city council co-sponsored the bill and voted unanimously for the park to be renamed Walter Anderson Memorial Park. Seen here are various Anderson/Monroe family members, celebrating the unveiling of the new sign.

Six

Community Life

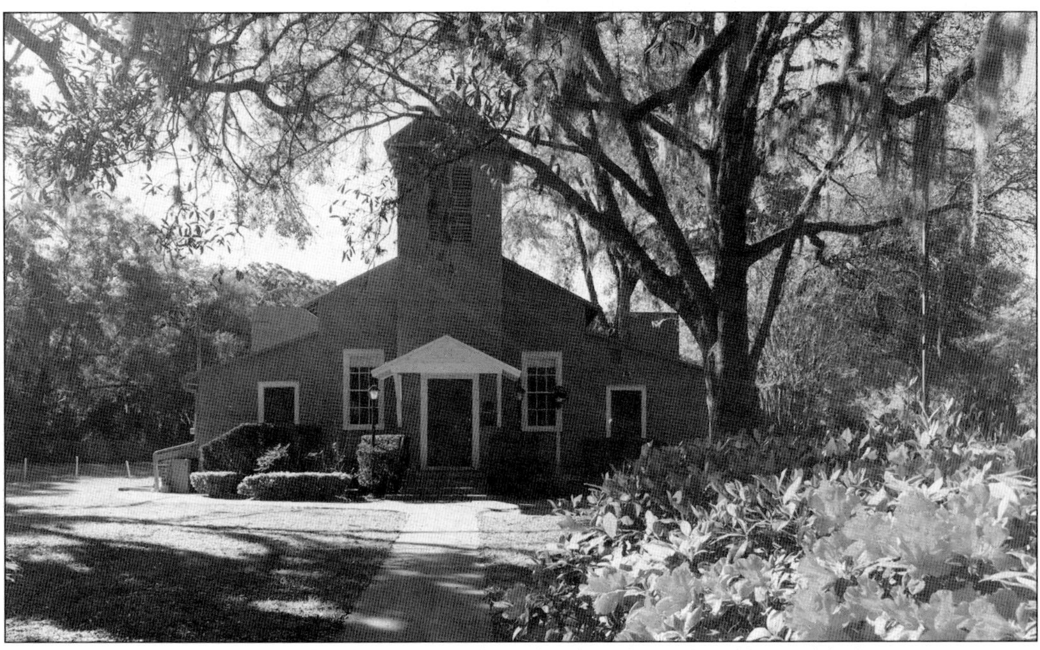

One of the centers of community life for Mandarin has long been the oldest public historic structure: the Mandarin Community Club. The building was originally erected in 1872 and served as the Mandarin School. It also served as a worship space for citizens until the Church of Our Saviour was built. During World War I, it housed the local Liberty League activities and after the Mandarin Community Club was established in 1923, the building became the club's home. It continues to serve Mandarin's community today as an independent nonprofit organization.

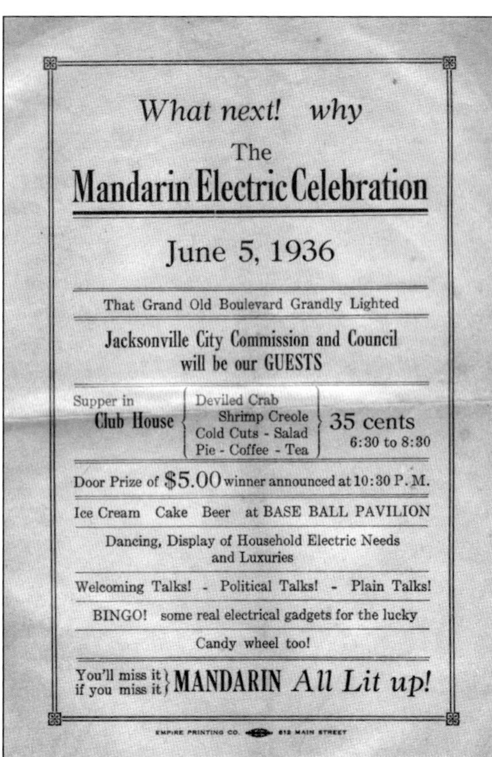

What next! why

The

Mandarin Electric Celebration

June 5, 1936

That Grand Old Boulevard Grandly Lighted

Jacksonville City Commission and Council will be our GUESTS

Supper in **Club House** { Deviled Crab, Shrimp Creole, Cold Cuts - Salad, Pie - Coffee - Tea } 35 cents 6:30 to 8:30

Door Prize of $5.00 winner announced at 10:30 P.M.

Ice Cream Cake Beer at BASE BALL PAVILION

Dancing, Display of Household Electric Needs and Luxuries

Welcoming Talks! - Political Talks! - Plain Talks!

BINGO! some real electrical gadgets for the lucky

Candy wheel too!

You'll miss it if you miss it } MANDARIN *All Lit up!*

EMPIRE PRINTING CO. 612 MAIN STREET

One of the goals of the community club was to get electricity to Mandarin. Since Mandarin was rural, residents lived without electricity until 1936. To celebrate this big event, the live oak trees along Mandarin Road were lighted with strands of light bulbs and a happy celebration ensued along the "Grand Old Boulevard." However, the service did not immediately cover all of Mandarin, leaving many residents to wait even longer for lights.

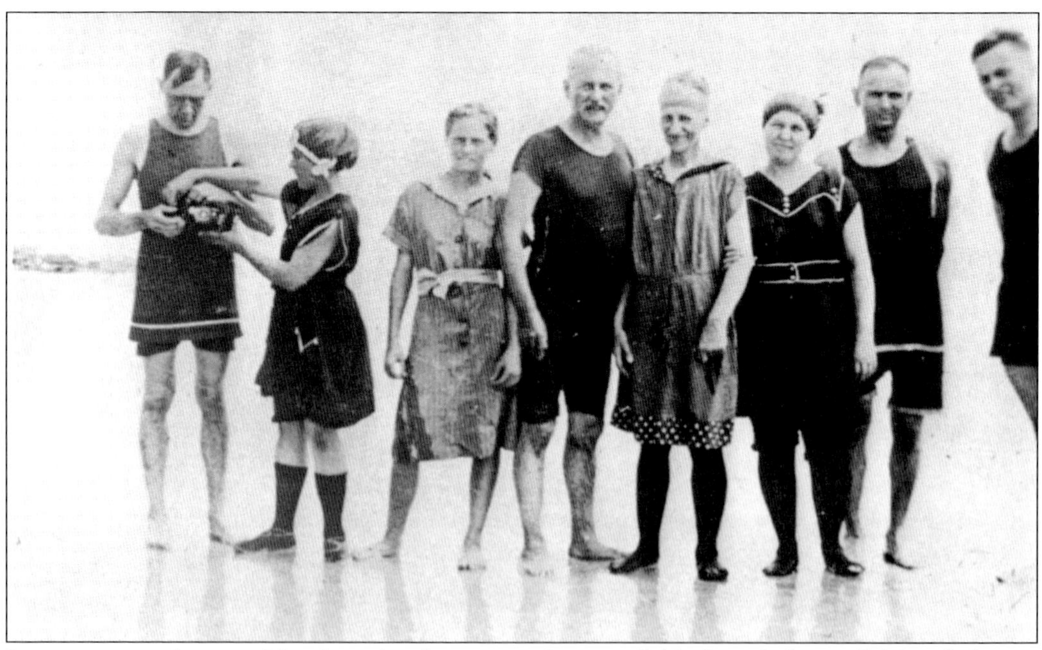

It was common for some Mandarin families to spend time at Pablo (now Jacksonville) Beach during the summer, despite the long trip. Here, the Walter Jones family and friends are seen in the 1920s, from left to right, two unidentified persons, Mabel Jones, Walter Jones, Edith Mary Jones, Agnes Jones, and two unidentified men. At that time, there were no direct routes from Mandarin to the beaches like there are today and the roads were poor.

This photograph was identified as the 1917 "Girls Basketball" team. They are having fun in the St. Johns River, but little is known about them, and none are identified. Perhaps they are celebrating a win. (Courtesy of Anne Morrow.)

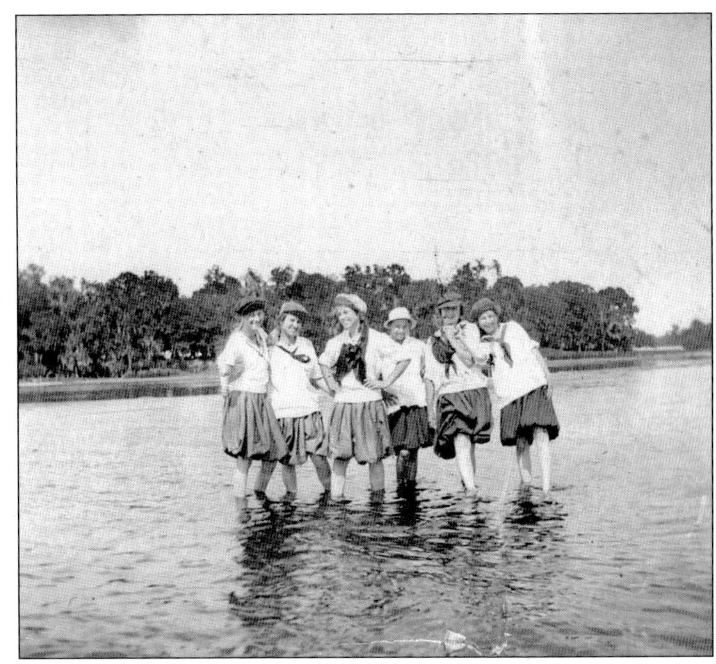

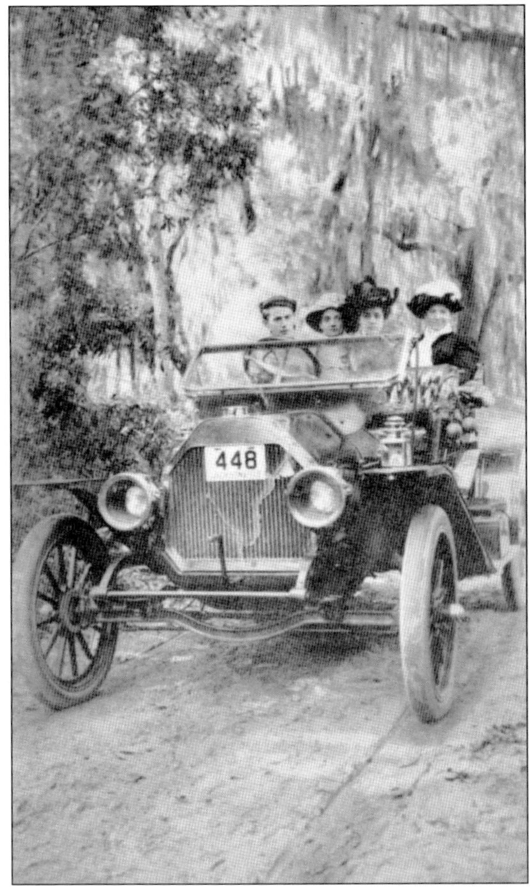

In the early 20th century, Mandarin residents were excited that the roads were hardened enough with oyster shells to actually move from horses to automobiles as a new mode of transportation. This change also heralded the beginning of the end of the steamboat era, which had been so vital to Mandarin residents.

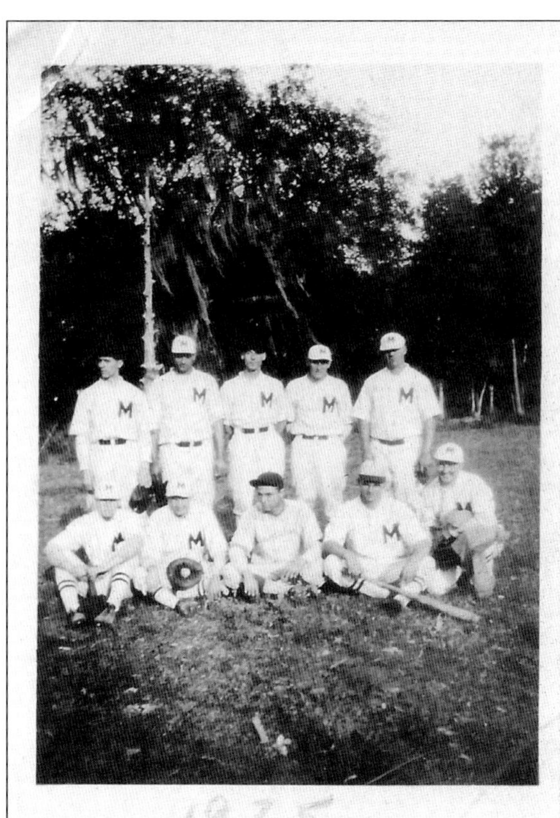

The Mandarin Orange Pickers provided baseball fun from 1925 until 1956. They played Jacksonville area teams on the grounds of the Mandarin Community Club and later at Alberts Field. People from the community came out on Sundays to sit in the bleachers, eat a picnic lunch, watch them play, and honk their horns as runs scored. It was fun for everyone, especially when the team won, which was often. In 1949, they won the North Florida Championship.

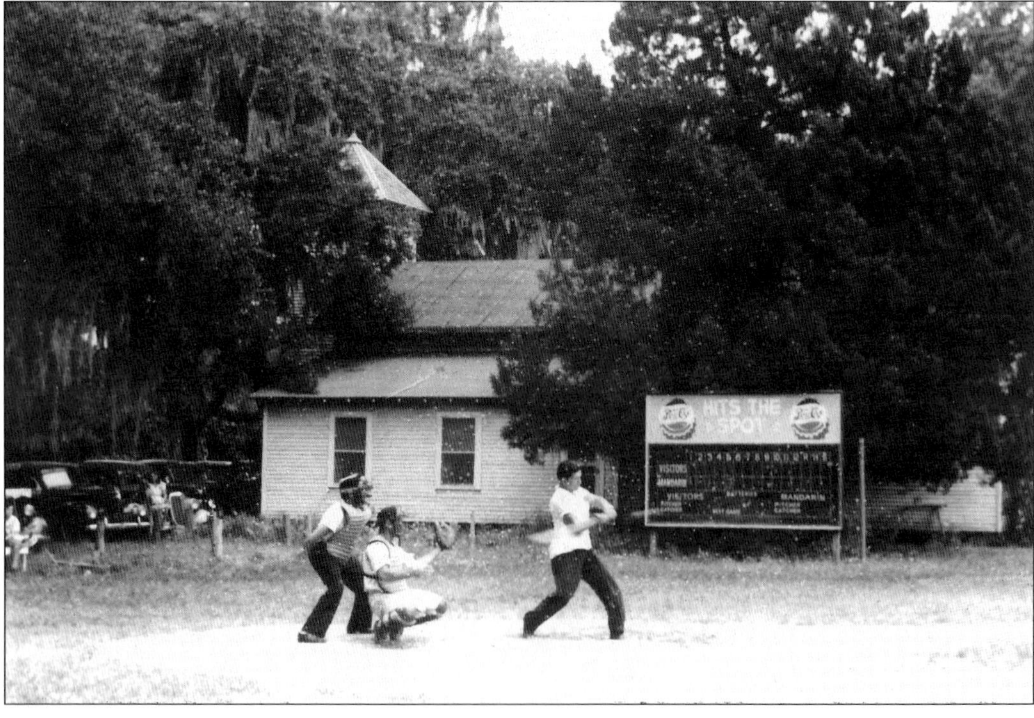

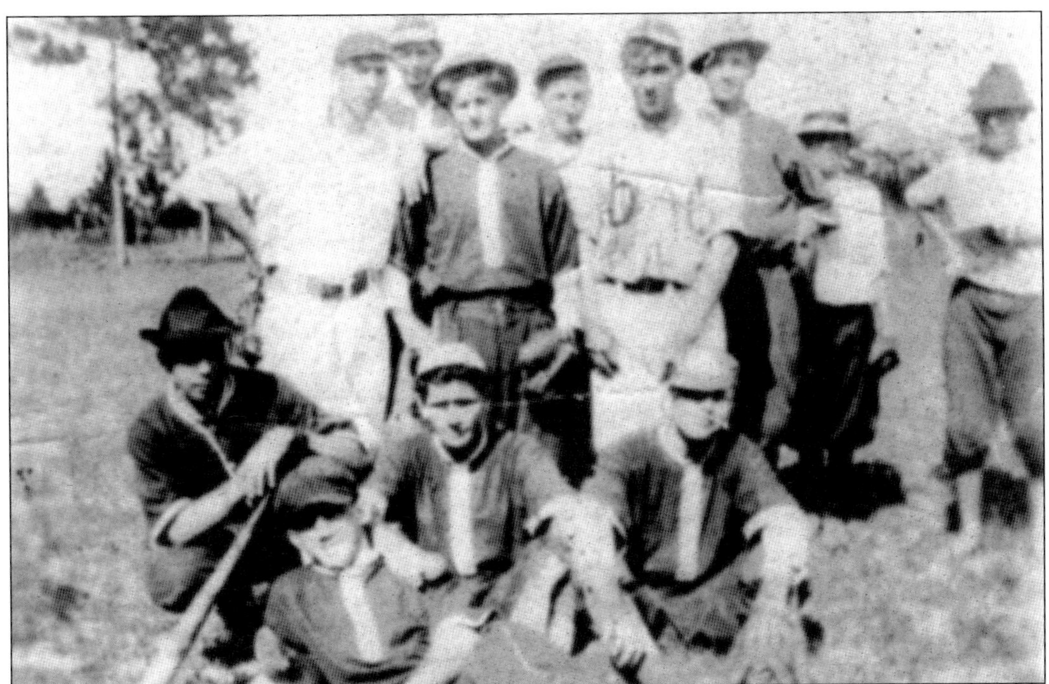

The Loretto community had a softball team, but we know little about them. The man in the middle with "DAD" written on his shirt is Tom Wilson; the rest are unidentified. (Courtesy of Tom "Tommy" Wilson.)

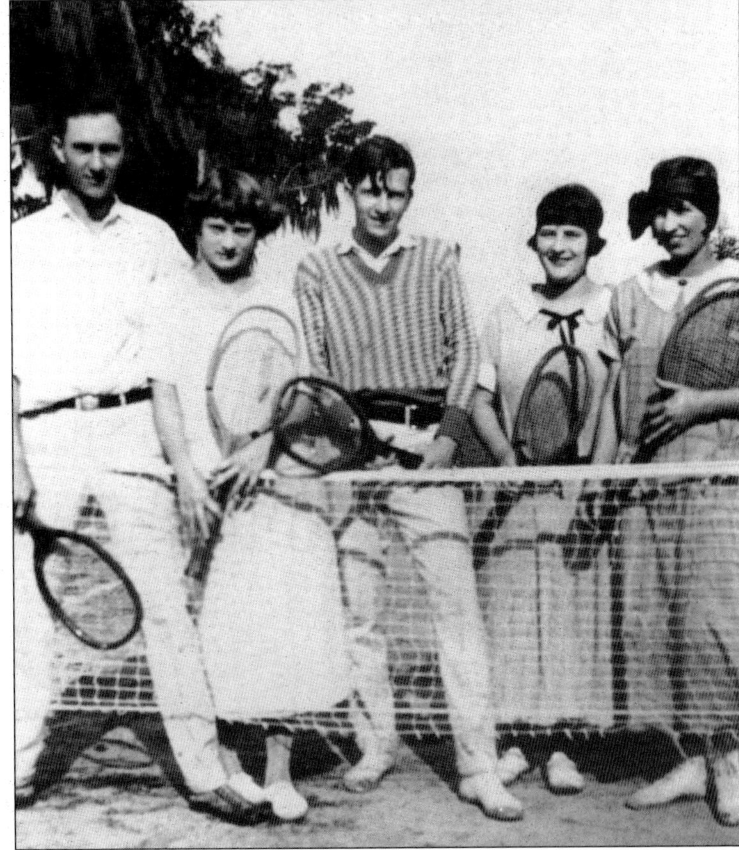

The Walter Jones family had a tennis court built in front of their home that was used by friends and neighbors who would drop by. At times, they kept a score sheet and had very serious tournaments. But mostly, it was a social group of Mandarinites enjoying the game. Identified here in 1925 are Charlie Brown in the middle and Aggie Jones, second from right; the rest are unidentified.

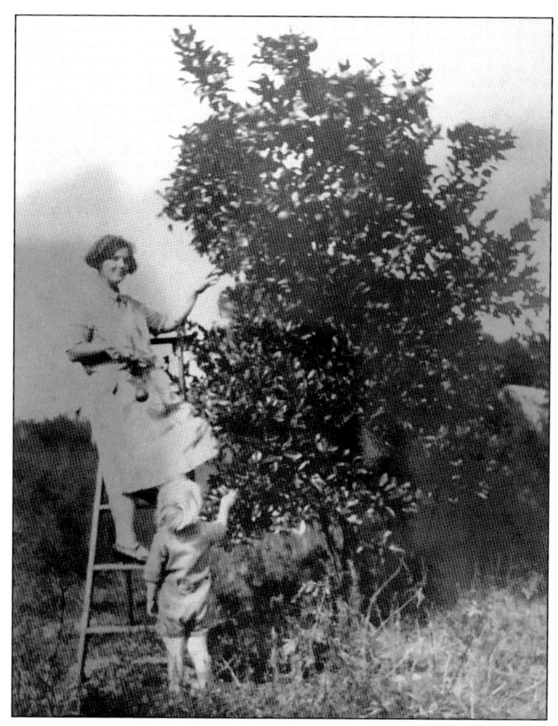

Grace Victoria Hartley is pictured with her son Eugene McDonald around 1923. After the great freezes of the 1890s, the citrus industry greatly decreased. However, there were still some nice groves in Mandarin that sold to the public and many that had backyard groves for their own use. Mandarin was known as a place to get citrus until the 1980s. (Courtesy of Martita McDonald Scheibe.)

The Mandarin Garden Club was established in 1945 at the Mandarin Community Club. Later, they met in people's homes, and in this photograph, the club is holding a flower show at the Athletic Club at Alberts Field in 1953. Finally, in 1967, the club opened its own building on Loretto Road. The Garden Club's primary goal is beautifying Mandarin. The Athletic Club also hosted dances, live music, and other special events. (Courtesy of Annie Morris.)

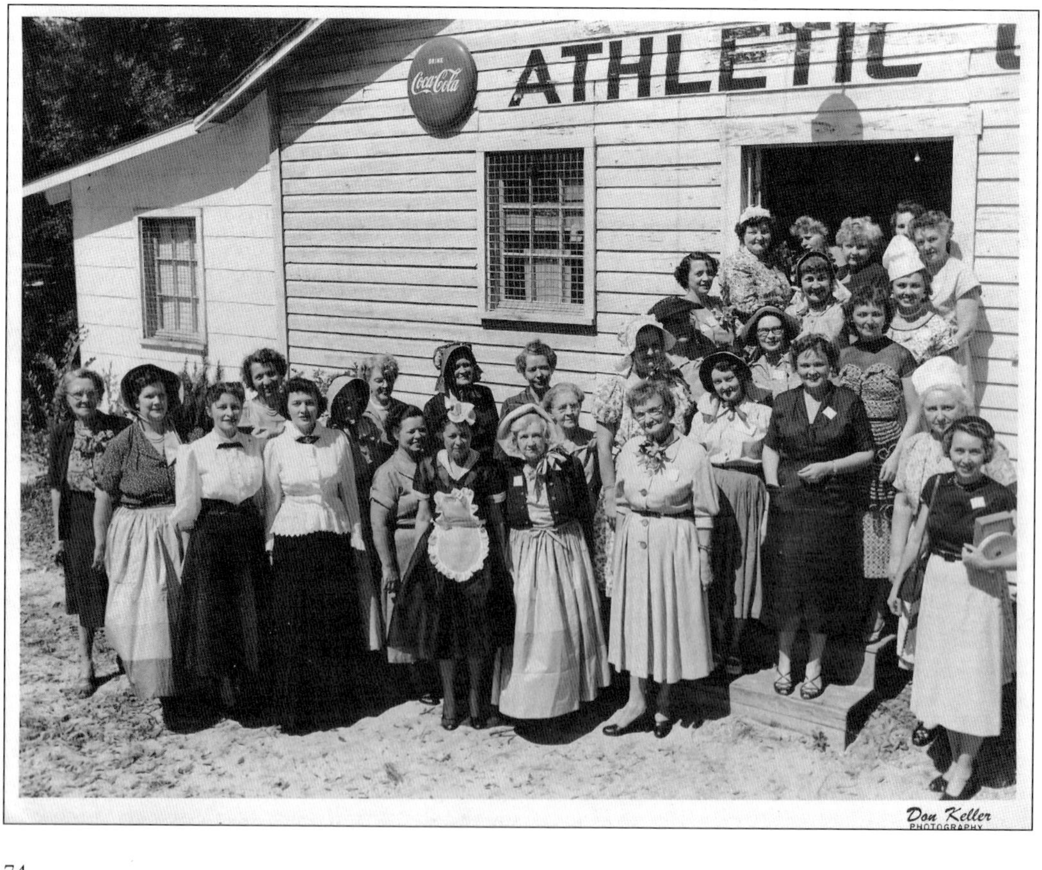

Following in the footsteps of the Mandarin Amateur Drama Association of the 1870s, the Mandarin Players, sponsored by the Mandarin Community Club, started a volunteer theater group in 1949, with Roy Meischner as the first director, followed by Anna Marie Wilford. A new stage was built at the club, and it served the players and several other groups offering local theater for many years. This 1954 play was called *The Cheerful Idiot*.

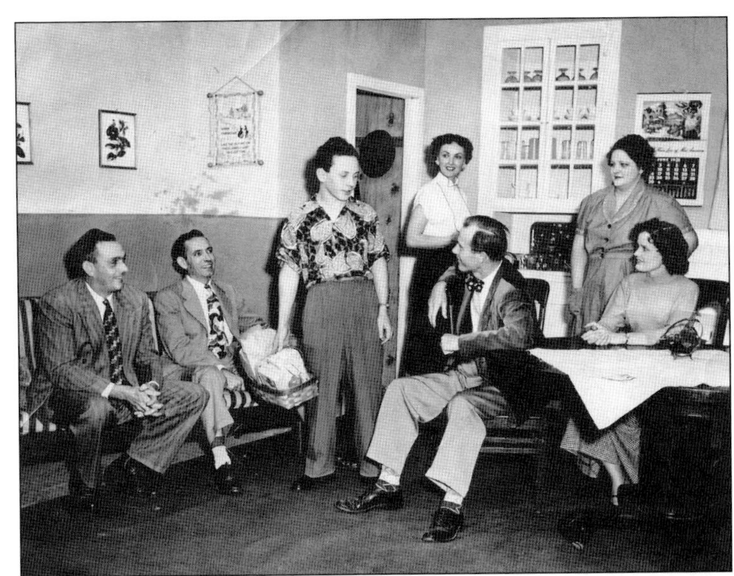

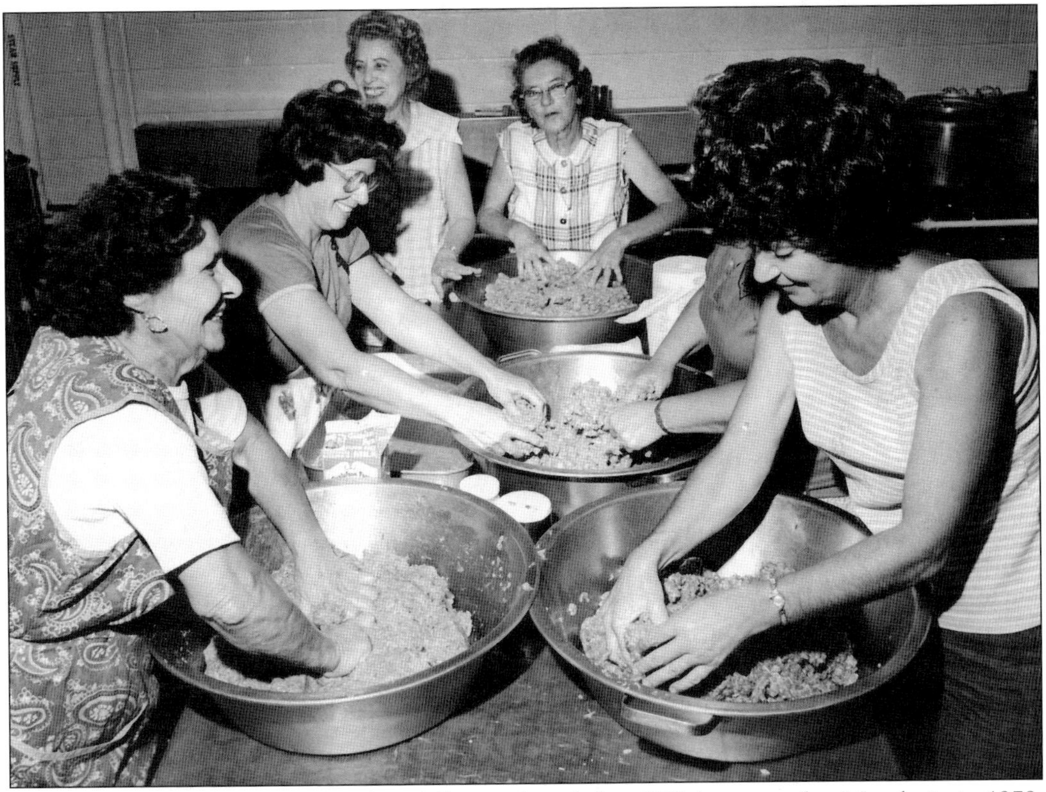

The Italian American Club of Jacksonville was founded in 1951 but moved to Mandarin in 1978. The thing most Mandarin folks associate with the club is the "Spaghetti-To-Go" dinners that have been available to the public for decades. Seen here, rolling meatballs, from left to right, are (first row) Lucia Giardino and Helen Hamm; (second row) Pauline Canto and Vivianne Marinucci; (third row) Margaret Puleo and Lillian Bureau. (Photograph by Rocco Morabito, courtesy of Italian American Club.)

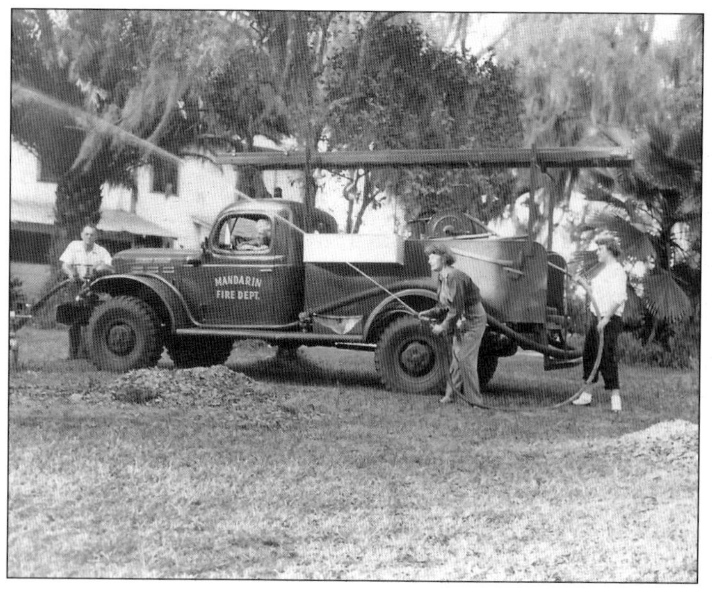

Volunteerism was necessary to provide needed services in Mandarin. Thus, the president of the Mandarin Community Club organized a meeting to form a fire department in 1950. By 1951, the department was organized and had a pumper truck. It was named the Mandarin-Loretto Volunteer Fire Department in 1956, and a station was built. It even had a Ladies Auxiliary. Seen here from left to right are Paul Dempsey, Ivy Nicholl (in the cab), Dot Landiss, and Marjorie Folds.

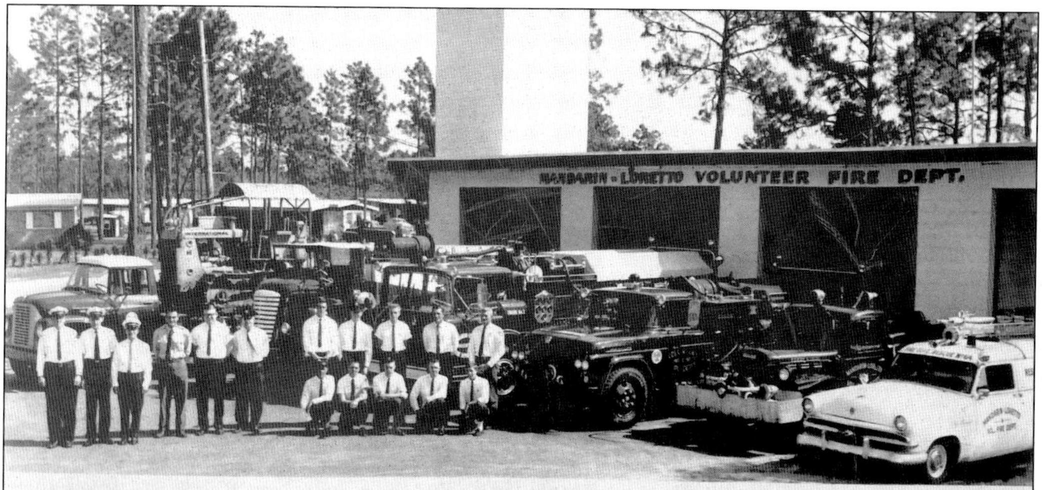

MANDARIN-LORETTO VOLUNTEER FIRE DEPT.

DUVAL COUNTY
MANDARIN-LORETTO VOLUNTEER FIRE DEPARTMENT
Station No. 64 Organized 1950
1965 ROSTER

CHIEF
W. L. ROARK

Deputy Chief, R. L. Flynn
Assistant Chief, B. M. Torelli
Captain, Wm. Rodriguez
Captain, T. D. Pound
Lieutenant, H. D. Hutt
State Forestry, W. L. Rehberg
Auxiliary Police, B. B. Bethel

FIREMEN

M. D. Fletcher, L. E. Stiffler, W. A. Winslow, Jr., C. E. Greenwood, Brian Long, R. E. Miller, C. H. Parker, W. A. Winslow, Sr., Wray Edwards, P. R. Marlin, Bobby Bethel, B. L. Bragg, Jessie Dunn, Mike Miller, K. F. Price, George Price, E. J. Urban

The first president of the group was Billy Barwald. His wife, Peggy, Braddy Wilford's wife, Anna Marie, and several others manned a phone tree to alert the firemen to a reported fire. By 1965, the equipment and station had grown greatly, and the service was eventually taken over by the City of Jacksonville after the consolidation of the city and county. (Courtesy of Evans Howard.)

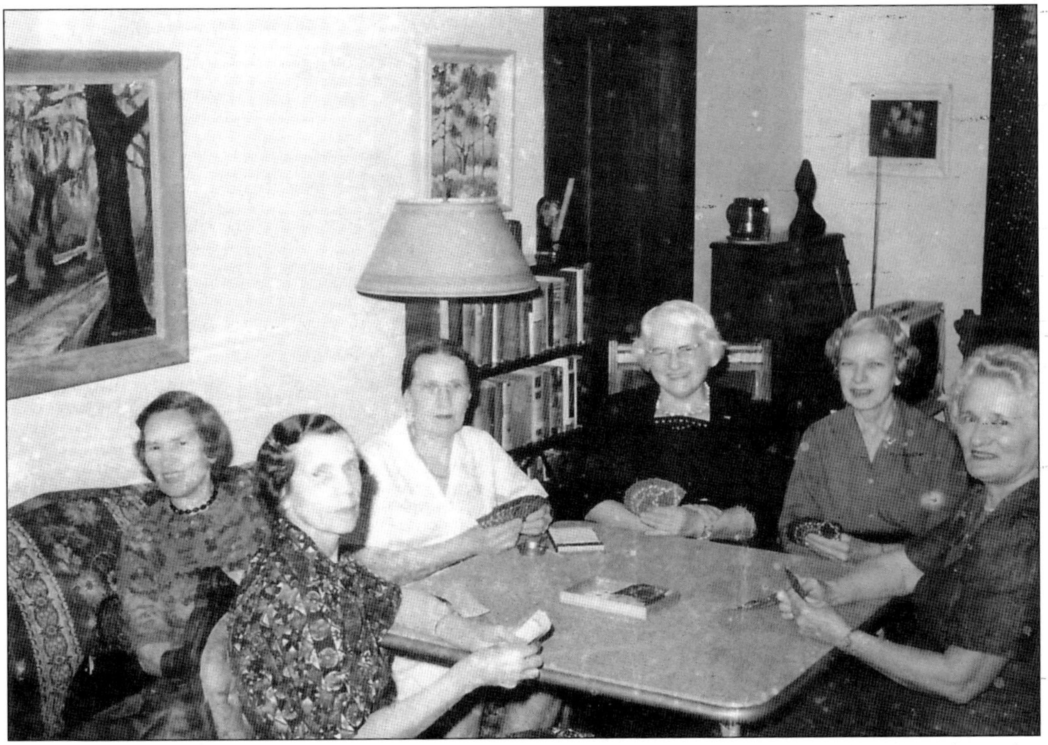

A popular social activity of the 1950s and 1960s was to get together with a group of friends to play cards. This is a photograph inside the Brown house (notice early paintings by Charlie Brown on the wall). Pictured from front to left are Mary Brown, Eleanor Brown, Adalyn "Deenda" Brown, Agnes Jones, Fannie Brown, and Mamie Jones Woolfe.

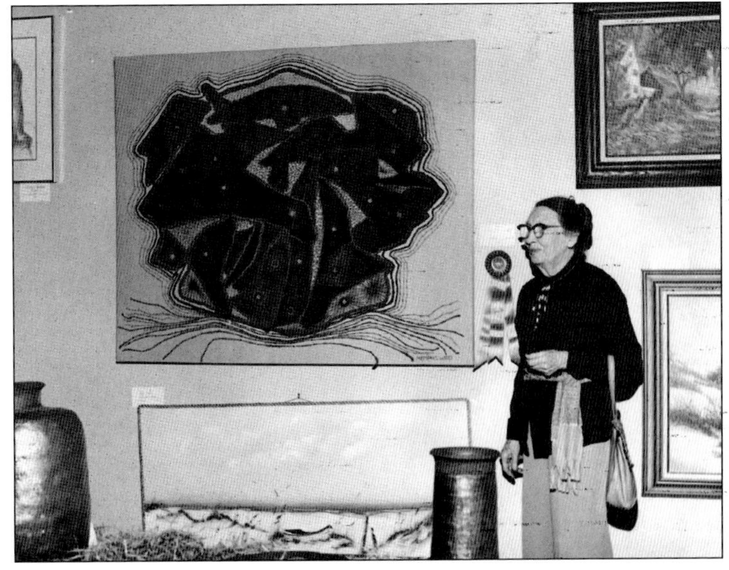

The Mandarin Art Festival was founded in 1968 at the Mandarin Community Club. Artist Memphis Wood (seen here) wanted to create a venue for local artists to show and sell their work. Rosemary McCorkle was the founding chairperson, followed for many years by Judge Ed Westberry. It has become one of the most respected art festivals in the region, bringing thousands of visitors to Mandarin on Easter weekend. (Courtesy of Horace Glass.)

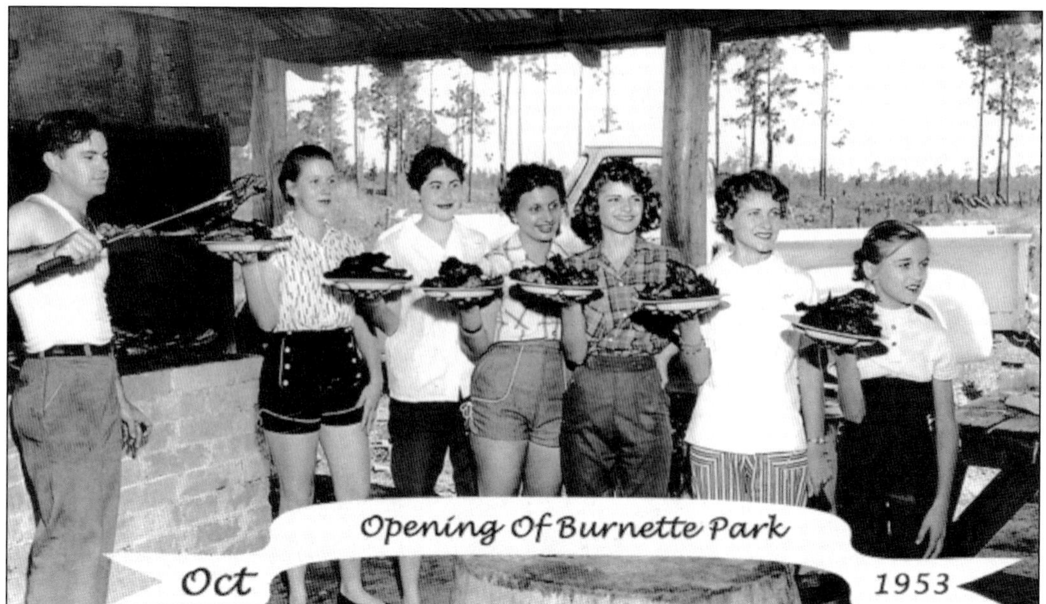

Burnett Park was opened by the Greater Loretto Improvement Association. It was a busy place in the mid-1900s, hosting Loretto School Halloween carnivals, a community center, the Southside Saddle Club, and sports activities. Helping open the park in 1953 are, from left to right, Bob Ortagus, unidentified, Beverly Williams, Maggie Brown, Jean Wilford, Frances Wilford, and Barbara Wilford. (Courtesy of Barbara Wilford Gentry.)

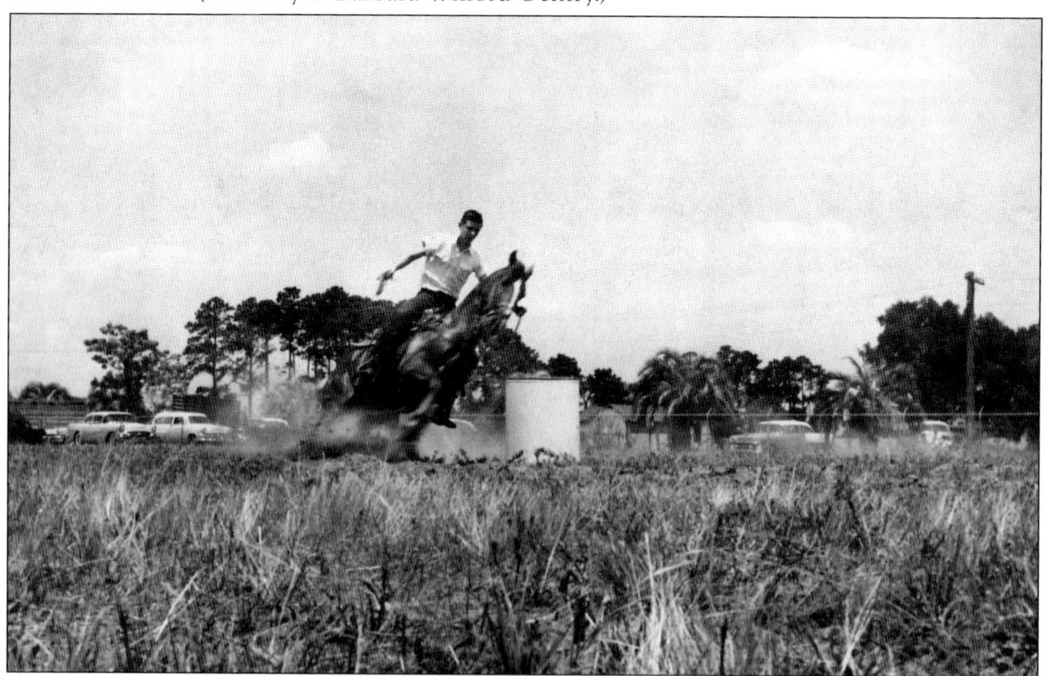

So many young people had horses that the Southside Saddle Club was created in 1957. It was located at Burnett Park. Many people would swarm the park on rodeo nights to watch the kids barrel race. Seen here is Jim Arnold barrel racing on his famous horse Red. They also hosted very popular trail rides in the area. (Courtesy of Megan Arnold.)

Seven

Mandarin Artists

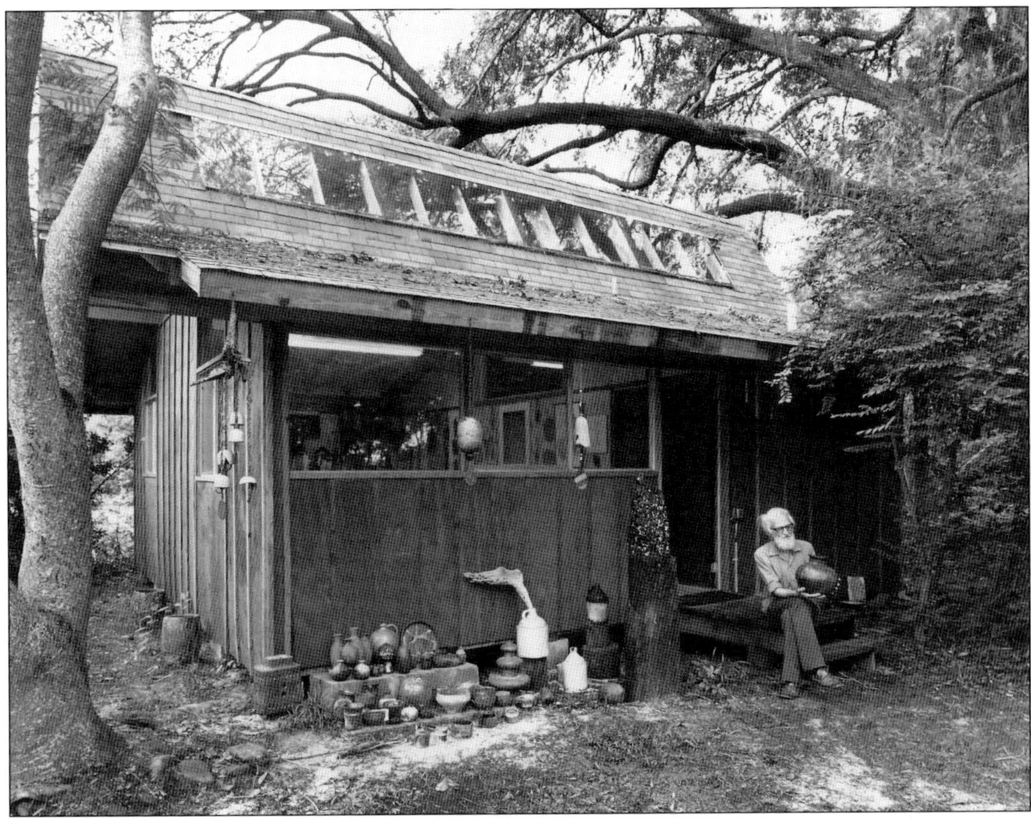

Mandarin was once considered a little art colony of sorts. The beauty and history of the area seemed attractive to creative people—a perfect place for artistic inspiration. Among those many artists, the one that seems to be the most remembered is potter Charles (Charlie) Moses Brown (1904–1987) on Mandarin Road. It was always a delight to visit and talk with Charlie in his studio and take home a special object: "I love clay!—the way it looks—the way it feels when I mix it with my hands—the first glimpse of a glowing pot when the kiln is opened. I even enjoy the back-breaking task of digging it. I suppose, then, that it is perfectly natural that I have become so absorbed with the making of clay objects that it has become my very life—My greatest wish is that I will leave behind me a few statements in clay that have a timeless and precious quality which makes for endurance."

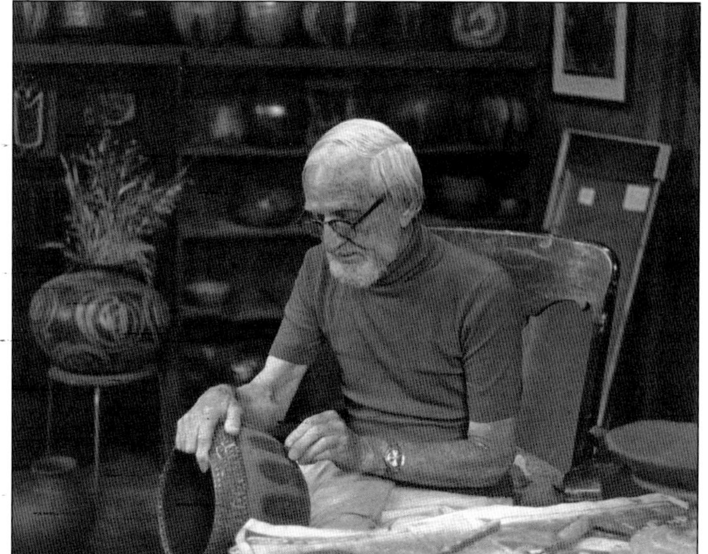

Brown's first artistic interest was in painting landscapes, but in 1951, he met Memphis Wood, who encouraged him to take a pottery course. He fell in love with the feeling of clay in his hands so much that at age 58 he left his job as a CPA to become a full-time potter. All of his pottery was formed by hand and decorated using natural objects like sweetgum balls.

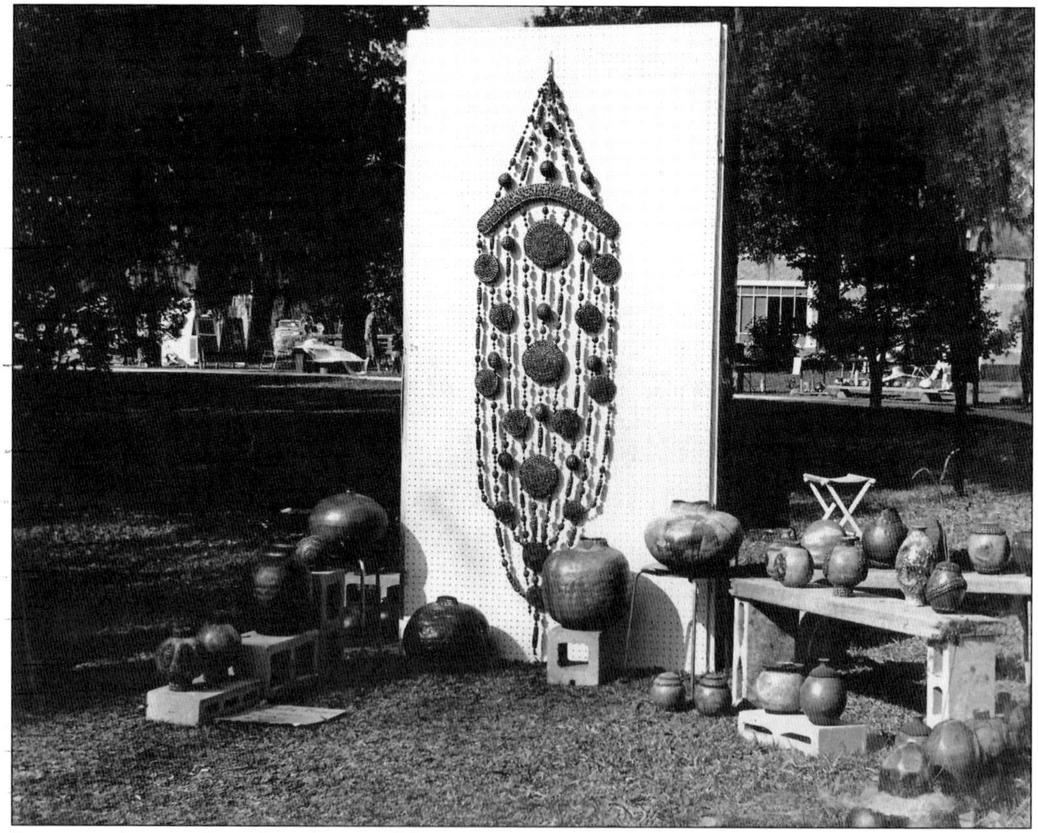

Brown made everything from huge wall hangings to pots, bowls, necklaces, and Christmas ornaments. His signature style was raku, a technique where the pottery is pulled red hot from the furnace and placed in organic matter—in his case, sawdust. His works are found in major collections including the Smithsonian and the Johnson Wax Collection. The Mandarin Museum also has a large and diverse collection of his work.

Memphis Wood (1902–1989), a longtime resident of Mandarin, was at one time affectionately known as Jacksonville's "First Lady of Art." Wood was an artist and teacher who excelled in drawing, painting, stitchery, pottery, jewelry, fabric construction, and fiber art. She was one of the founders of the Mandarin Art Festival.

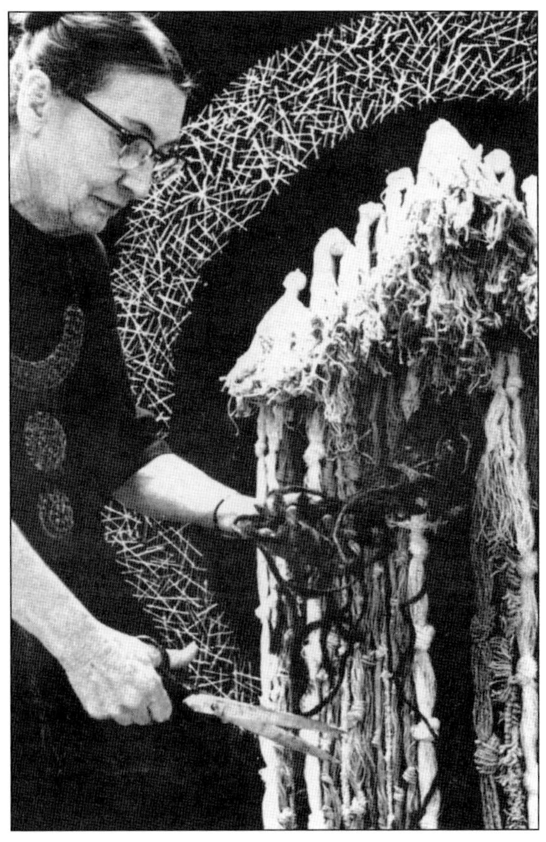

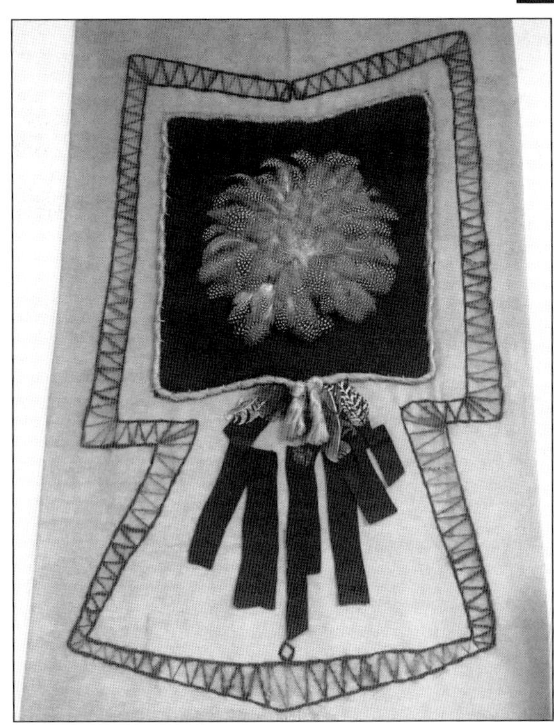

Wood taught art at Landon High School and Jacksonville University. She was known for having a strong influence on many artists in the region, including her lifelong friend Charlie Brown. Many of Memphis' works are found in museums and corporate, private, church, and university collections across the country. Mandarin Museum is fortunate to own a large collection and variety of her art, including this beautiful piece.

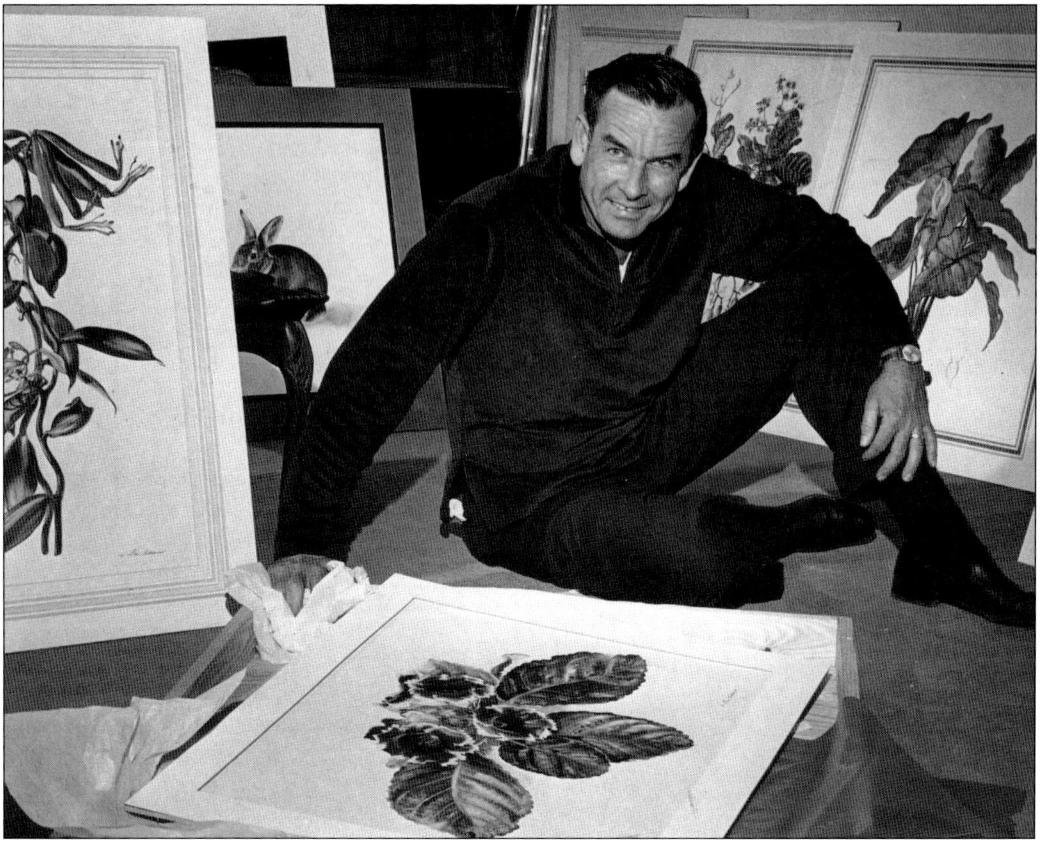

Lee Adams (1922–1971) was known for his nature work, but also his large murals, including *Ribault's Landing* (1959), which was in the old Sears store in Jacksonville. Thankfully, the mural was saved and restored and can still be seen at the Main Jacksonville Public Library. Following that, the State of Florida Commissioned him to paint 11 murals for the 1964 World's Fair in New York. He is seen here working in his studio. (Courtesy of the Jacksonville Public Library, *Florida Times-Union Editorial Archive*.)

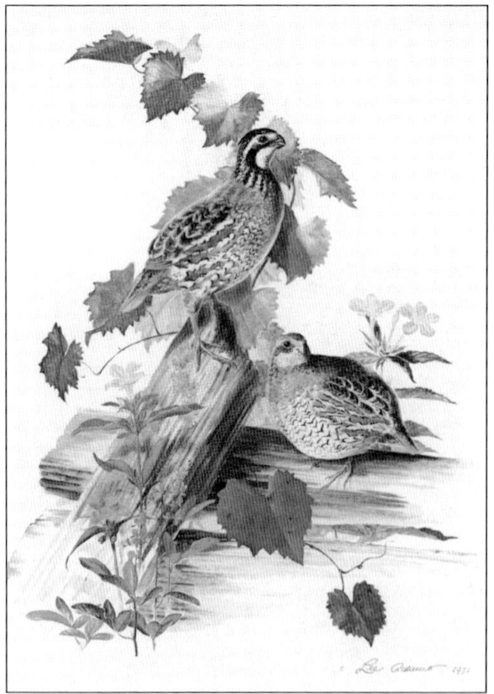

Adams was a self-taught artist who loved the outdoor world, painting plants, flowers, birds, and other creatures. This print is illustrative of his bird prints that were very popular. Sadly, in 1971, Lee and his wife, Mimi, a well-known environmentalist, tragically died in a car accident. At the time, he was one of the foremost botanical and wildlife artists in the United States.

Bruno Alberts (1888–1970), a Louisville native, is probably most remembered in Mandarin because of his orchid business, Alberts & Merkel Bros. Inc., and his donation of the land for a ballpark that is now called Alberts Field. However, he was also a very talented and highly regarded painter and stained-glass artist. This image is a self-portrait. (Courtesy of the Filson Historical Society.)

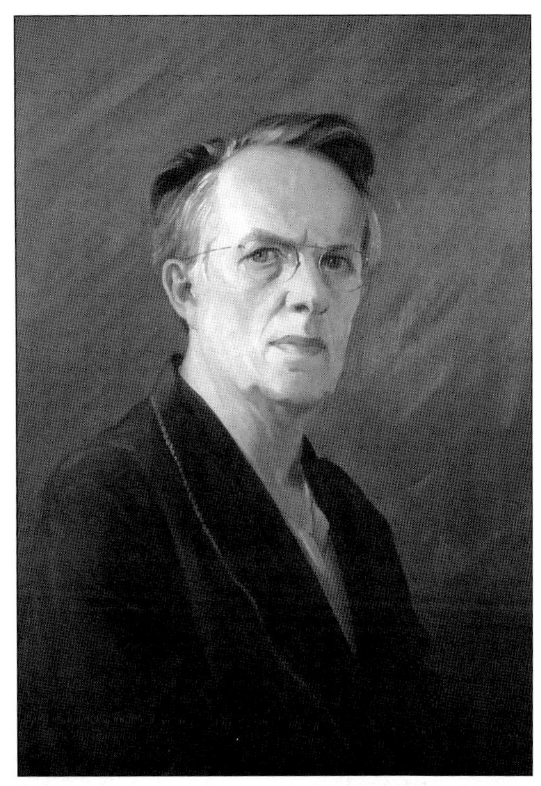

Bruno Alberts and his wife, Ann, moved to Mandarin in the 1930s to focus on orchid growing. They were very active in community life and their church, the Episcopal Church of Our Saviour, where there is a stained-glass window dedicated to Bruno. They moved back home to Louisville in the 1960s. The Mandarin Museum owns one of his paintings, seen here, a beautiful still-life, painted in 1962.

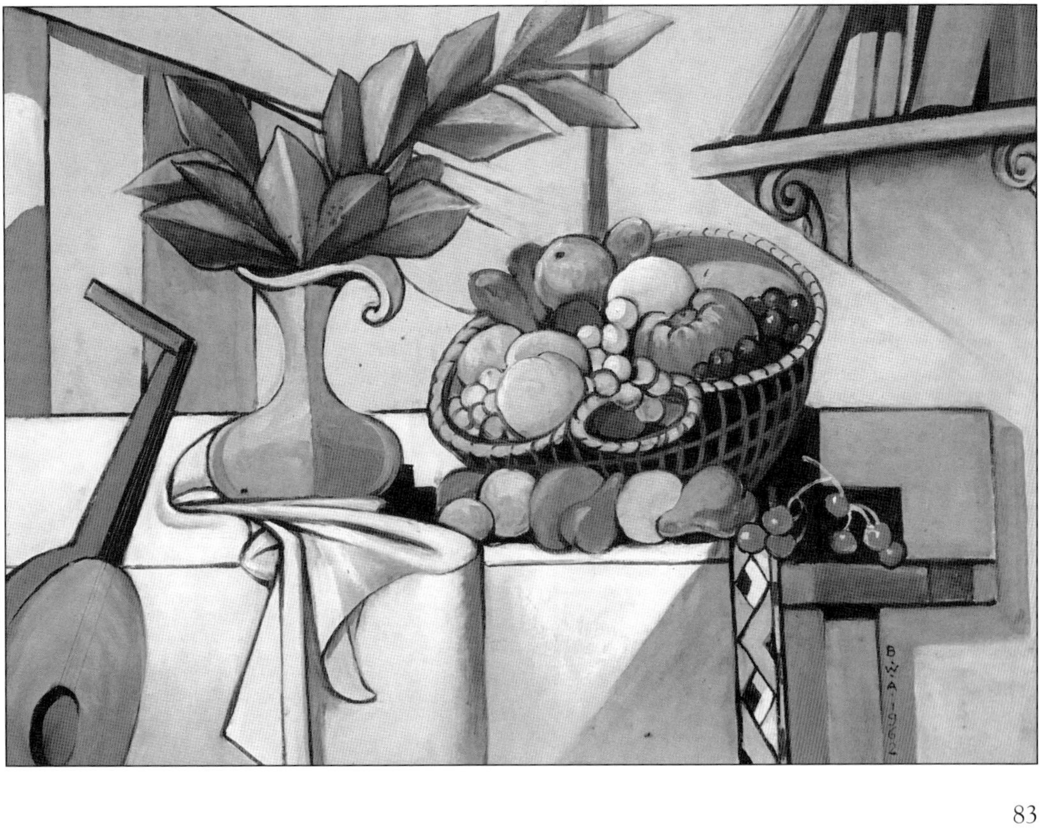

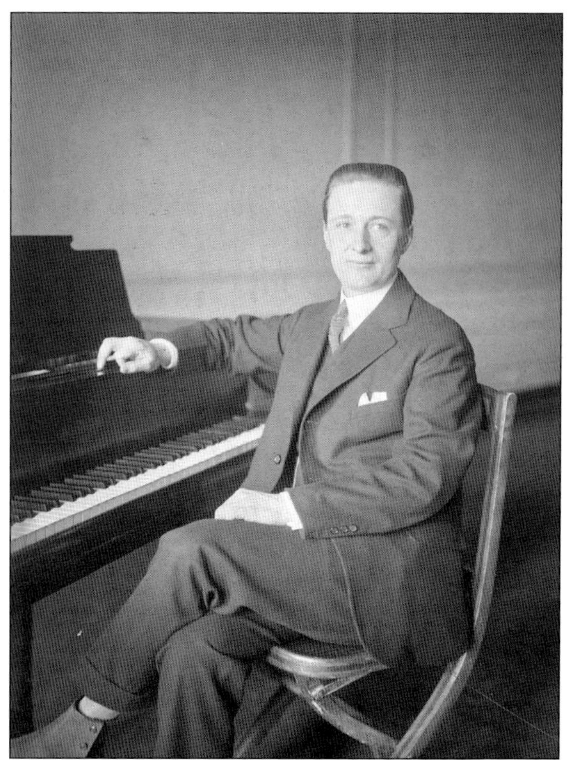

Hans Barth (1897–1956), considered a child prodigy, was awarded a scholarship at the age of six to the Royal Conservatory of Music of Leipzig, Germany. But the family emigrated to New York and it was in America that he made his first recital. He went on to perform over 500 recitals in the United States and Europe, including at Carnegie Hall. Barth was also a composer and made seventeen recordings with Victor Records. He also invented a quarter-tone piano. He and his wife moved to Jacksonville in the mid-1940s and lived on Mandarin Road at the time of his death. He taught piano to many students privately and at Jacksonville College of Music (now Jacksonville University). (Courtesy of the Library of Congress.)

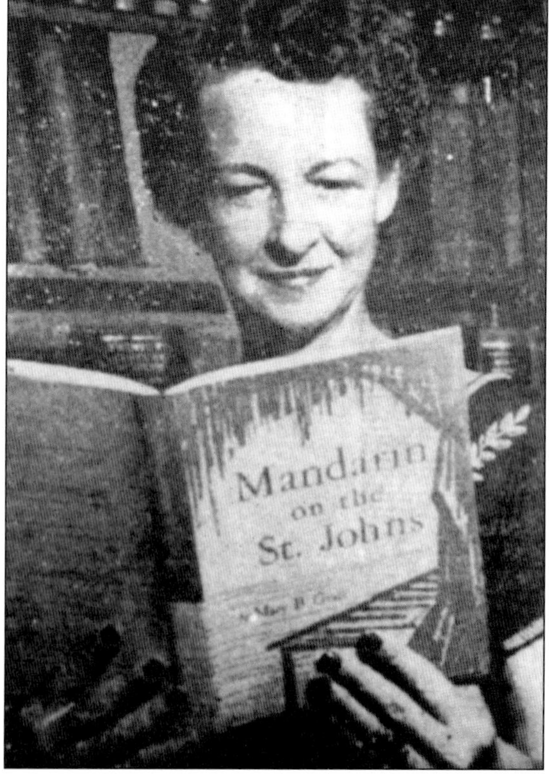

Mary Graff (1908–1994) was the first person to write a book entirely devoted to Mandarin's history, *Mandarin on the St. Johns* (1953). She was a teacher and historian, and at one time head of the social sciences department at Robert E. Lee High School. Originally from Iowa, she came to Mandarin in the 1930s to be a companion to her aunt Nellie Bird, and she fell in love with the history of the community. Her book documented Mandarin's history from the 1560s to the late 1940s.

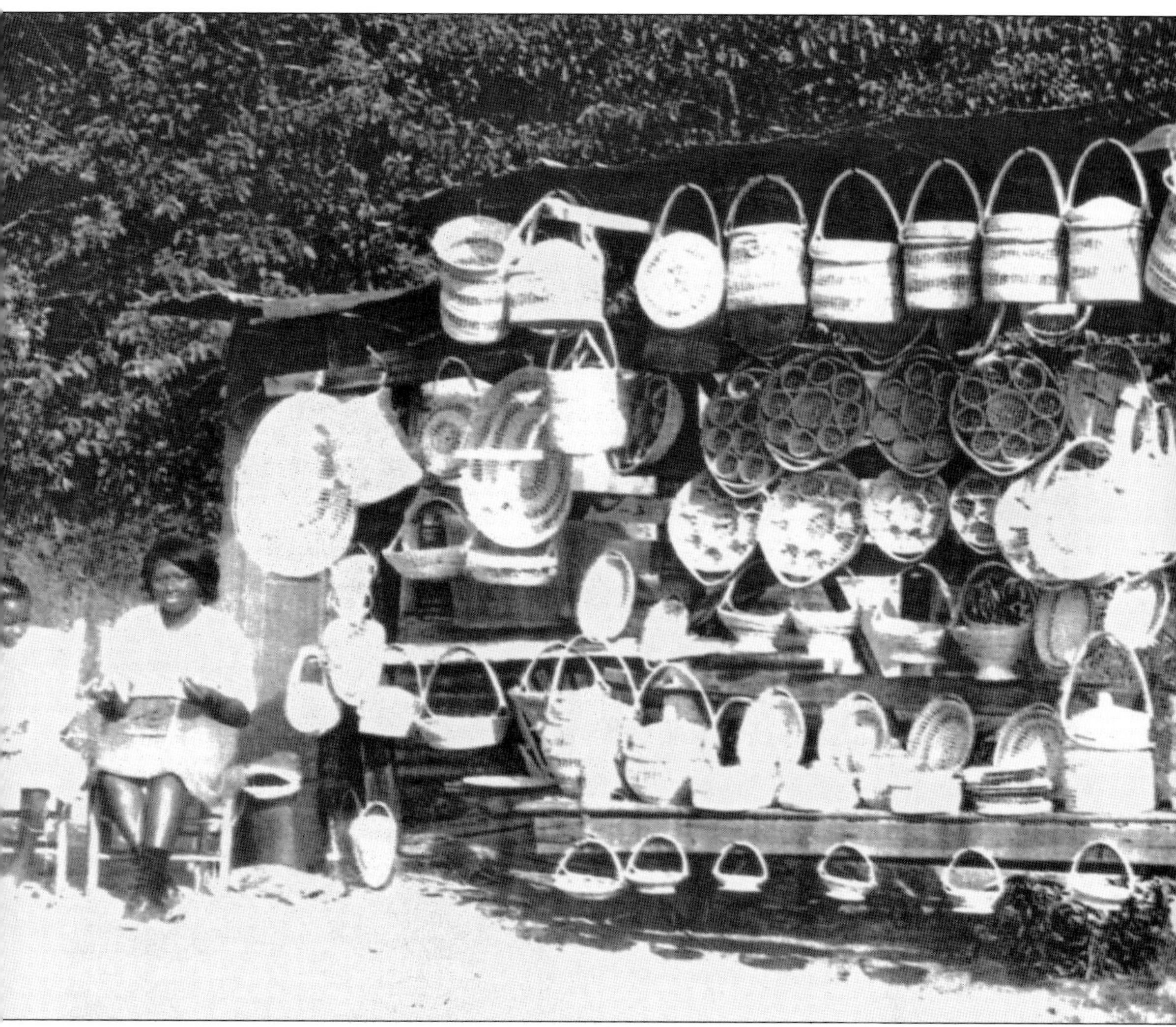

Mary Foreman (1923–2001) brought a unique artistic talent to the Mandarin community: sweetgrass basketry. Born in Mount Pleasant, South Carolina, she was surrounded by people who carried on the tradition of weaving baskets and other objects from sweetgrass, pine needles, and bulrush—all materials that grew in the Lowlands of South Carolina. The tradition was first brought to the area by enslaved people from West Africa and is popular within the Gullah Geechee heritage. When Foreman moved to the Edisto area of Mandarin, she became very well-known and respected for her natural artistic creations. She was a regular exhibitor at the Mandarin Art Festival as well as other many other art shows, winning numerous awards for her work. She is seen here with her daughter Regenia, selling her products along the "Sweetgrass Basket Maker Highway"—US Route 17 in Mount Pleasant. She passed on the love and skill of her craft to her daughters Mary Foreman Passmore and Regenia Foreman Woodie, who followed in her footsteps as basket weavers. (Courtesy of Regenia Foreman Woodie.)

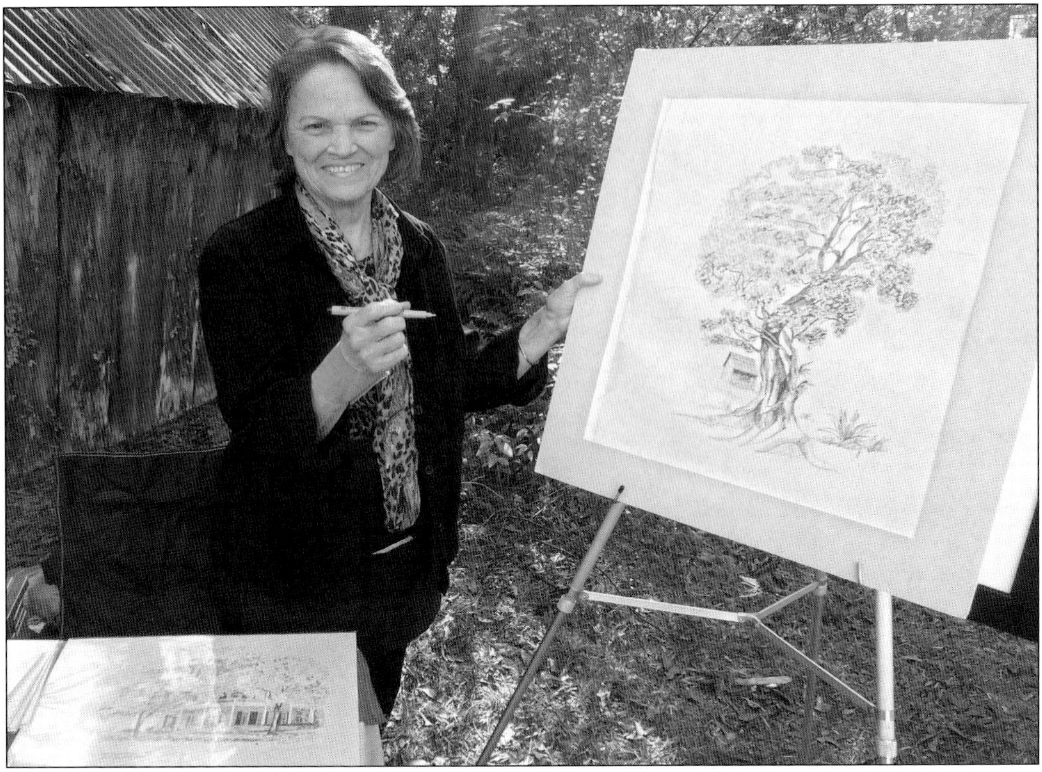

Lucinda Halsema (1942–2020) became an artist in the late 1970s, doing watercolors and etchings, but became best known for her pen and ink drawings of historic places in Jacksonville. She was very involved in the community, serving as president of the Mandarin Community Club, assisting with the Mandarin Art Festival, and serving her church, the Episcopal Church of Our Saviour. She also taught many children to draw and paint.

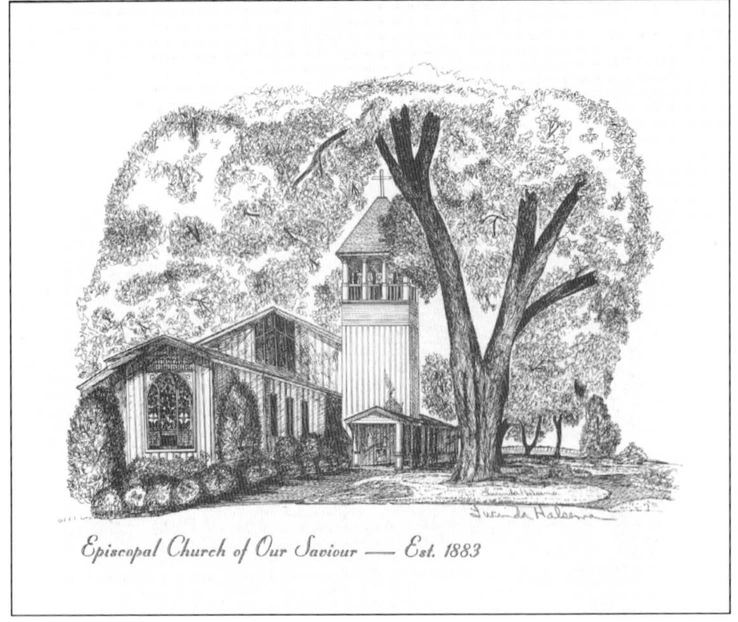

Halsema's pen and ink renderings were very detailed. She did them in black and white but also hand-colored them. Since she lived in Mandarin and loved the history of the area, she decided in the 1980s to do a series of drawings of the historic structures in the community. She also produced a beautifully illustrated book for the Jacksonville Symphony that was written for children to learn about different instruments.

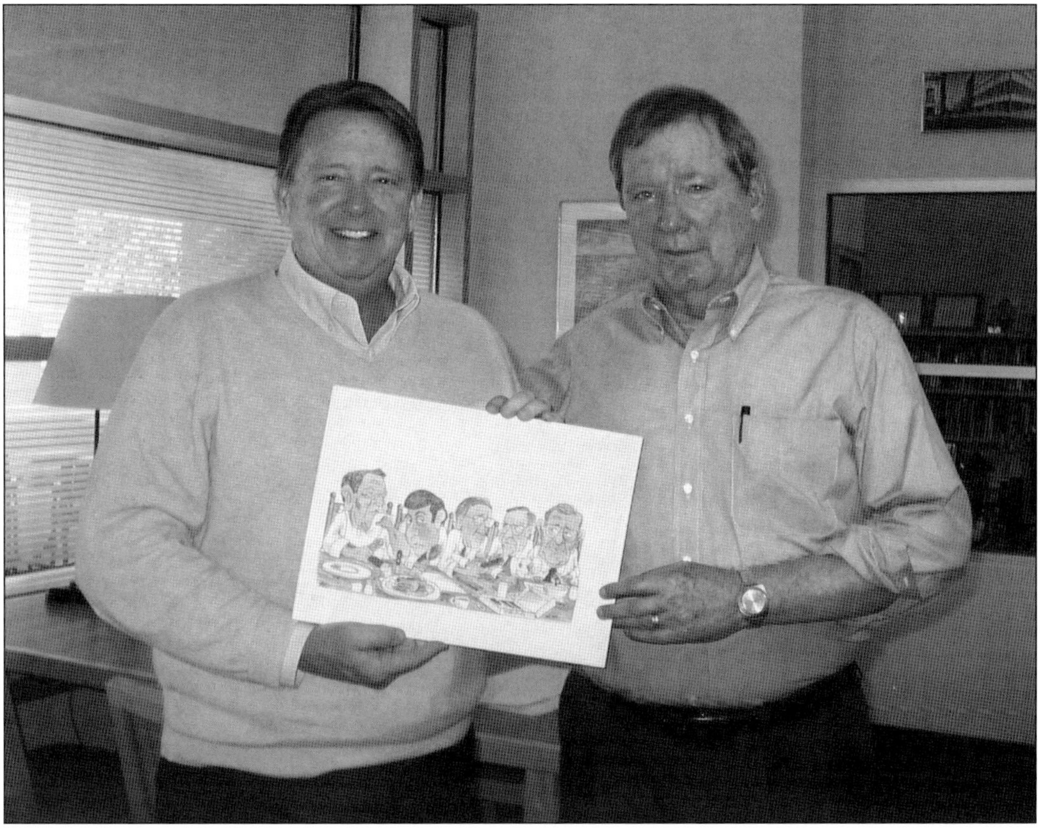

Ed Gamble (born in 1943) was an editorial cartoonist for the *Florida Times-Union* from 1980 until 2010. An award-winning political cartoonist, he has been nationally syndicated, and his cartoons have been published in newspapers and exhibits all over the United States and the world. He has won more than 50 national, regional, and state awards for his cartoons. Gamble is seen here on the right with former mayor of Jacksonville John Delaney.

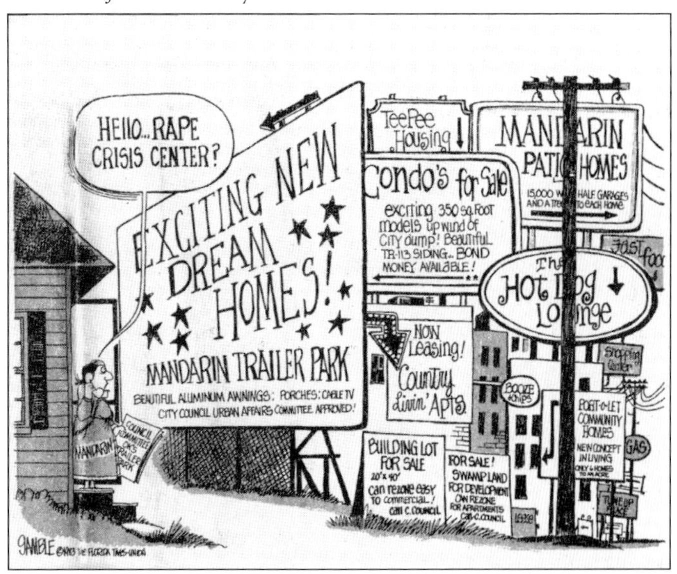

This original drawing was given to Mandarin Museum by Ed Gamble. It clearly depicts the changes in Mandarin caused by growth and development in the area. A special collection of his digital images may be viewed at the Thomas G. Carpenter Library at the University of North Florida, which houses over 2,000 of Gamble's cartoons on local and state events.

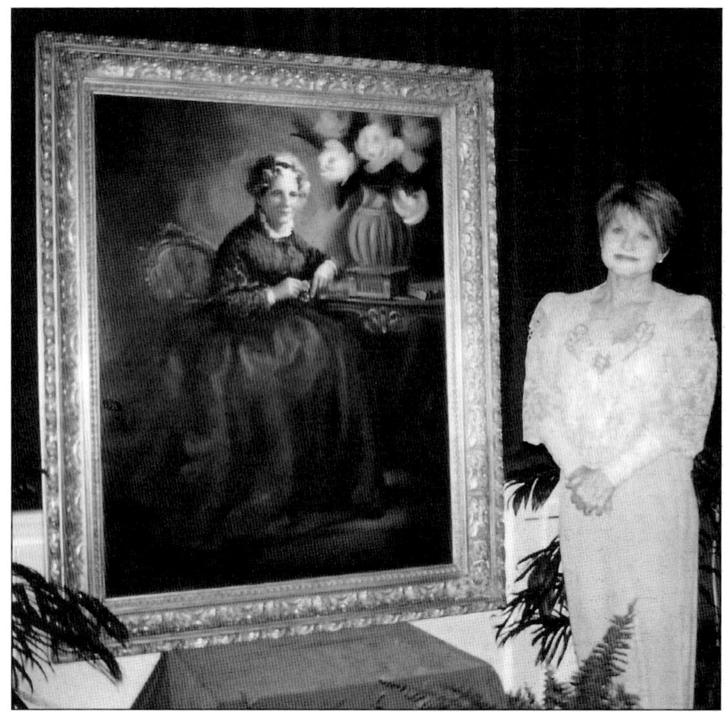

Ann Manry Kenyon is a classically trained and highly acclaimed portrait artist who has been steadily working her craft in her studio off Mandarin Road since the 1990s. She learned to paint as a young child, taking art lessons from watercolor artist Harold Hilton, who was regarded as one of Florida's best during his time. She works in oil, watercolor, and pastels and is sought after as a teacher in these media.

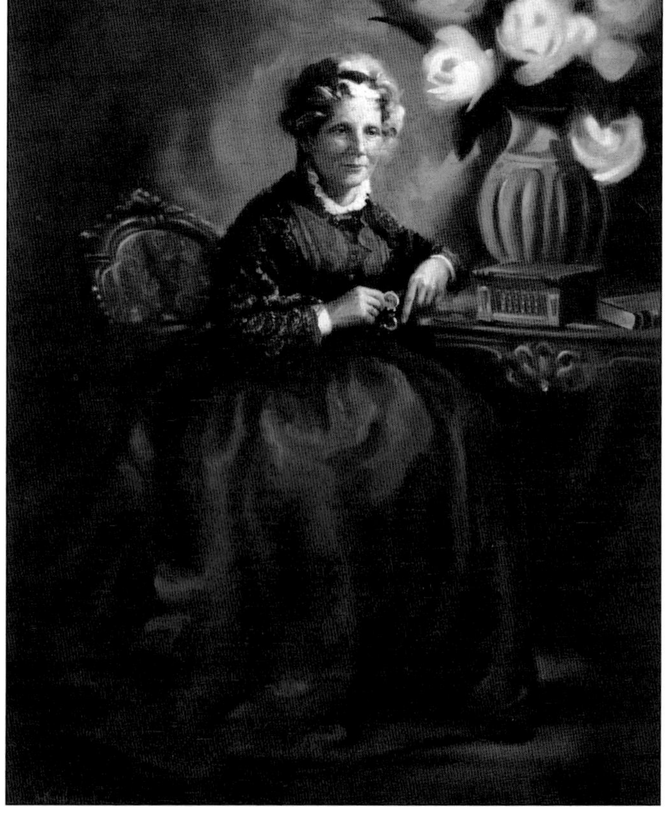

Ann is known for her portraits of government officials, families, and even famous professional golfers (in her series "Golfing Greats"). However, one that is beloved in this community is of Harriet Beecher Stowe. This portrait was donated by her to the Mandarin Community Club in 1998. It is in a perfect spot because the community club building was erected as a schoolhouse in 1872 with the fundraising assistance of Stowe.

Brenda Mauney Councill (born in 1956) moved to Mandarin with her family from North Carolina when she was four years old and was already drawing. She says that being an artist has always been her life's goal. She now lives in North Carolina again and specializes in public art like large murals, sculptures, and domed ceilings. She has won numerous awards for her work. But Councill also kept part of her heart in Mandarin.

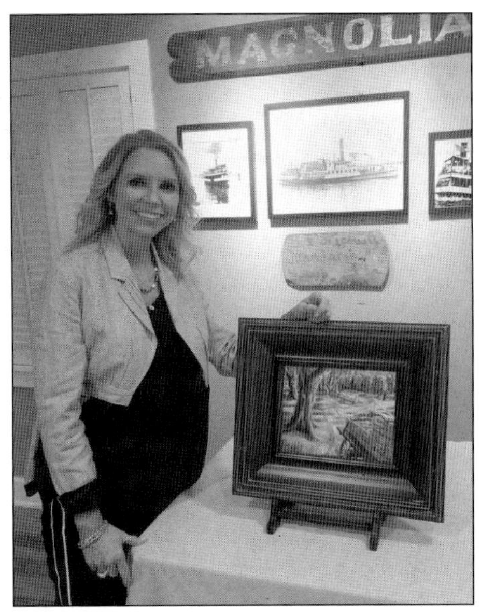

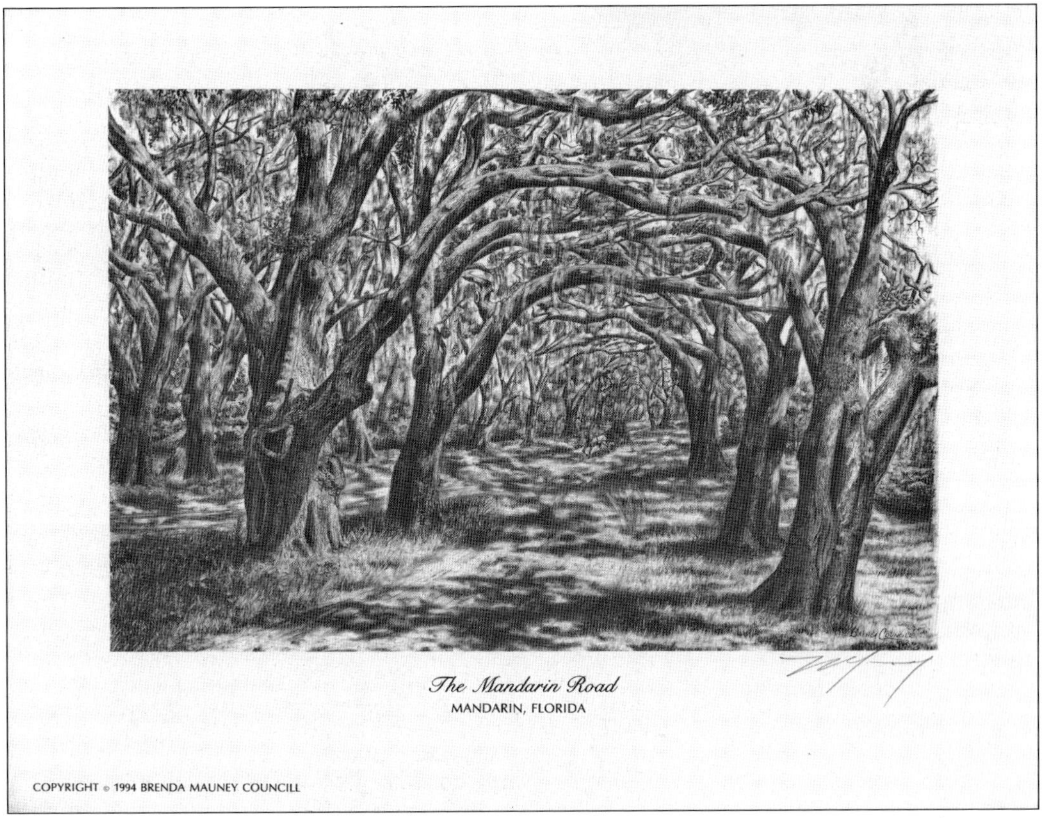

The Mandarin Road

MANDARIN, FLORIDA

An interest in historic preservation led to "The Mandarin Series," a collection of award-winning drawings featuring many historic landmarks in Mandarin. These prints were very popular in the 1980s and 1990s and are still in demand today. The late Charlie Brown praised the collection, saying, "I have seen many, many pencil drawings in my long life, but never anything to compare with a magnificent drawing by Brenda Councill."

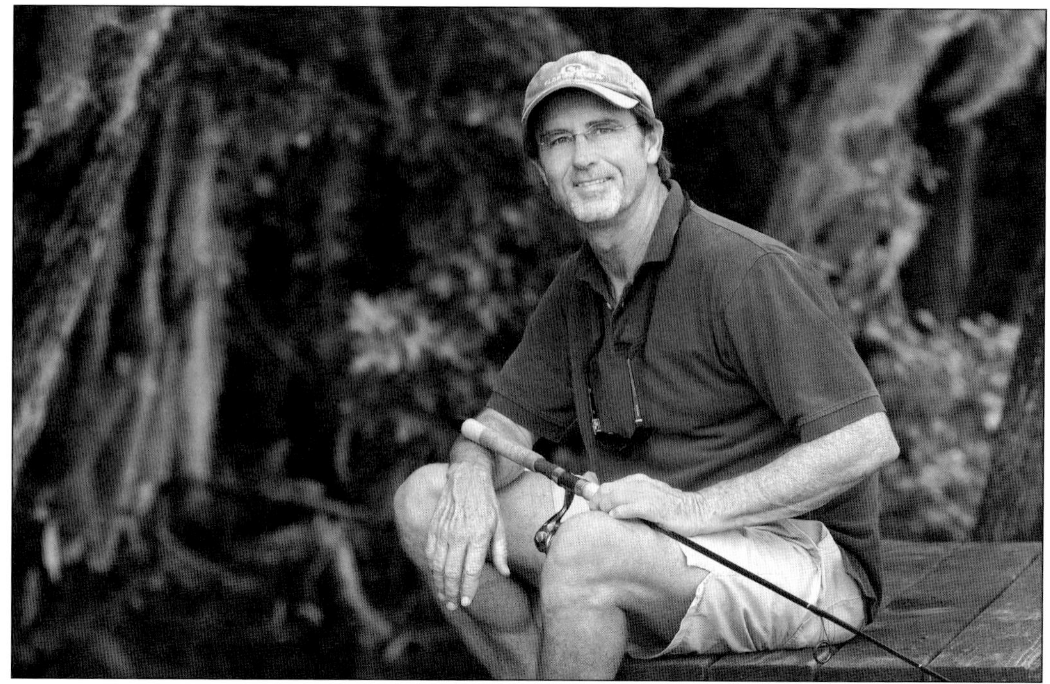

C. Ford Riley (born in 1952) has spent much of his life wandering the forests of northeast Florida and being awed by the beauty of the natural world. He has studied wildlife and natural environments and has had an illustrious career painting those subjects in watercolor, oil, and acrylics. He has received national and international awards. Working from his studio in Mandarin helps him stay close to his subjects and gives him inspiration (Courtesy of C. Ford Riley).

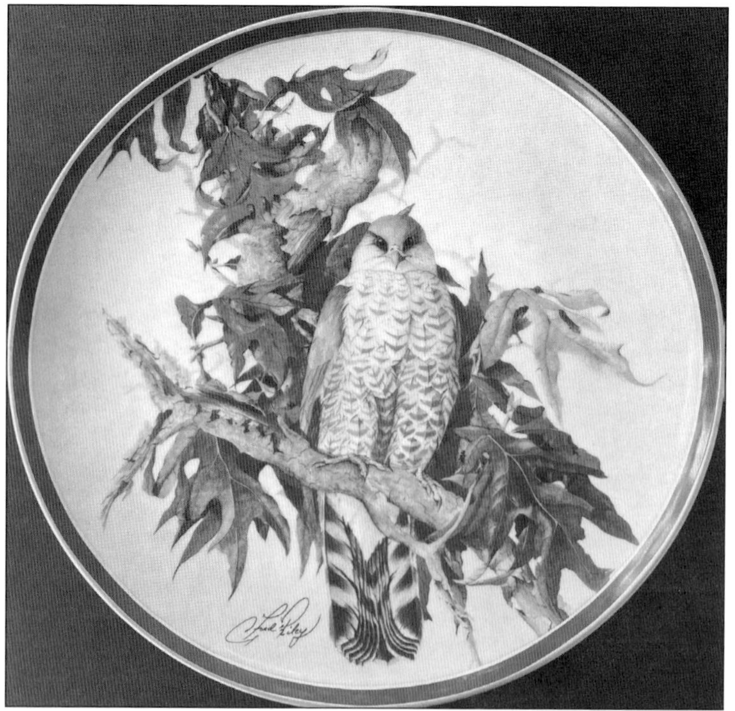

Much of C. Ford Riley's early work included birds and local trees and flowers. He was called the "Audubon of the 1980s" because his drawings were so perfect, built on years of observing and studying wildlife habitats and sketching birds and small animals. His bird prints were very popular, and some, like this one of a Cooper's hawk, were featured in a series of Hamilton Collection plates. His motto has been "I paint what I know."

John Kenning (born in 1950) grew up in Mandarin and Fruit Cove and took painting classes at age six from Barbara Anderson. His first complete painting with her was of the Church of Our Saviour. Because he was a local boy, he had the fortune to be mentored and influenced by Memphis Wood and Lee Adams. Bob Broward, an architect, taught him how to draw structures. He is seen here drawing along with the finished product.

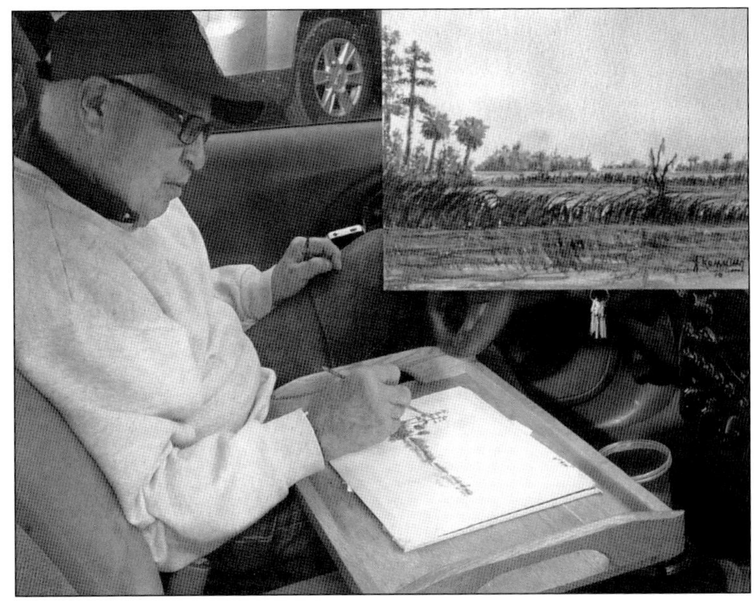

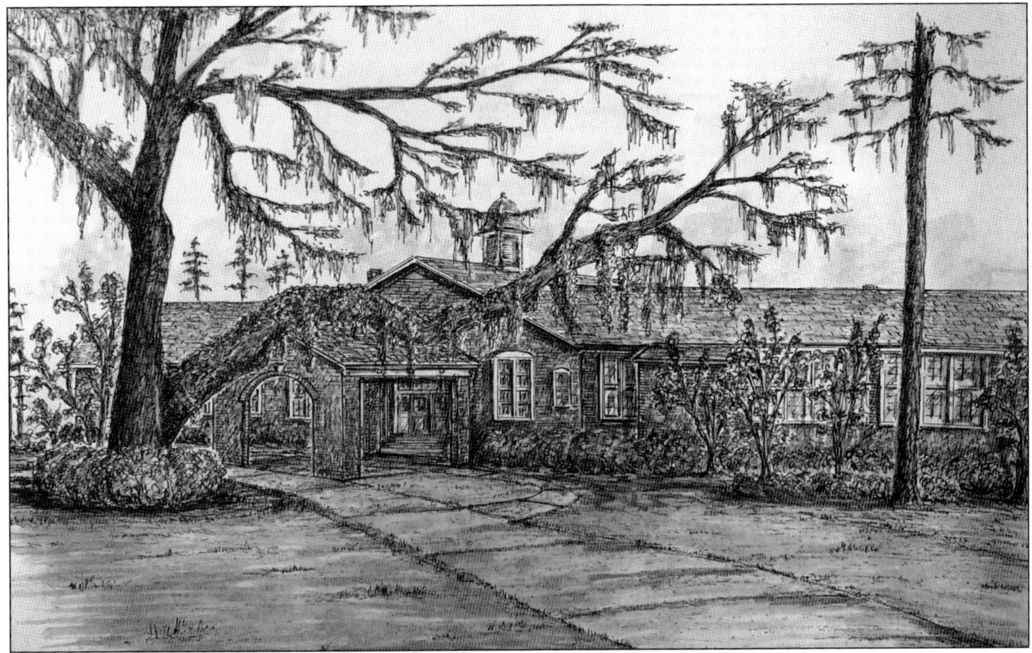

Kenning went on to earn a BA at the University of Arkansas, did graduate work in studio art, and has continued to paint his whole life. Some of his favorite subjects are historic buildings, like the Loretto Elementary School (seen here) in Mandarin. He also did two views of the *Maple Leaf* (Civil War shipwreck) from an underwater perspective—one of the shipwreck and one of the diving operation.

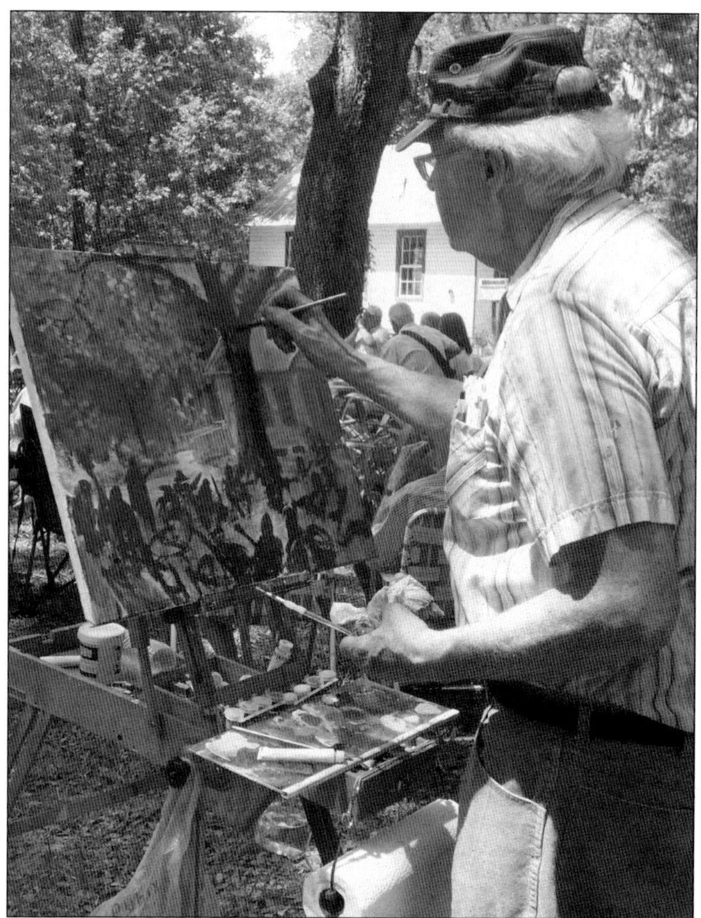

Gary Garrett (born in 1949) grew up on Jacksonville's Southside but moved to Mandarin in 1987. He, too, started painting by age six, when his mother gave him a watercolor set. He was guided and inspired by Mandarin's Memphis Wood, who was his art teacher at Jacksonville University. He especially credits her with helping him learn to use colors skillfully and in exciting ways.

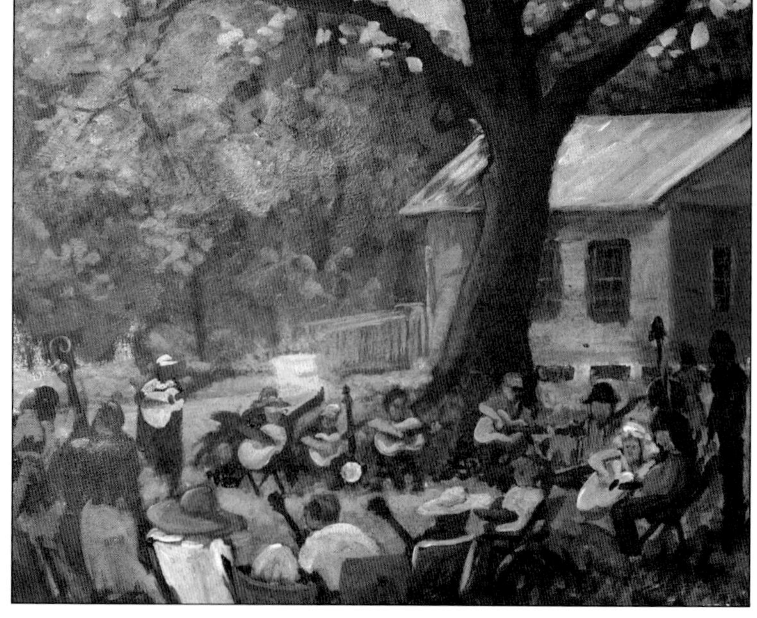

Walter Jones Historical Park is one of Garrett's favorite places to paint. This painting of the "Under the Oaks" music jam captures the event perfectly. The painting was a gift to Mandarin Museum. A very diverse artist, he also plays guitar, drew cell animations, has built guitars in his workshop, and had a career in television production. Now retired, he is very active with the First Coast Plein Air Painters, art shows, and festivals.

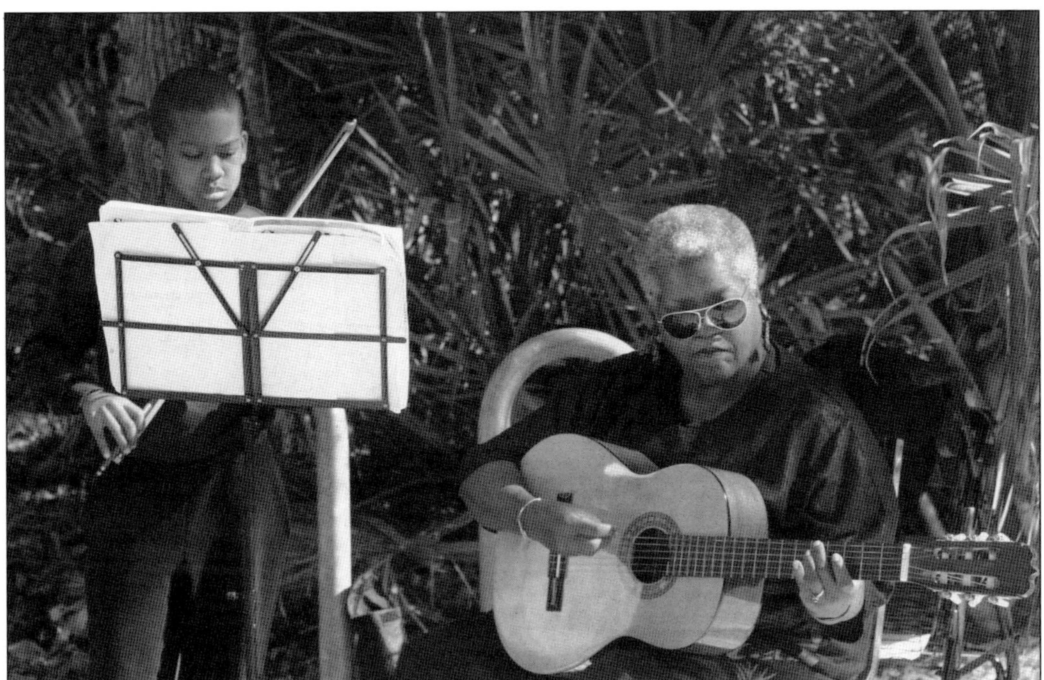

Johnese Lennon (1947–2018) lived in Mandarin since 1983, quietly raising a family, playing music, and painting. She received a degree in fine arts from Jacksonville University. Lennon especially found pleasure in painting things around her—portraits of family and friends, murals, flowers, and places that were special to her. She is seen here playing guitar with her grandson Jonathan at the 2010 Winter Celebration at Walter Jones Historical Park.

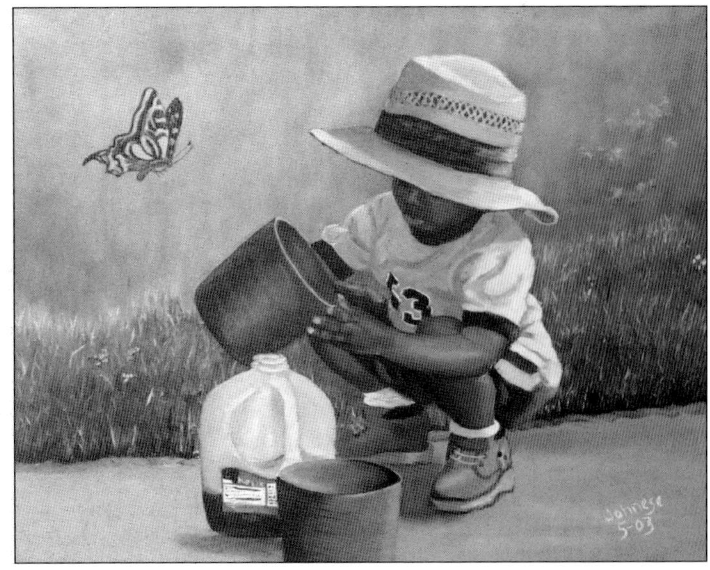

This portrait was of Johnese Lennon's grandson Jonathan. Johnese's daughter Katryna says, "Her grandson was her muse. From the moment he was born, she constantly photographed and painted him." Lennon not only sold her paintings on her website and at art shows, but also gave many of them away to friends. Her home still bears a large mural she painted of fishermen on County Dock. Fishing was one of her favorite things to do with Jonathan.

Olis Garber, a professional photographer for 50 years, was inspired by the work of Ansel Adams with his dynamic black and white scenes of wildlife, salt marshes, and birds. While working a career in IT development, he also had a career as a wedding photographer. That transformed over time into portraits and landscapes and traveling to remote places around the world, winning many awards. He is seen here shooting in Patagonia. (Courtesy of Olis Garber.)

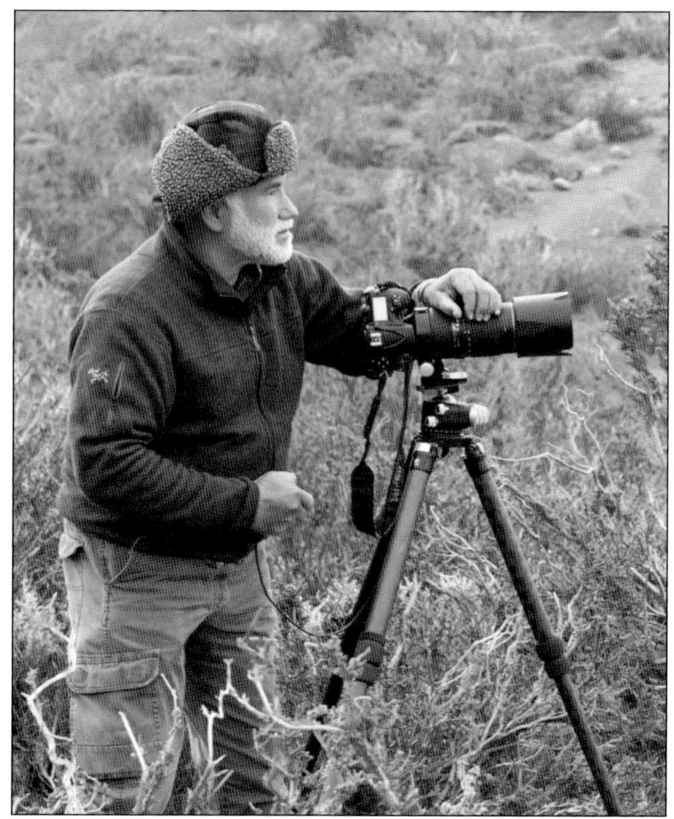

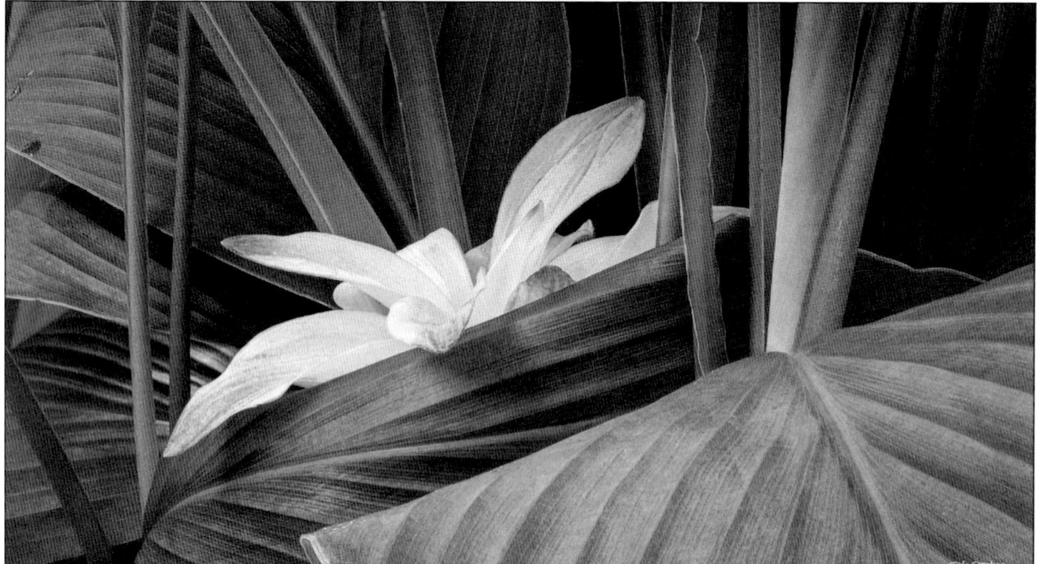

Garber loves to observe flowers closely; this one is of a turmeric plant in Mandarin. He says that when he looks at a flower, "I'm thinking about a portrait of a person's face, the direction of light, and the background." The results are stunning. In 2021, he took on a very important project for Mandarin Museum & Historical Society, photographing every historic building and home in Mandarin for a photographic record. (Courtesy of Olis Garber.)

Eight

Businesses

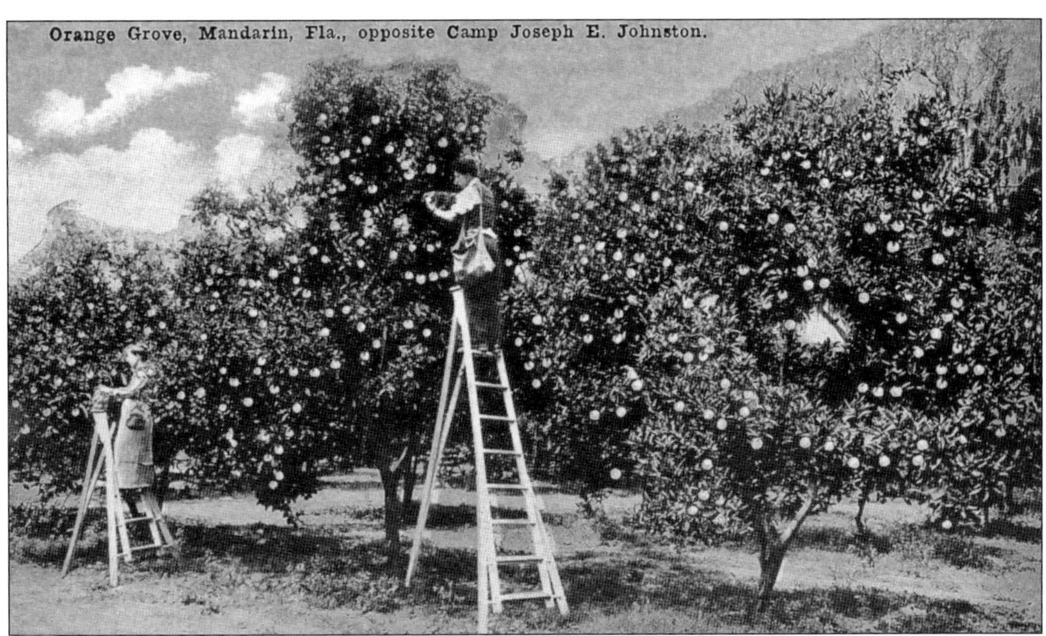

The primary industry in Mandarin in the late 19th century was citrus. The freeze of 1899 destroyed the groves and they never came back at the same level, but citrus has always been part of the Mandarin scene—and is why this village was named "Mandarin." The pickers carried large and heavy burlap bags to collect the fruit, which is usually ripe after the first cold spell.

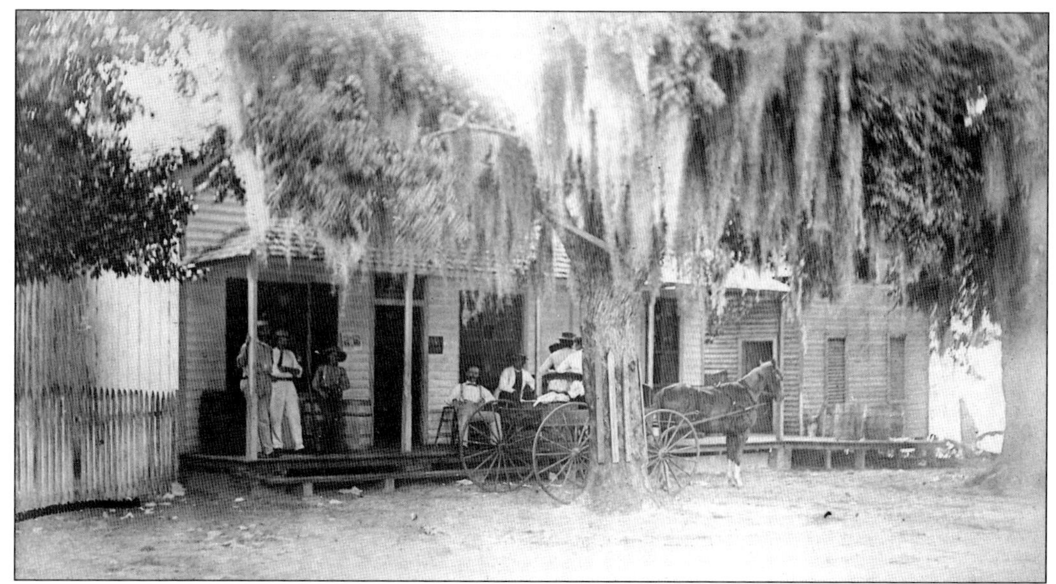

Mandarin's first general store and the post office were located at the Mandarin Wharf because all goods and services were connected with steamboat transportation, which brought the mail, goods for the store, and passengers. This was located on "Store Lane." This area was also the community gathering place where one learned the news of the day and how everybody's crops were faring.

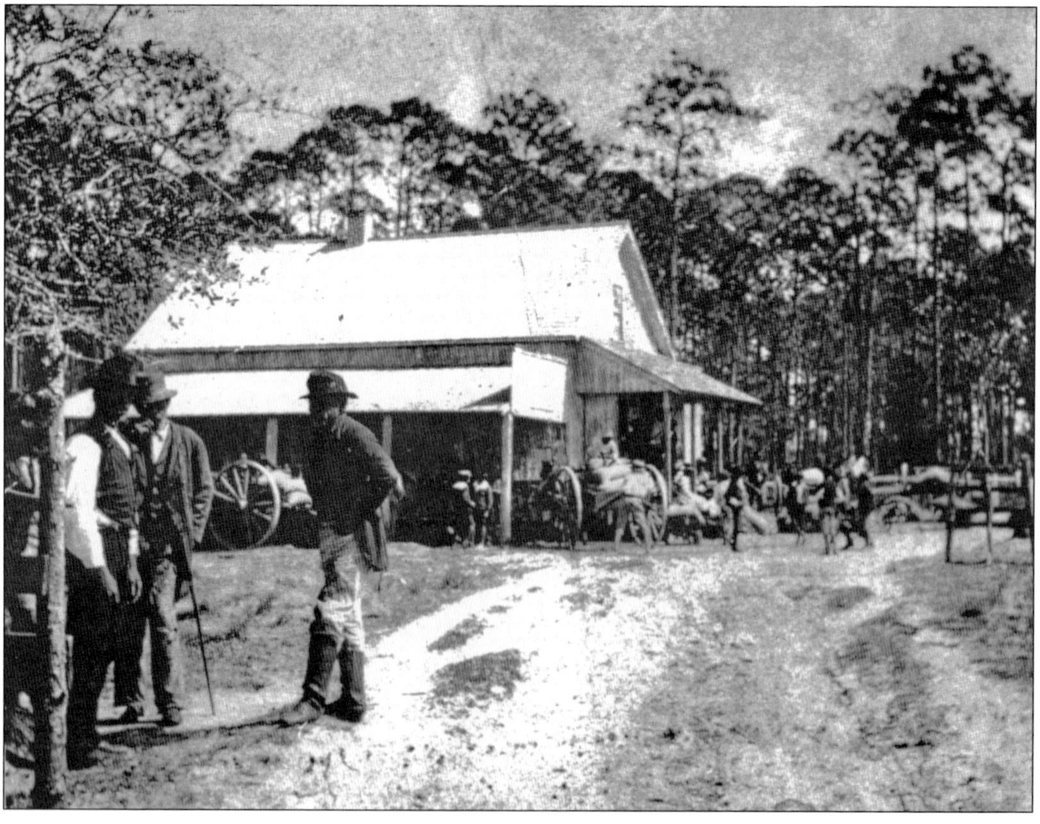

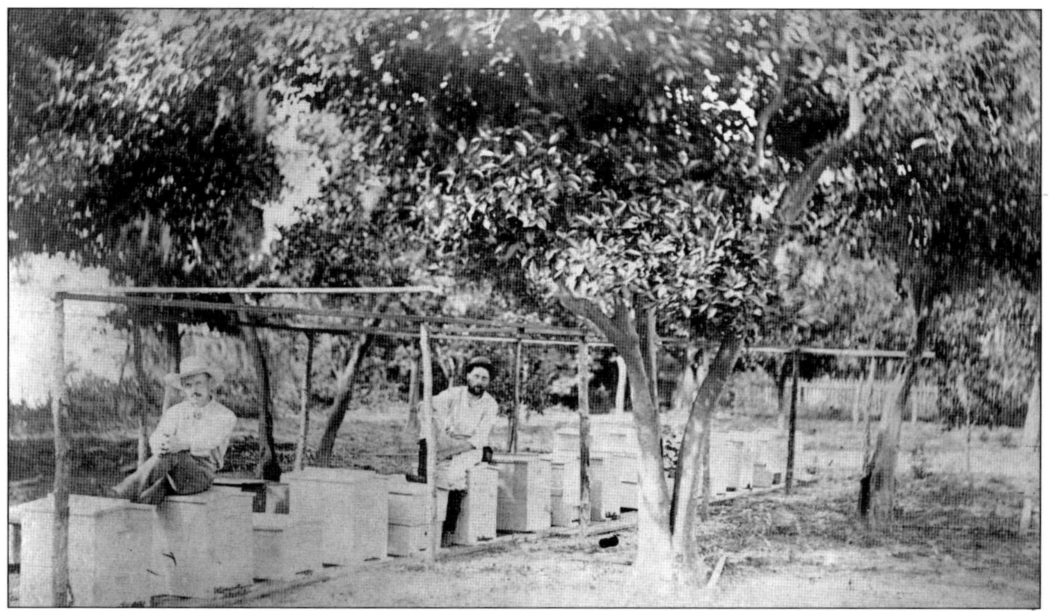

W.B. Dismore (right) sits with an unidentified friend at some apiary boxes along the river. People built their beehives among the citrus trees to help pollinate the citrus blooms and make better honey. Beekeeping in Florida was a very common source of extra income. (Courtesy of the Mary Graff Collection, Jacksonville Historical Society.)

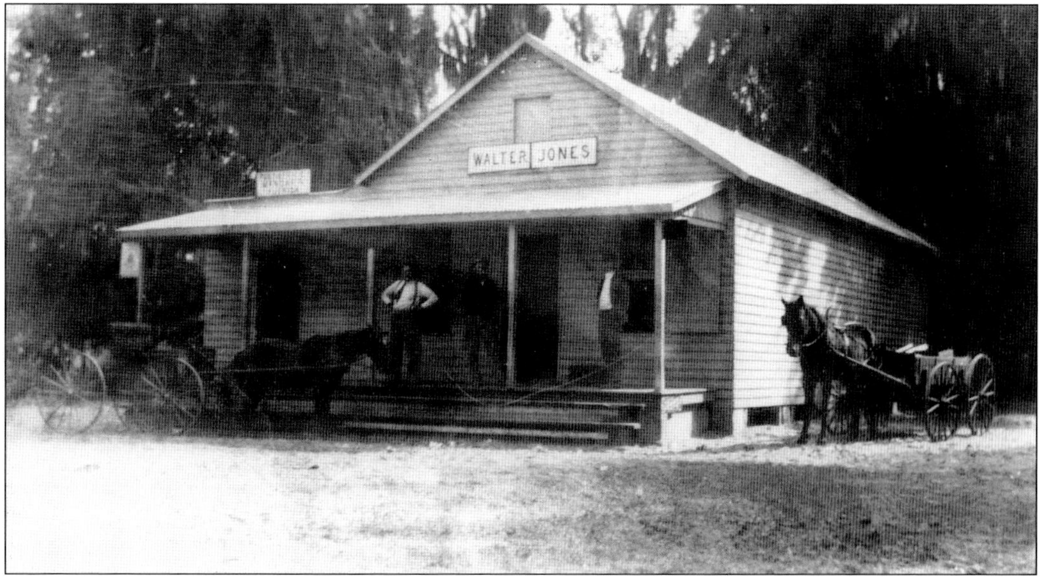

As the 20th century brought better roads, the hub of the village moved away from the river to what is now called Mandarin Road. In 1911, Walter Jones, the postmaster, had local builder William Monson build the Walter Jones Store and US Post Office. This building is in the National Register of Historic Places and serves today as a museum operated by the Mandarin Museum & Historical Society, through a partnership with the Mandarin Community Club, which owns the building.

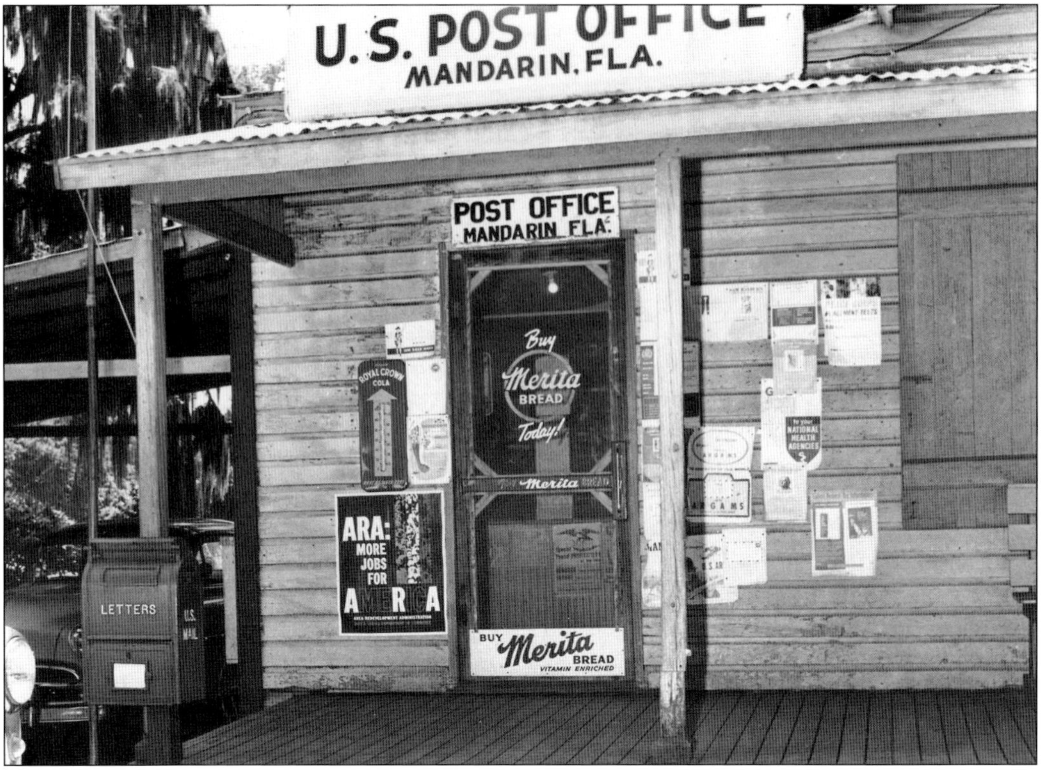

This view is from the early 1960s. Agnes Jones held the position of postmistress for the longest time, up until a new and more modern post office was built on San Jose Boulevard in 1963. This building was then closed but used later for other purposes. From 1978–1982, it was the home of the *Mandarin Weekly Advertiser* newspaper and the first Mandarin Historical Society, both operated by Mandarin resident Horace Glass.

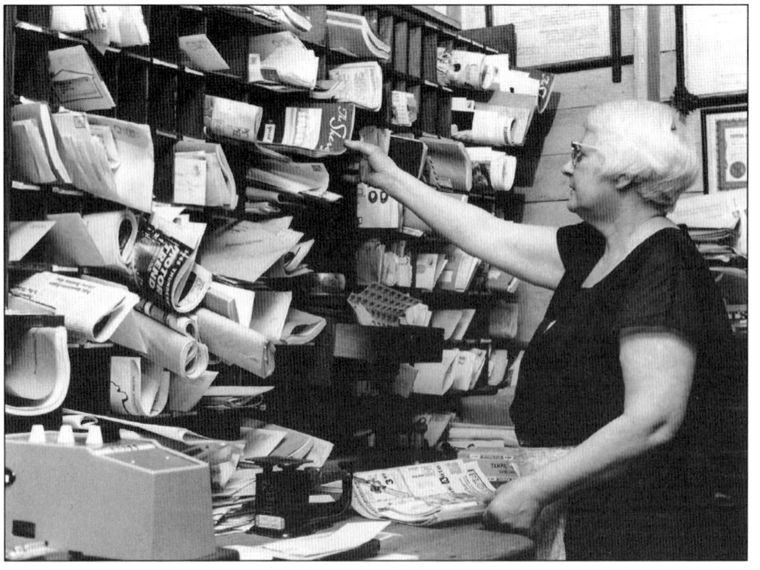

Agnes Jones, or "Miss Aggie," is shown hard at work sorting the mail. This building was where people came to get and send their mail as well as buy goods, use the phone, post a message to the bulletin board, listen to the sports and news on the radio, trade magazines and papers, catch the school bus, and learn the latest Mandarin gossip. It truly was the heart and soul of the community on the peninsula.

Dr. George Kennedy's office was located on a piece of land called Triangle Farm, where he lived with his wife, Letitia Jacks Kennedy, and their daughter Jean. Dr. Kennedy (1880–1923) was known as a very caring and dedicated doctor. Jean remembered him rowing across Julington Creek to care for a sick boy. He died at a very early age and is buried at the Mandarin Cemetery. (Courtesy of the Morrow family.)

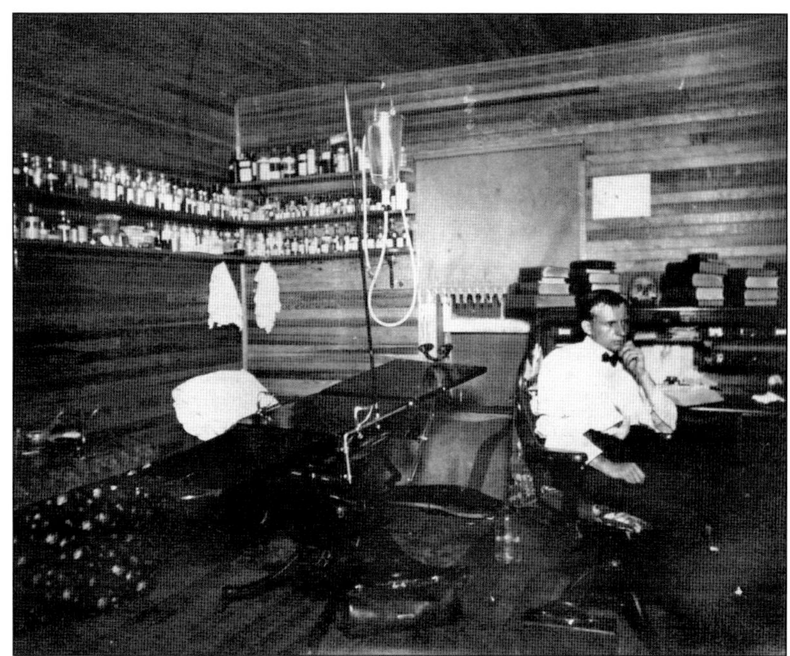

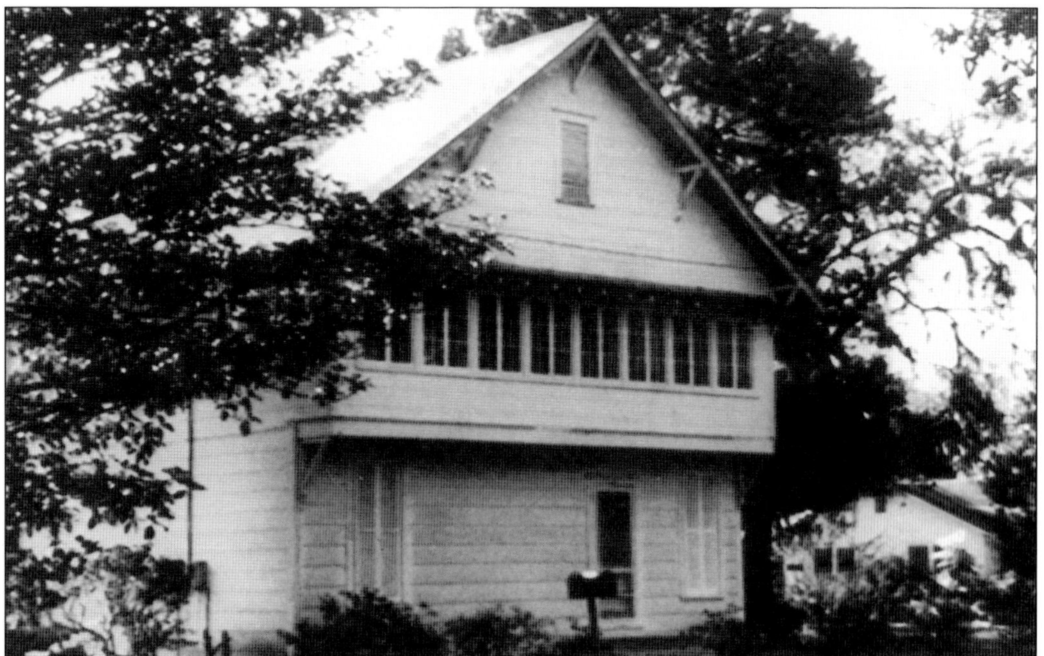

Just east on Loretto Road from Triangle Farm was the Flynn Feed & Seed. According to an oral history by Theodore Flynn, his father, James J. Flynn, bought the store from the widow of his brother in 1911. "After my father's death, my mother and I operated the store, until I bought her out in 1946." It remained a store until 1958, when he opened a new one on State Road 13.

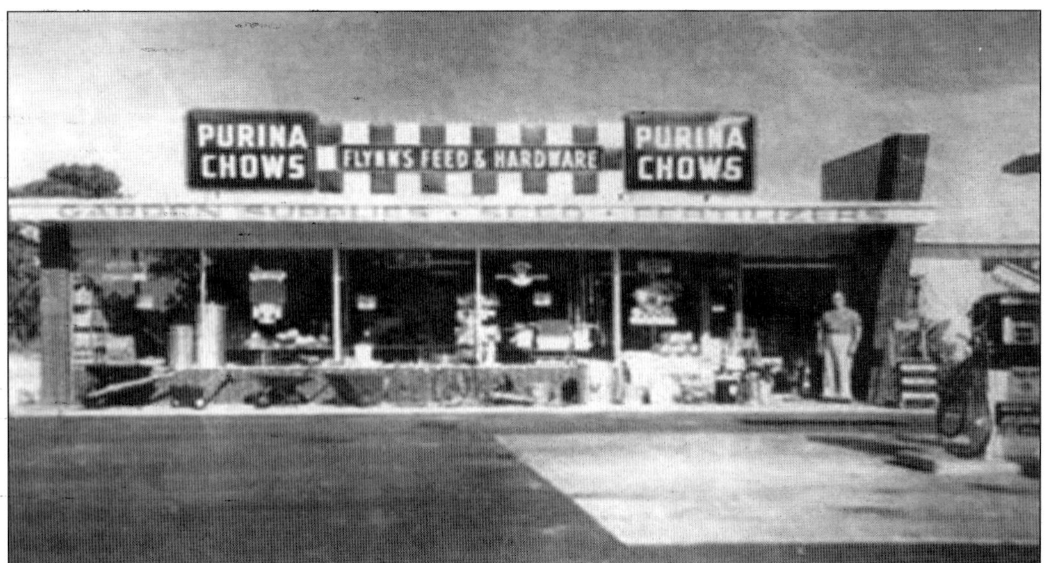

The new store, Flynn's Feed and Hardware, was modern and much larger. It was located at the corner of State Road 13 and Westberry Road. It was a welcoming store, a busy place where everyone knew each other's names. Theodore Flynn retired in 1973, and his son Ronald Lee Flynn Sr. ran it until it was sold out of the family to Hagan Ace. Theodore is seen standing at the door.

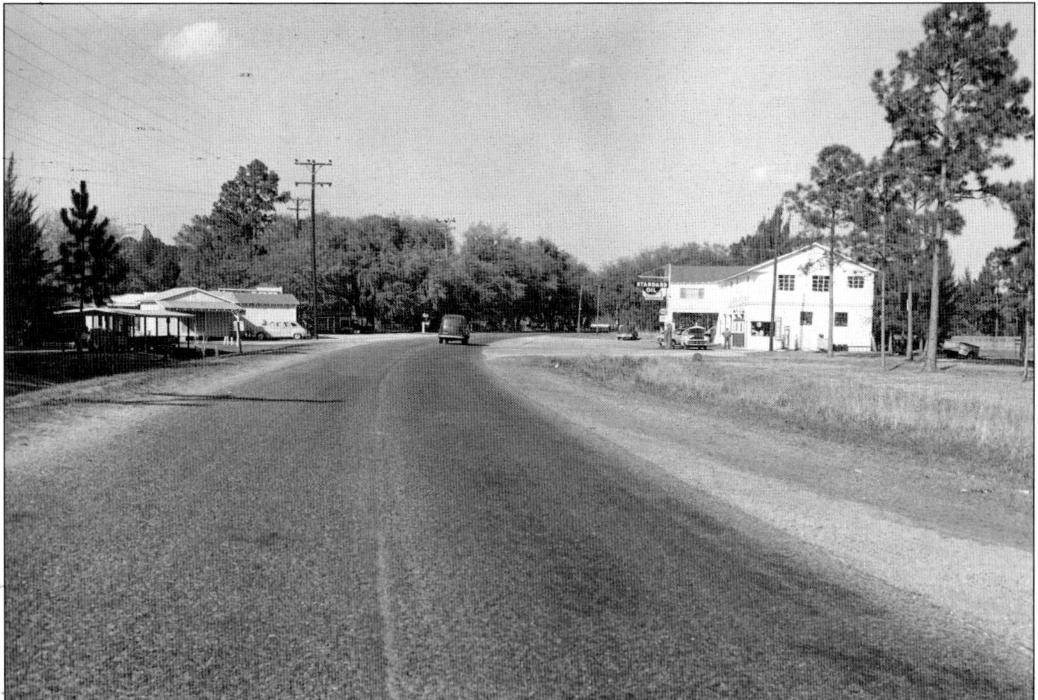

Looking north on State Road 13 in 1954 (now called San Jose Boulevard) toward Mandarin Road is Wilford's Garage on the right and Ruth Flynn's store on the left. The area where the "Little Train" was located can also be seen on the left. Today, this road is a six-lane highway with traffic lights and traffic jams and stores and other businesses lining the entire route. (Courtesy of the State Archives of Florida.)

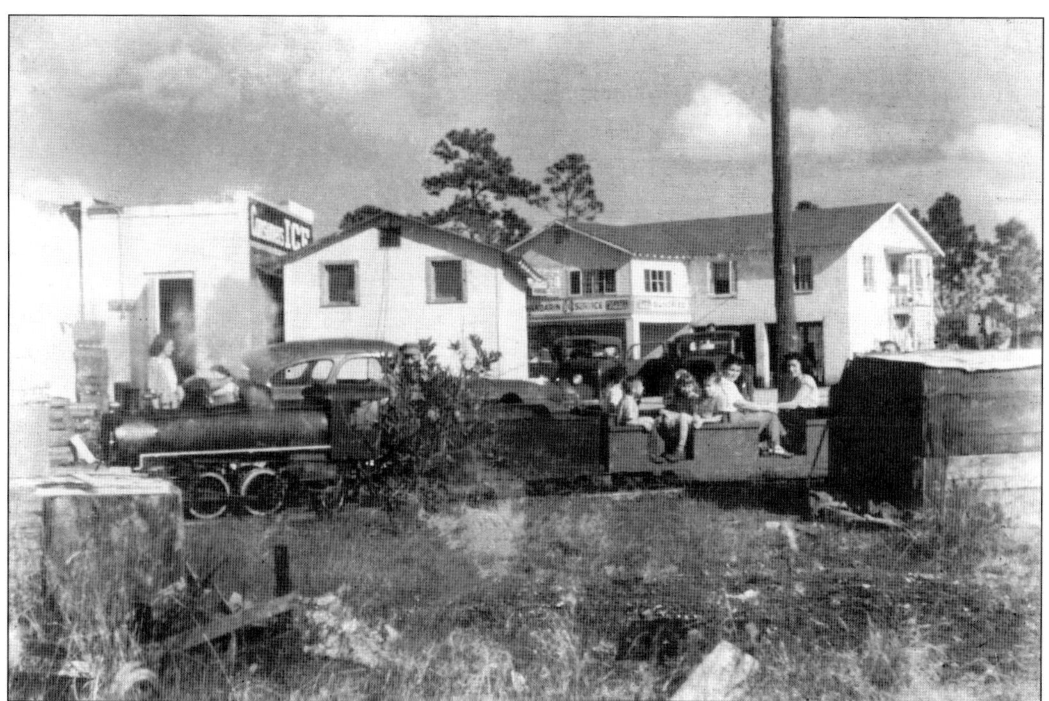

The Little Train ran behind Flynn's Store and Icehouse and into the woods. According to Wilford descendant Barbara Wilford Gentry, that store was started by Gress and Evelyn Wilford and later run by Gress's sister Ruth Wilford Flynn and her husband, Earl. Most people remember it as Ruth Flynn's store or sometimes the "Banner" store and, later, Mandarin Super. Braddy Wilford's Garage and Texaco station are seen across State Road 13.

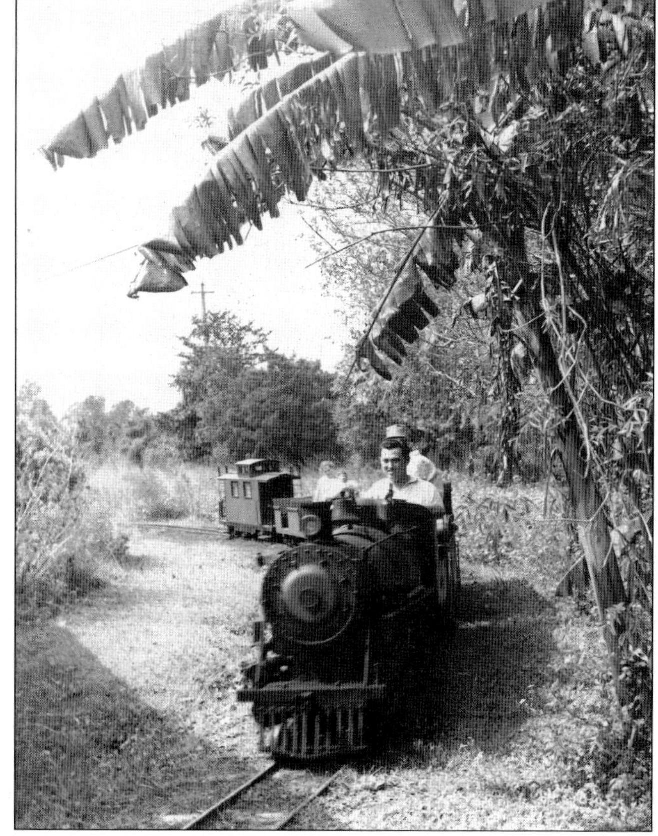

The tiny St. Johns & Eastern Railroad operated on State Road 13 from the mid-1940s until 1968. E.C. Ward built the steam locomotive in his garage. It was open Sundays and holidays and it cost 10¢. Mandarin resident Ronald McKinney is driving the train here, with Ward right behind him and Ronald's wife, Helen, and daughter Francie in the rear of the train. (Courtesy of Francine McKinney Igou.)

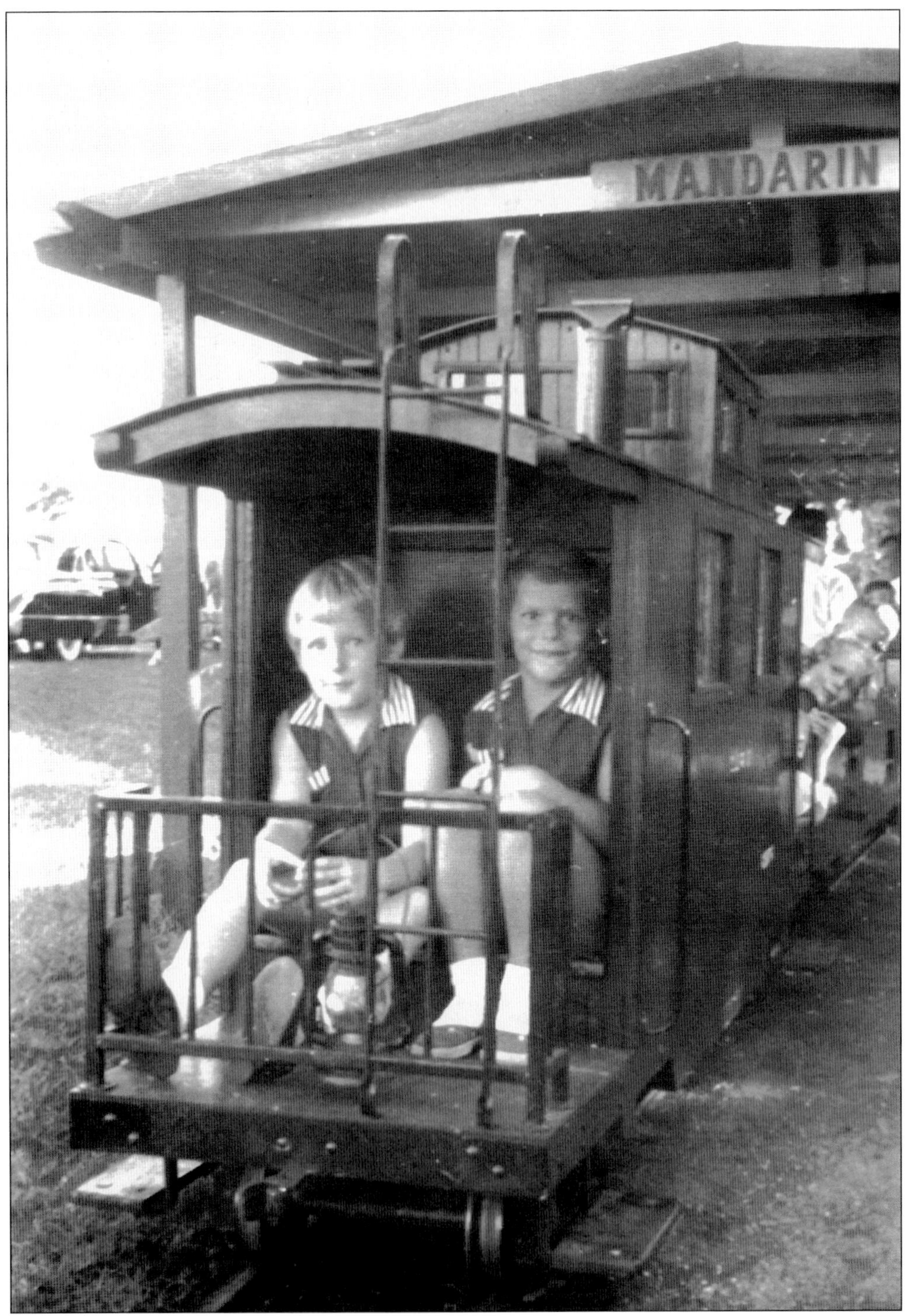

Pulling into the station are visitors from the San Jose area; from left to right are Helen Margaret Joost, Sharon Malone, and looking out from the back, Rita and Hobie Joost. People came from all over Jacksonville, making the long drive to the country to ride the train and buy oranges, grapefruit, and satsumas from the citrus groves in the area. (Courtesy of Mary Kight.)

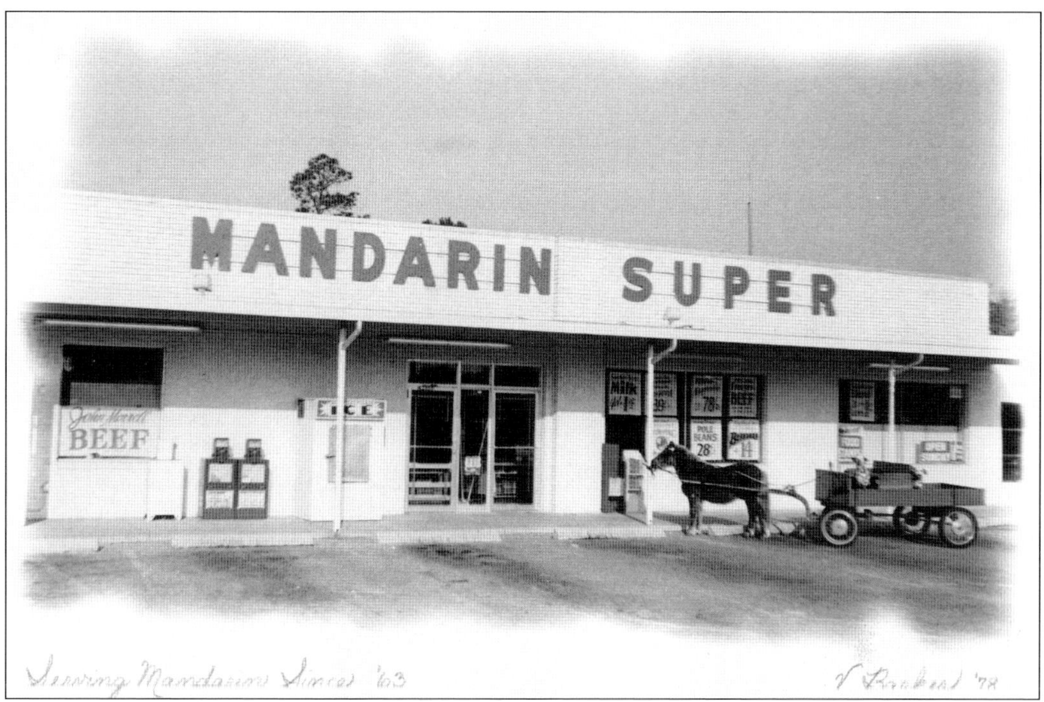

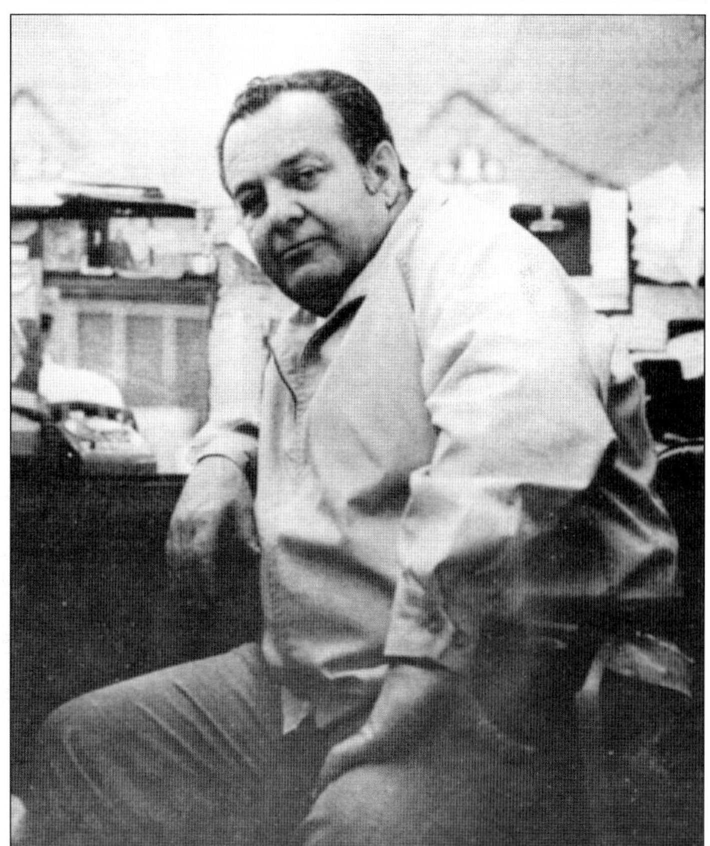

The Mandarin Super building was originally built by Earl and Ruth Wilford Flynn on the southwest corner of Mandarin Road and State Road 13, where a Publix now exists. It was sold to Joe and Betty Cury, who owned it from about 1967 to the early 1990s. In those days, many people had open accounts where you could shop, sign, and pay with one check at the end of the month. While the Curys owned it, they hosted a yearly holiday party in December with free food, drinks, and a live band. Toward the end of his life, Joe became a celebrity of sorts for fighting JEA rates and running for city council. (Above, courtesy of Virginia Barker; right, courtesy of *Rolling Stone*.)

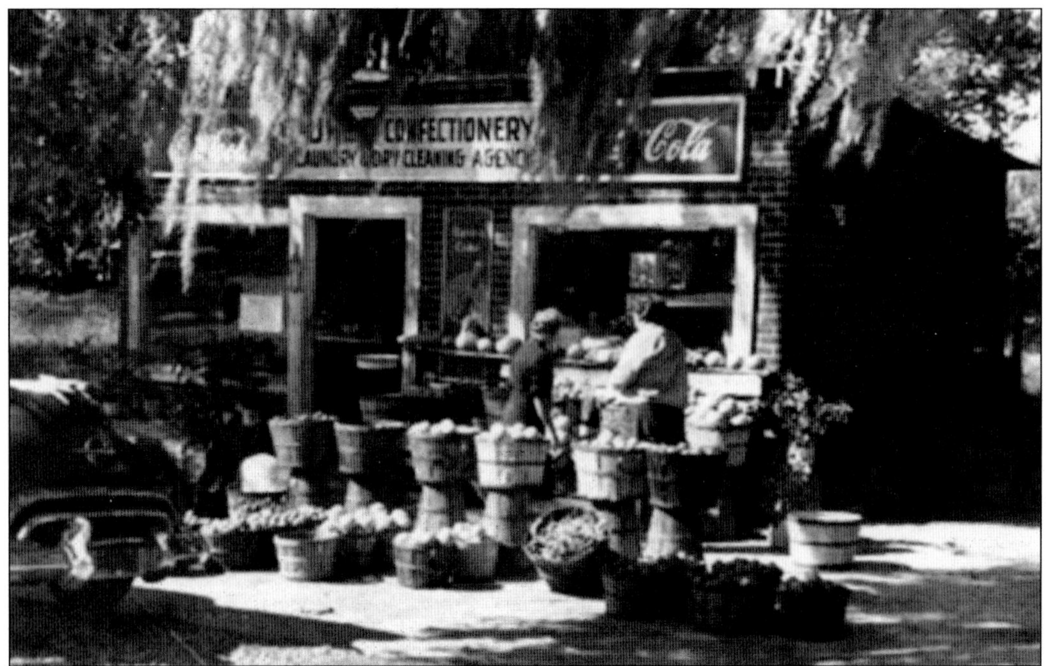

Just across Mandarin Road from Flynn's store was Dukes Confectionery, selling fresh citrus, produce, and a variety of other items, as well as taking in laundry. The Dukes family owned and lived on the property, which is now the Gates of Olde Mandarin shopping center.

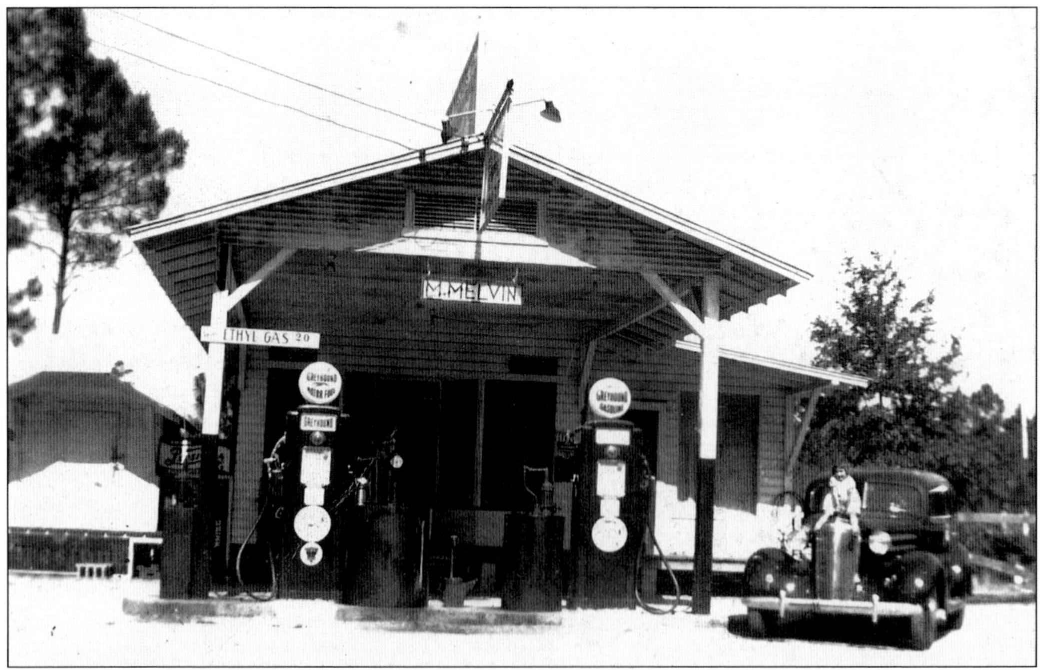

Further north on State Road 13, near where Interstate 295 now connects to the Buckman Bridge, was Melvin's Store. It was owned by Melvin O. Melvin and his wife, Pearl Flynn Melvin, and they lived right behind it. Their daughter Imogene is sitting on the hood of the car. In the 1960s, they sold the store to Marcus Acosta. (Courtesy of Donald Bowden.)

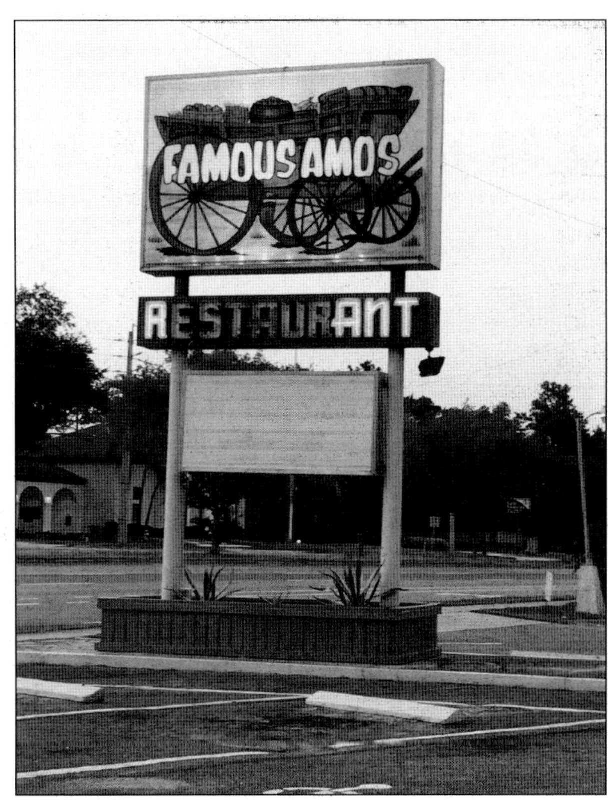

Famous Amos, on San Jose Boulevard at Oak Bluff Lane, was a local chain restaurant that also served as a well-known meeting and conversation place. It had been in Mandarin since 1977 before closing in 2019. The family-friendly restaurant served southern food in a western atmosphere. Many remember it fondly for its country cooking, all-night hours and all-day breakfasts, general friendliness, and the jukebox machines at each table.

This view of State Road 13 was taken in 1954 looking north from just south of Loretto Road. On the right is Stanley and Alma Flynn's Amoco station, and on the left is Epp Wilford's produce stand. There is still a gas station where Flynn's Amoco was on the right, and where the produce stand was on the left, became the Mandarin Pharmacy, and later a Taco Bell.

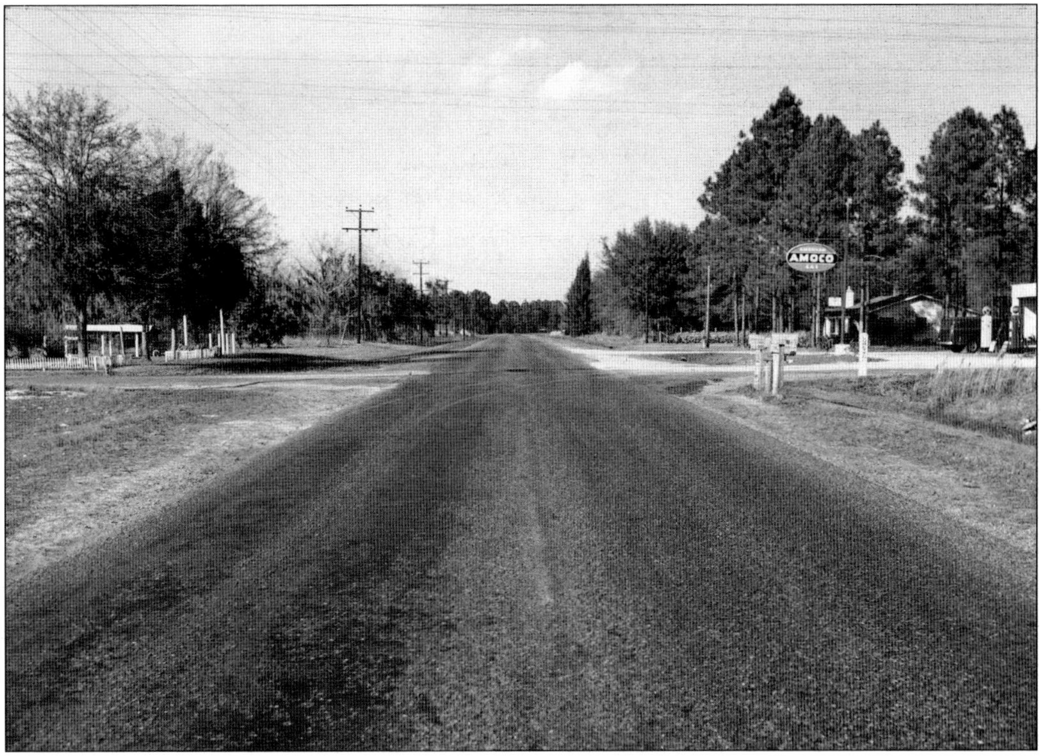

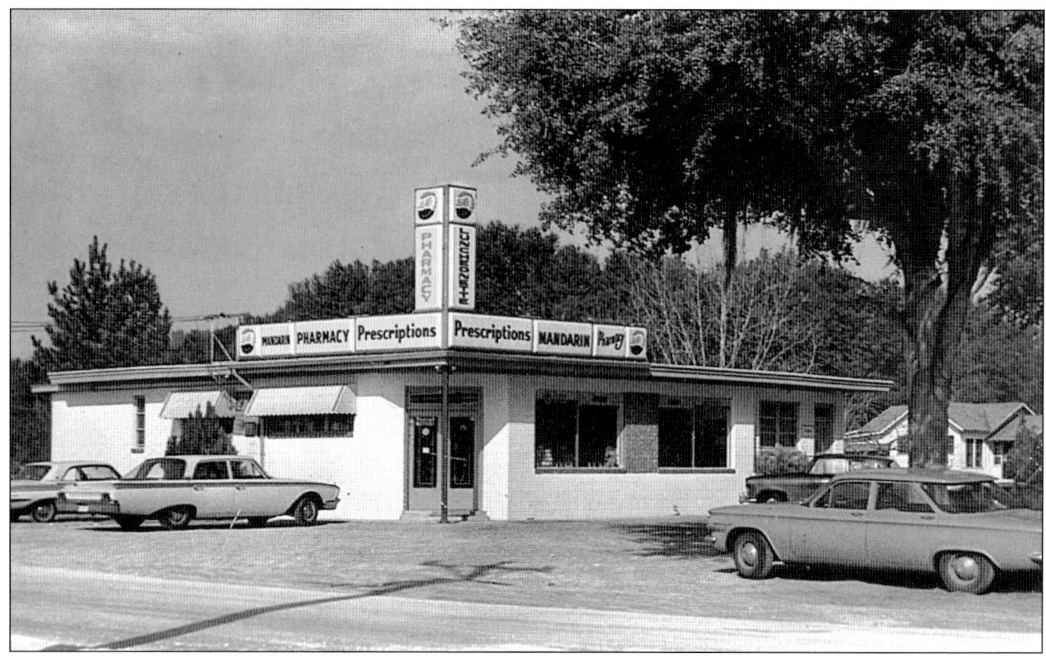

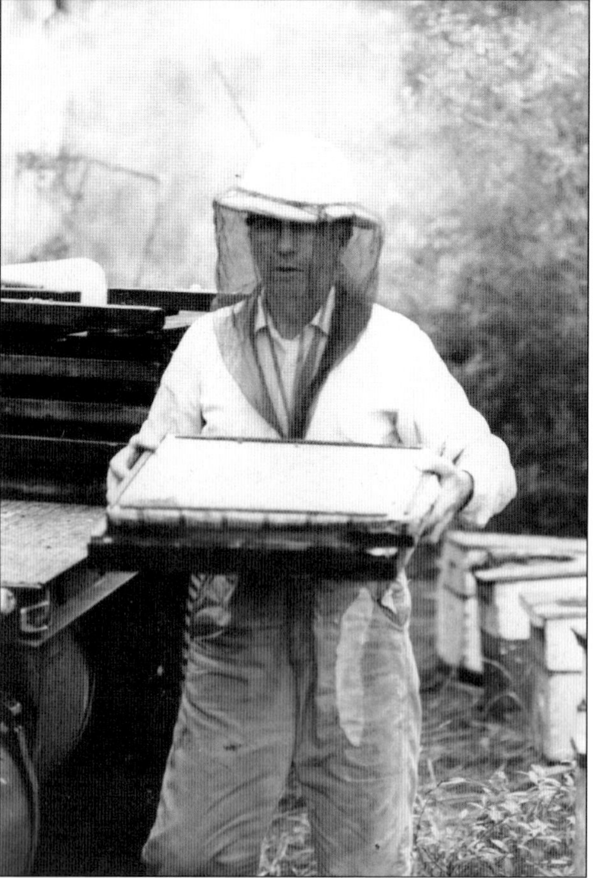

The Mandarin Pharmacy opened in 1960. It was a drugstore with a soda fountain and sundries. It even had a hitching post for customers who came on horseback. The first pharmacist was Don Scott, and the last was Calhoun Harris. On the right side was the first office of Dr. S. Joseph Bailey and, later, the office of the Justice of the Peace Ed Westberry.

Southeast of Loretto Road was Waldoch's Apiary and Honey Stand. George Waldoch, the "Honey Man," or his wife, Ruth, would man the stand, which was in front of their home. They also had a box for people to put their money in when they stopped to buy honey. George became the region's expert on beekeeping and honey. He passed away one day shy of his 100th birthday in 2019.

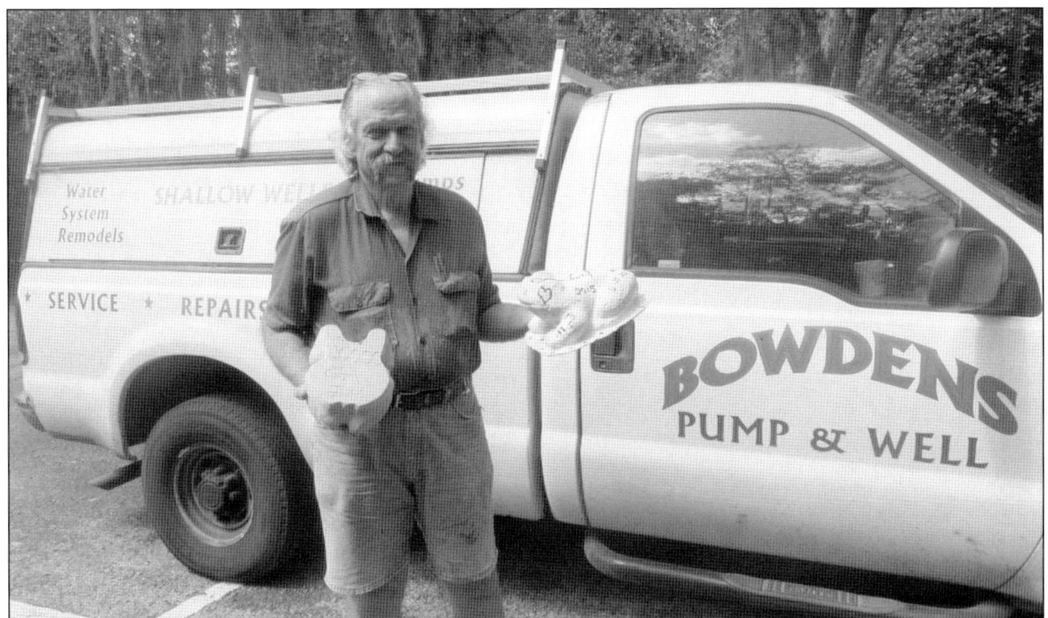

Donald Bowden ran his well-known pump and well business from 1976 to 2015. In 2022, he continues to drive this truck, but it is now full of concrete frogs. Mr. Bowden is now known as the "Mandarin Frog Man." He is seen here holding the mold and the 10,000th frog that he has cast. The frogs are painted and sold to benefit the Mandarin Museum & Historical Society, and have become a common sight in yards throughout Mandarin.

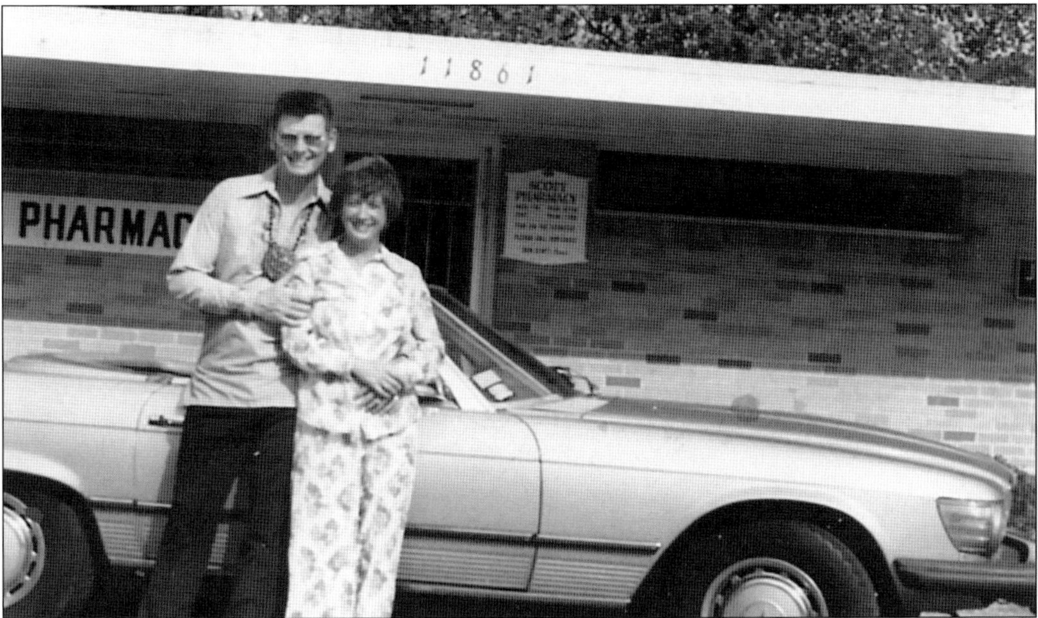

Don Scott, RPh, is seen in front of Scott Pharmacy with his wife, Barbara. Don was the pharmacist at Mandarin Pharmacy for Johnny Greenall in 1960 but moved with Dr. Bailey, who opened a new medical complex on San Jose Boulevard in 1962. Don was known for personal service and 24-hour delivery in his VW Beetle. The Scotts' daughter Susan also became a pharmacist and took over the practice after Don retired. (Courtesy of Susan Scott Earnhart.)

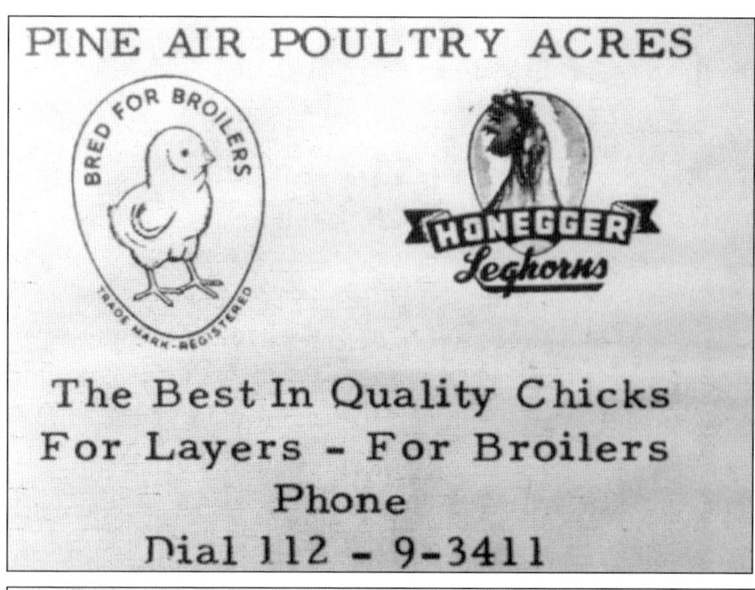

Off the beaten path at Loretto Road and Pine Acres Road was a poultry hatchery owned by Alton Belote, a member of the American Poultry & Hatchery Federation, which was organized in 1916. This hatchery existed until sometime in the 1960s. Also in the Loretto area, the Barkowski family owned a turkey farm.

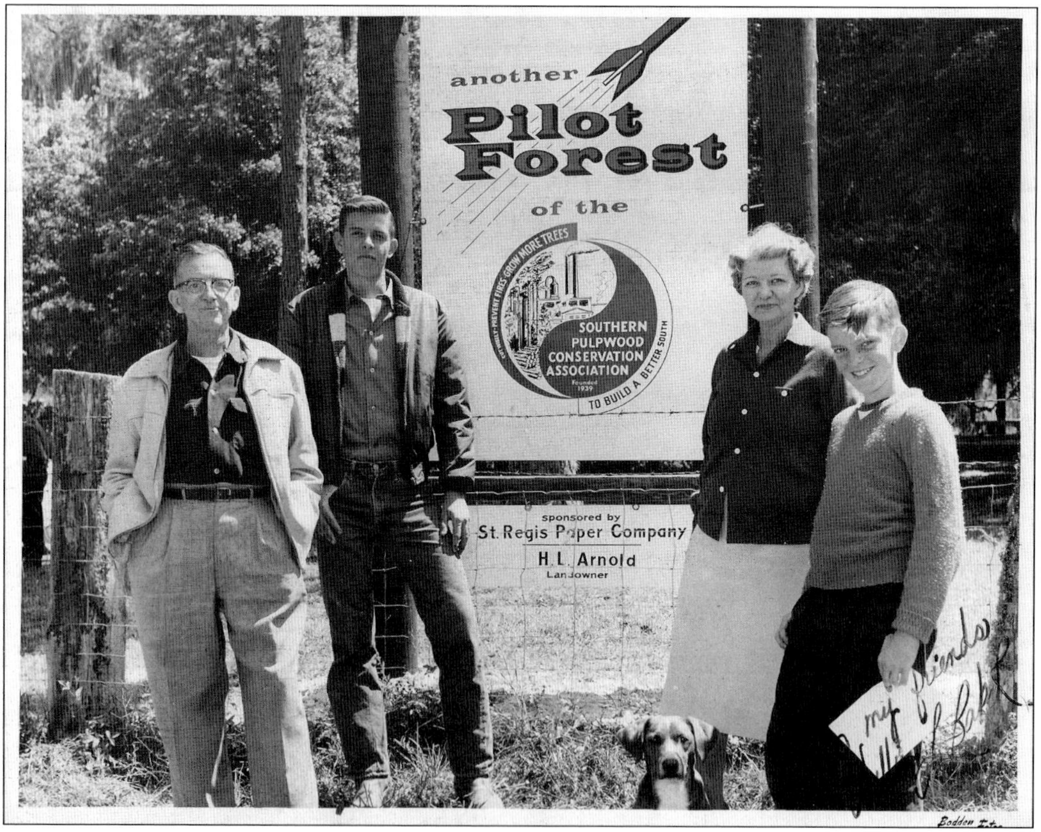

Just east of Pine Air Poultry on Loretto Road was the Arnold family's fern nursery. Elizabeth Arnold even propagated and patented a fern that was named for her, the "Frizzy Lizzie." The Arnolds also partnered with the St. Regis Paper Company to utilize some of their land as a "Pilot Forest"—a model of better forestry for the small landowner. From left to right are H.L. Arnold, son Jim, wife Elizabeth, and son David. (Courtesy of Megan Arnold.)

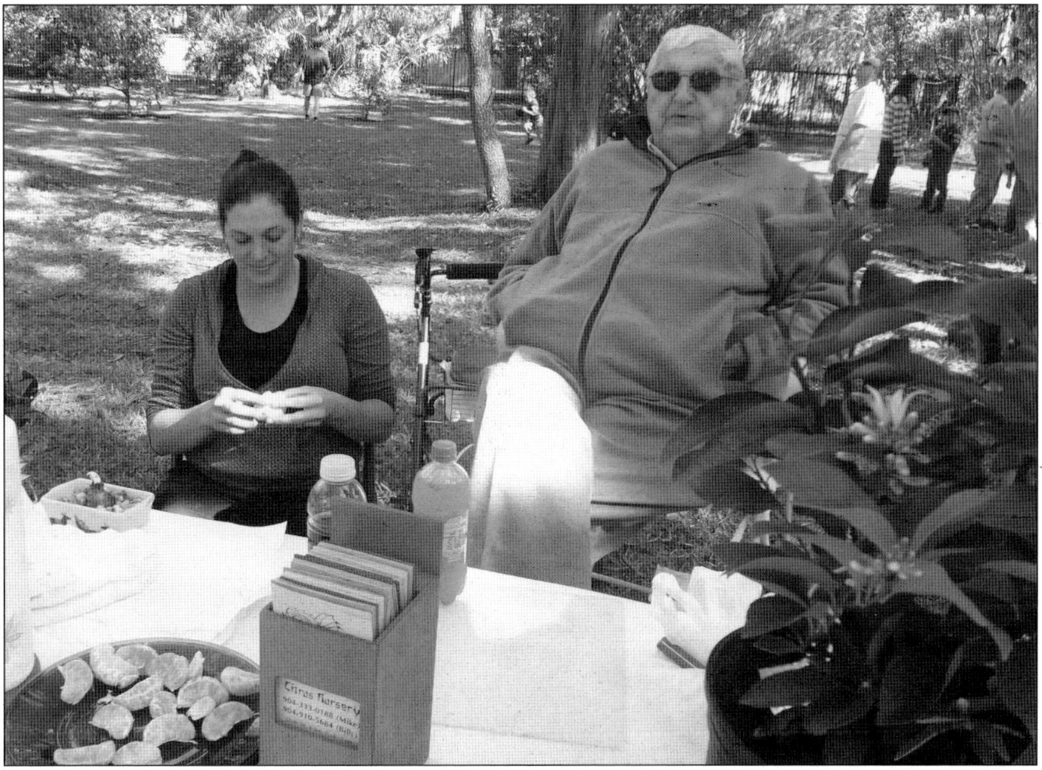

Billy Barwald was a member of the community since 1938. A landscape architect and citrus expert, he operated his business from his home on Loretto Road. In 1990, Billy and his son Mike opened Flying Dragon Citrus Nursery. He was an expert in the field, gave talks about citrus all around the state, and was elected to the Florida Nursery and Growers Association Hall of Fame in 2011. The nursery closed in 2019.

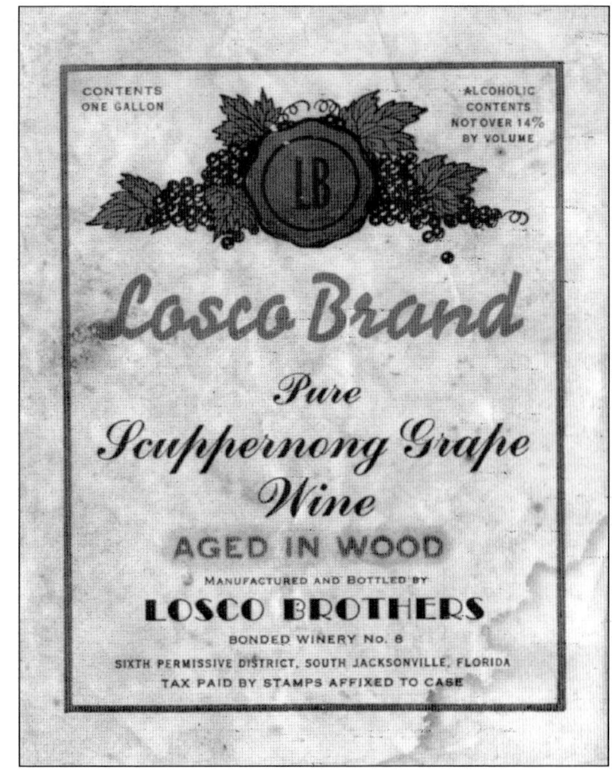

The Losco family settled in the place now known as Losco Road in the late 1800s. Francisco Losco and Dometilla Danese immigrated to America from Italy, married, and became farmers. They had a seven-acre scuppernong grape vineyard that produced about 40 barrels of wine a year. In 2007, when the family property was sold, the log cabin winery was donated to the Walter Jones Historical Park by David Losco.

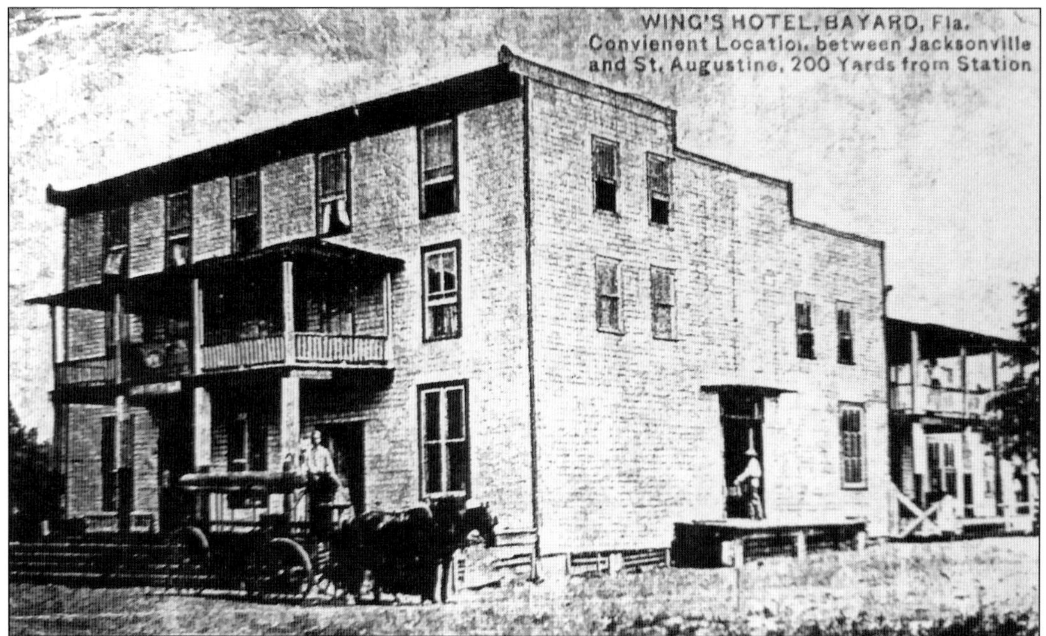

Southeast of Loretto, the community of Bayard grew up along the railroad track heading south through Florida in the late 1800s. It served as a train stop, but also sprung up with sawmills and a turpentine camp. W.W. Wing came to work at one of those sawmills and was soon killed on the job. Wing's Hotel was operated by his wife Juliette, son C.W., and other family members from 1899 until the 1950s. It had 12 rooms serving travelers and boarders. It later became the Bayard Country Store and eventually was torn down in 2004. (Courtesy of Richard Wing Turrill.)

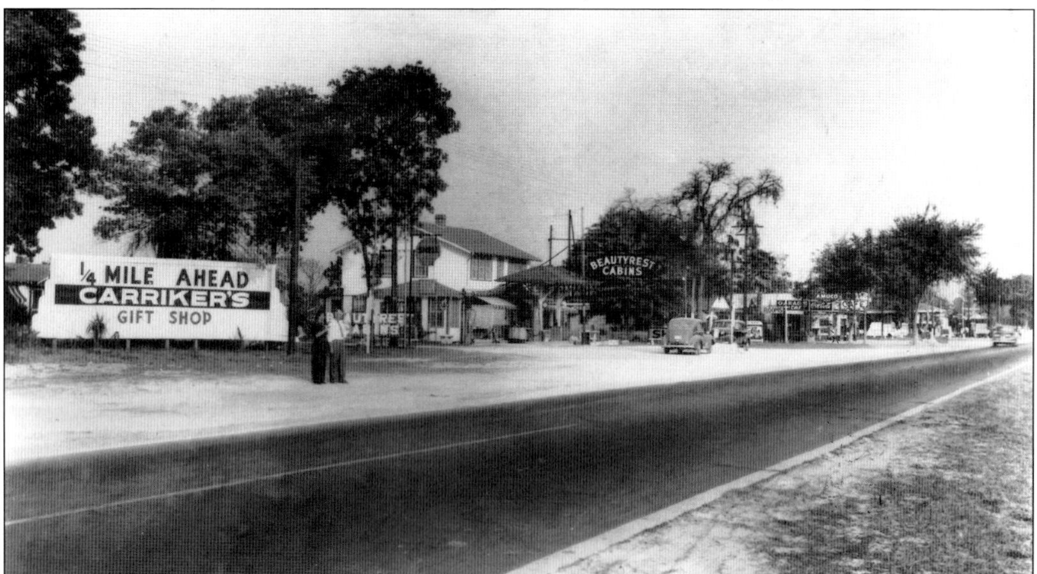

When the Dixie Highway (US Route 1) was completed in this area in 1934, business really started to boom in Bayard. It was the first paved highway along Florida's Atlantic coast. It is hard today to imagine it as a two-lane road. Bayard was considered the outskirts of Mandarin but always a vital community that is the eastern border of what is now considered Mandarin. (Courtesy of Marvin Neil Targonski.)

Another popular place in Bayard in the mid-20th century was Steve's Grocery-Café-Garage and Cabins. The Targonski family owned this hugely popular place for tourists to stop on their way south to Miami. Located on US Route 1, it provided everything a traveler would need. (Courtesy of Marvin Neil Targonski.)

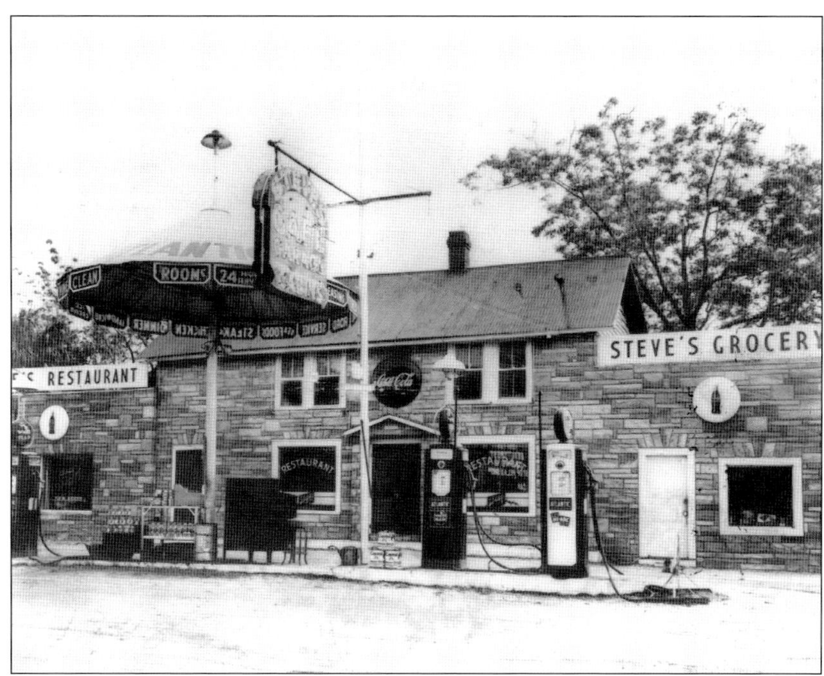

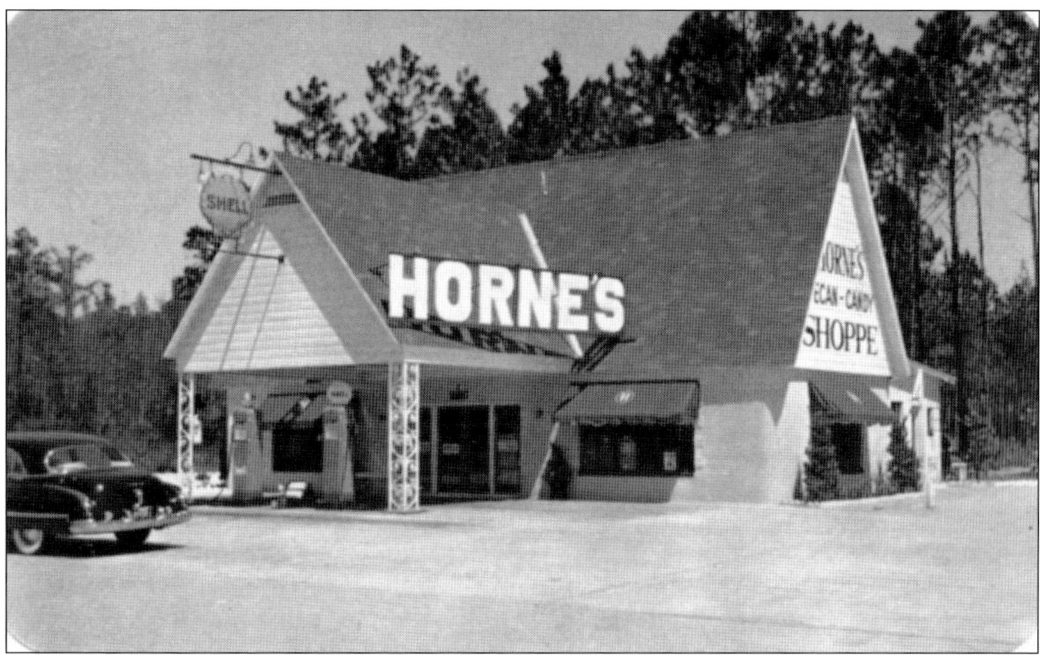

The A.I. Horne family opened Beautyrest Cabins in the 1930s in Bayard, followed in 1948 by their son Bob's first Horne's Candy Shoppe. Known for its delicious candy, the business grew and developed into a chain of 44 stores that included small cafes and other goods. It was a very popular stopping-off place along US Route 1 until the Interstate Highway System moved traffic west of Bayard. Horne's was purchased by the Greyhound Corporation in 1964.

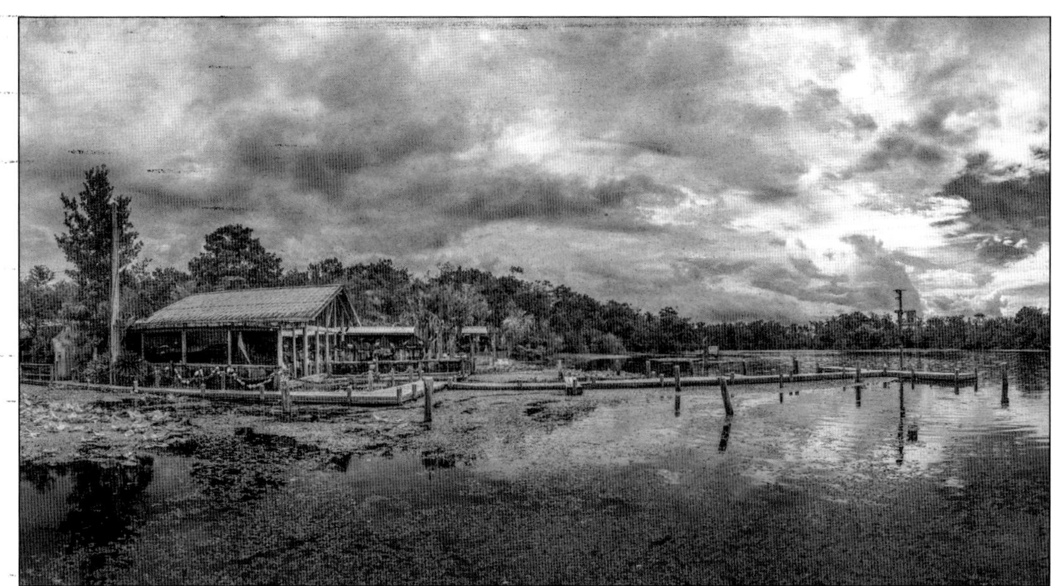

Many old-timers remember Clark's Fish Camp on Julington Creek as a place you could launch your boat and buy bait and a snack. But in the mid-1970s, the Clark family sold it to Jack and Joan Peoples, who enlarged it to become Clark's Fish Camp Seafood Restaurant. This rustic restaurant has patio seating and is filled with a huge taxidermy collection, which fascinates guests of all ages. (Courtesy of Olis Garber.)

FLORIDA MOTOR LINES

ANNOUNCES

NEW BUS SERVICE

"THE SCENIC ROUTE"

Jacksonville -- Mandarin -- Green Cove Springs

EFFECTIVE JANUARY 26, 1942

Schedules and Rates Subject to Change Without Notice

TO JACKSONVILLE

	DAILY EXCEPT [illegible]N.	DAILY	DAILY EXCEPT SUN.	DAILY EXCEPT SUN.	DAILY EXCEPT SUN.	MON. AND THUR. ONLY	SAT. ONLY
LEAVE	A.M.	A.M.	A.M.	P.M.	P.M.	P.M.	P.M.
Green Cove Springs		7:00					
Lee Field							
Orangedale		7:10					
Switzerland		7:20					
Fruit Cove Terrace		7:23					
Julington Creek	6:15	7:25	7:50	5:55	7:20	12:01	2:00
Mandarin P. O.	6:25	7:30	8:00	6:05	7:30	12:10	2:10
Flynn's Store	6:28			6:08		12:13	2:13
Gress' Store		7:32	8:02	6:10	7:32	12:15	2:15
Melvin's Store		7:33	8:05	6:12	7:35	12:17	2:17
Loretta	6:30						
Hartley's Store	6:33						
Jct. Sunbeam - 47 - St. Aug.	6:35	7:38	8:10	6:17	7:40	12:25	2:25
Goodby's Lake	6:38	7:40	8:12	6:18	7:42	12:28	2:28
San Jose	6:40	7:43	8:15	6:20	7:45	12:30	2:30
Clayton Hotel, So. Jax	6:45	7:45	8:17	6:22	7:48	12:33	2:33
Jax - (Over old bridge)	7:00	8:00	8:30	6:35	8:00	12:45	2:45
	A.M.	A.M.	P.M.	P.M.	P.M.	P.M.	P.M.

The Florida Motor Lines and later the Florida Greyhound Lines helped transport Mandarin residents to Jacksonville in the mid-20th century. This schedule is from 1942 and includes several of the existing business stops. Many Mandarin residents depended on this transportation to get to school and work. It touts Mandarin as "the Scenic Route." Being beautiful has always been one of Mandarin's claims to fame because of the giant canopy of live oak trees.

Nine

Churches and Schools

The earliest presence of an official Christian congregation in Mandarin was in 1834 when a Presbyterian Church was built, located where the Mandarin Cemetery is now. During the next years, the unrest of the Seminole Wars and poverty took their toll, and the little church closed. In the 1950s, the Mandarin Chapel was begun at the Mandarin Community Club, and in 1961, it became Mandarin Presbyterian Church on Mandarin Road east of County Dock Road (second sanctuary seen here). In 1994, Mandarin Presbyterian Preschool was started. In 2000, a new church complex was built on the old Triangle Farm at Loretto, County Dock, and Mandarin Roads and is called the Loretto Road Campus. The 1961 buildings are now called the Mandarin Road Campus.

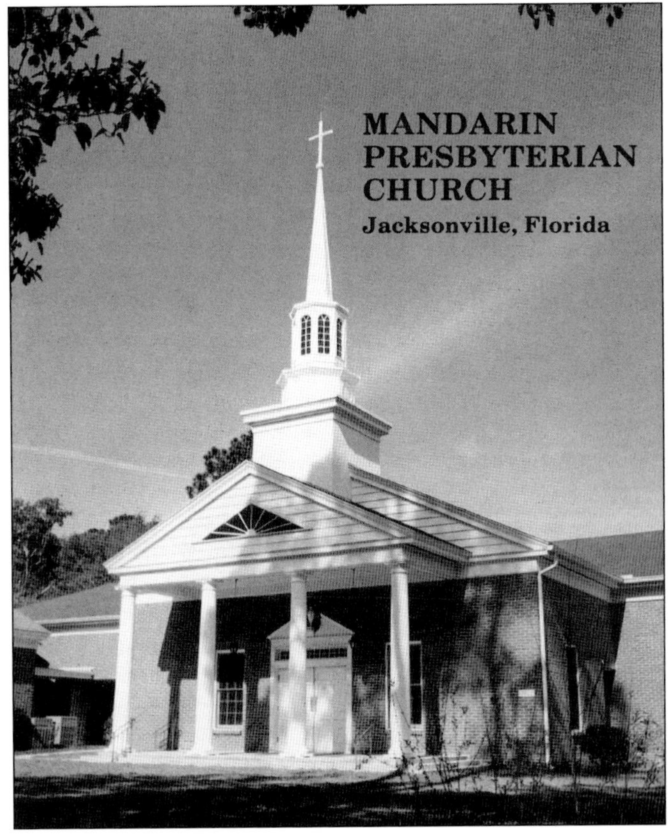

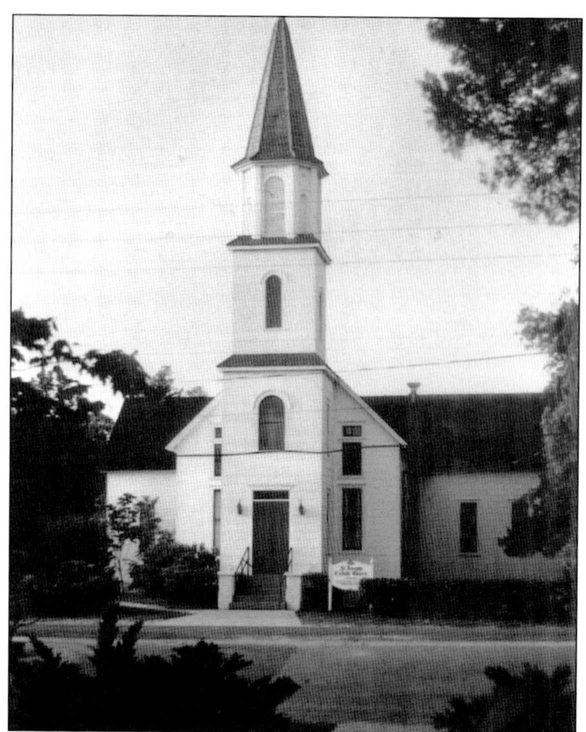

In the mid-19th century, the area once called "Honey Hill," but now called Loretto, was one of the stops for traveling Catholic priests. In 1850, the Rev. Bishop Verot purchased land from Charles Reed and received donated land from George Hartley, and a small chapel was built in 1858. Construction of the church seen here was begun by local builder William Monson in the late 1880s and opened in 1912. The "historic church," as it is often called, is listed in the National Register of Historic Places.

This building, the rectory, is just to the left of the church, and the academy is to the right. St. Joseph's provided education to the community beginning in 1868 when the Sisters of St. Joseph sent Sisters Julia Roussel and Mary Bernard to the wilderness of Mandarin to teach both Black and White children.

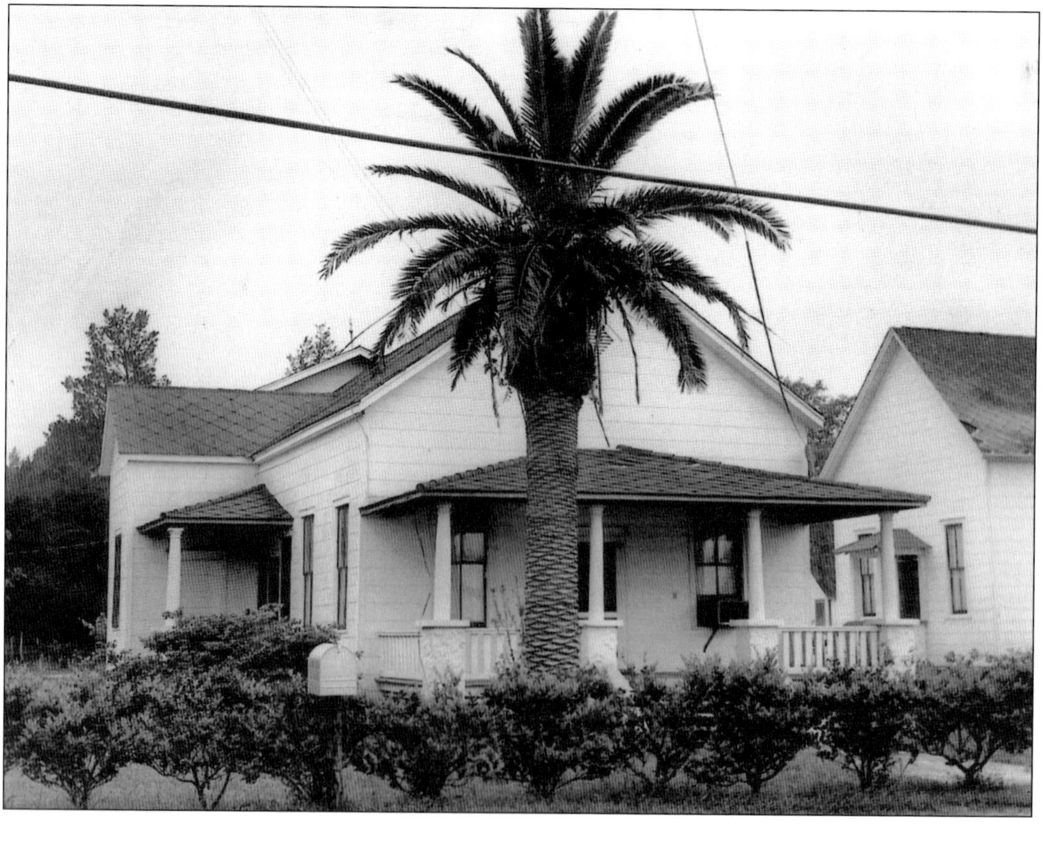

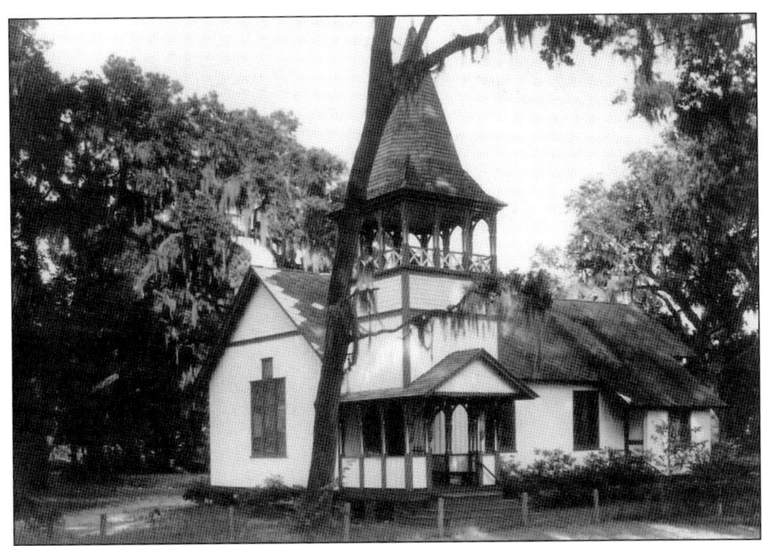

The congregation of the Episcopal Church of Our Saviour was formed in 1880 when Calvin Stowe held Bible readings and services in the Mandarin School building, which was used as a church on Sundays. This group, including many English families, built a small church on Mandarin Road, overlooking the St. Johns River in 1883. The land was purchased for $121.75.

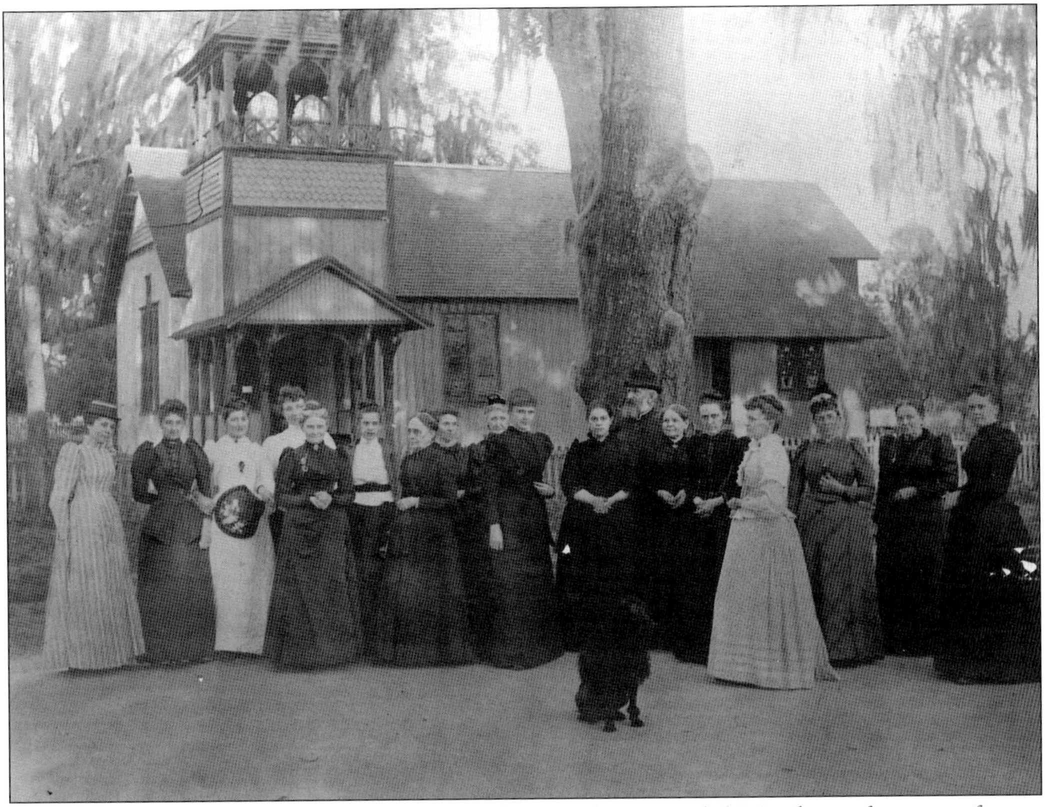

The congregation grew and was very active until 1899, when many left Mandarin after severe freezes destroyed the citrus industry. The church's status changed to "mission" with monthly services. After World War II, however, growth occurred again and this sanctuary was used until 1964 when Hurricane Dora destroyed the church, including the famous Tiffany stained-glass window that was in honor of the Stowes.

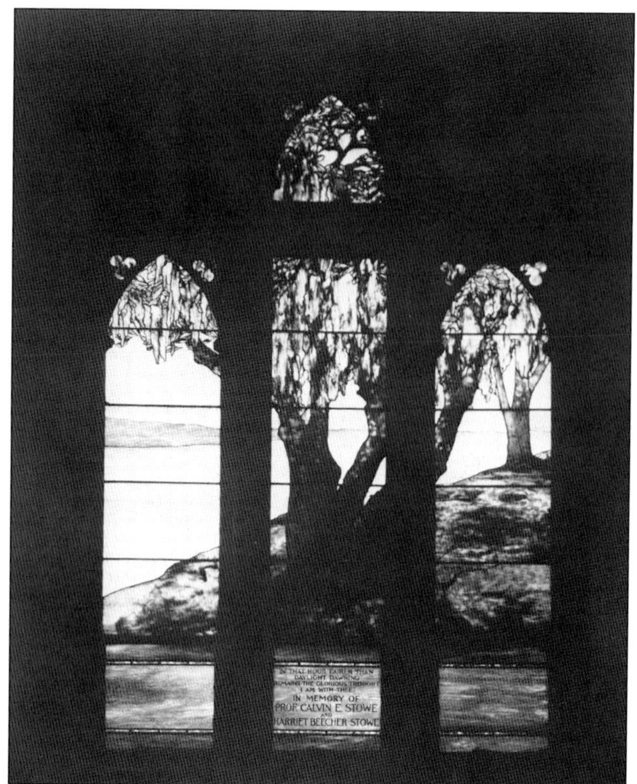

Reportedly, Harriet Beecher Stowe, after leaving Mandarin in 1884, asked that the church have a window made in honor of her husband, Calvin. After the Stowes had passed, the Stowe window was designed by Margaret Huntington Hooker, in honor of both Calvin and Harriet. A fundraising campaign took place, and Louis Comfort Tiffany agreed to make it. The window was complete and installed in 1916. It is said to represent the view from the Stowes' porch facing the river. (Courtesy of the State Archives of Florida.)

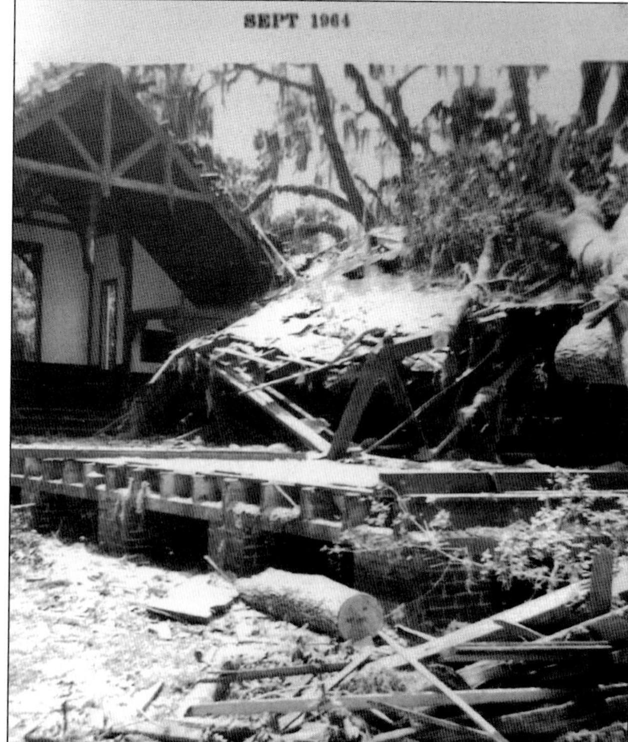

After the destruction caused by Hurricane Dora, the entire church had to be replaced in 1966. Thankfully, the other stained-glass windows, pews, and altar were saved and placed in a new and special small chapel at the back of the much larger new sanctuary.

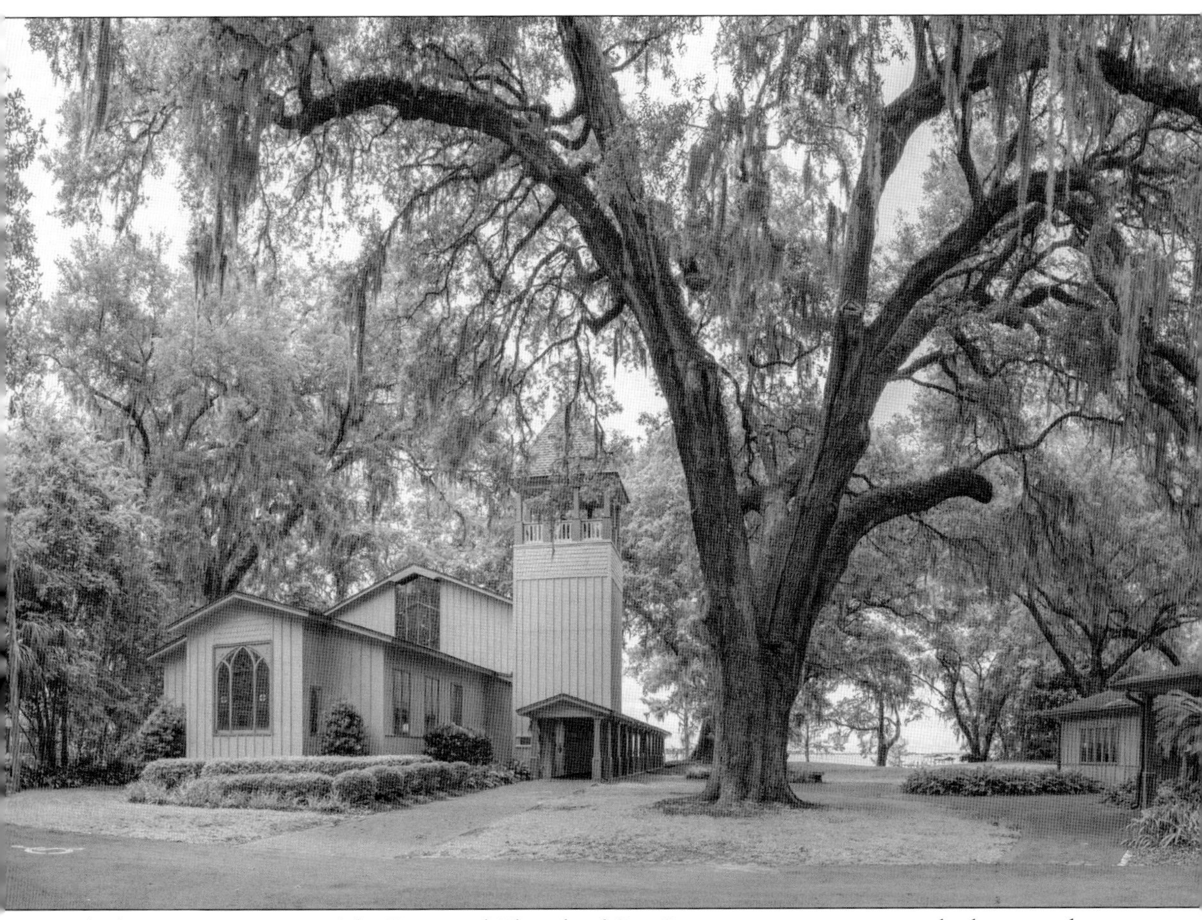

The large congregation of the Episcopal Church of Our Saviour remains active and relevant today. One of their most popular community activities is hosting live music on their grounds along the banks of the St. Johns River. (Courtesy of Olis Garber.)

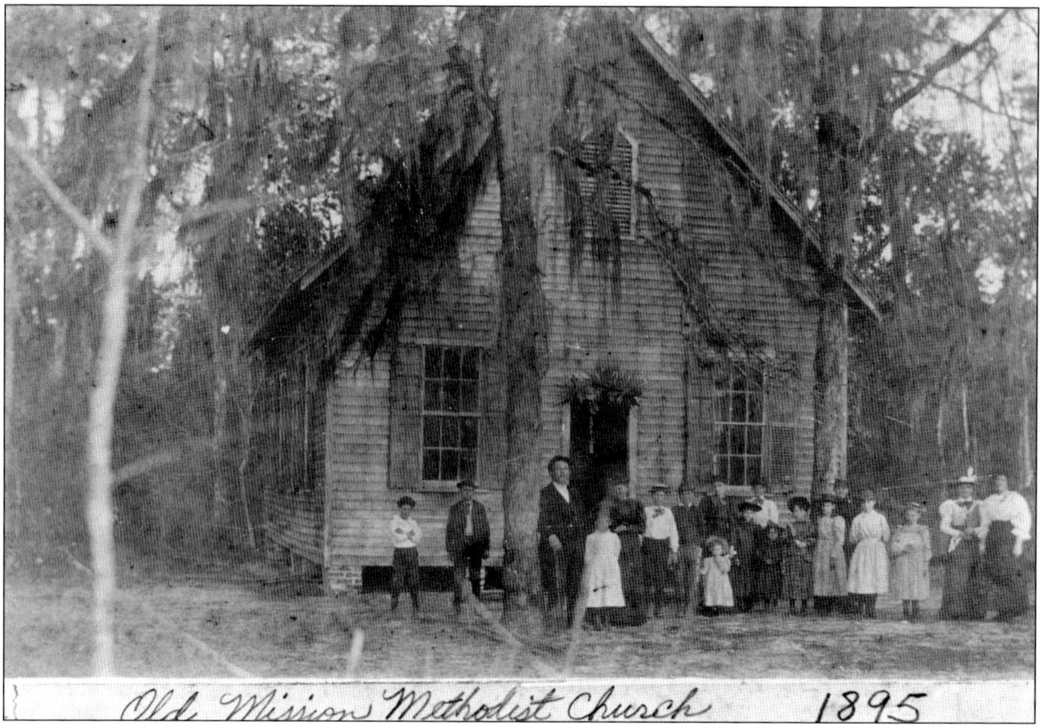

Old Mission Methodist Church 1895

The first Methodist congregation in Mandarin was started in 1874 as a mission located just south of the intersection of Loretto Road and State Road 13. It was a circuit church led by T.W. Moore of the Mandarin and Palatka Mission in the Jacksonville District. Circuit rider ministers traveled long distances and were called "saddlebag preachers." From 1874 to 1904, Mandarin was served by 13 different circuit riders. (Courtesy of Mandarin United Methodist Church.)

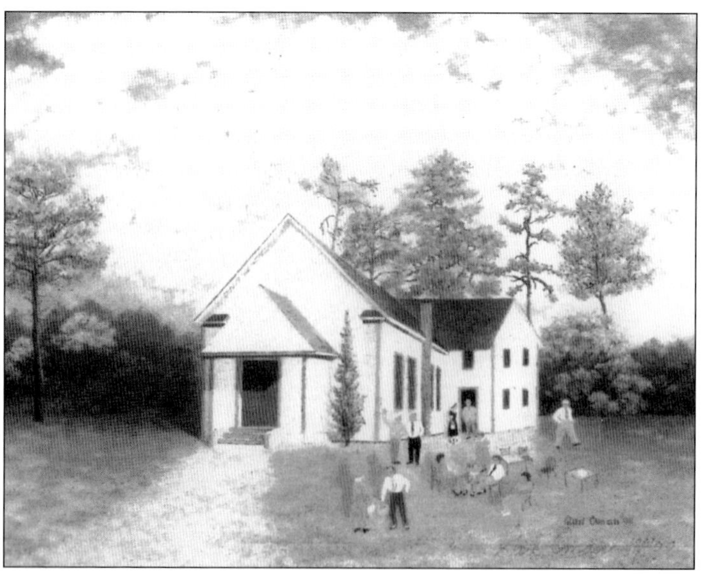

In the late 1890s, Bethel Methodist Church was started at St. Augustine Road and State Road 13. Eventually, members from the closed Mandarin Mission began to attend. Bethel later became Mandarin Roads Methodist and, eventually, Mandarin United Methodist Church (MUMC), which is a large congregation today. It is located on San Jose Boulevard just north of Mandarin Road, where the first sanctuary was built in 1960. (Art by Gail Oman, courtesy of MUMC.)

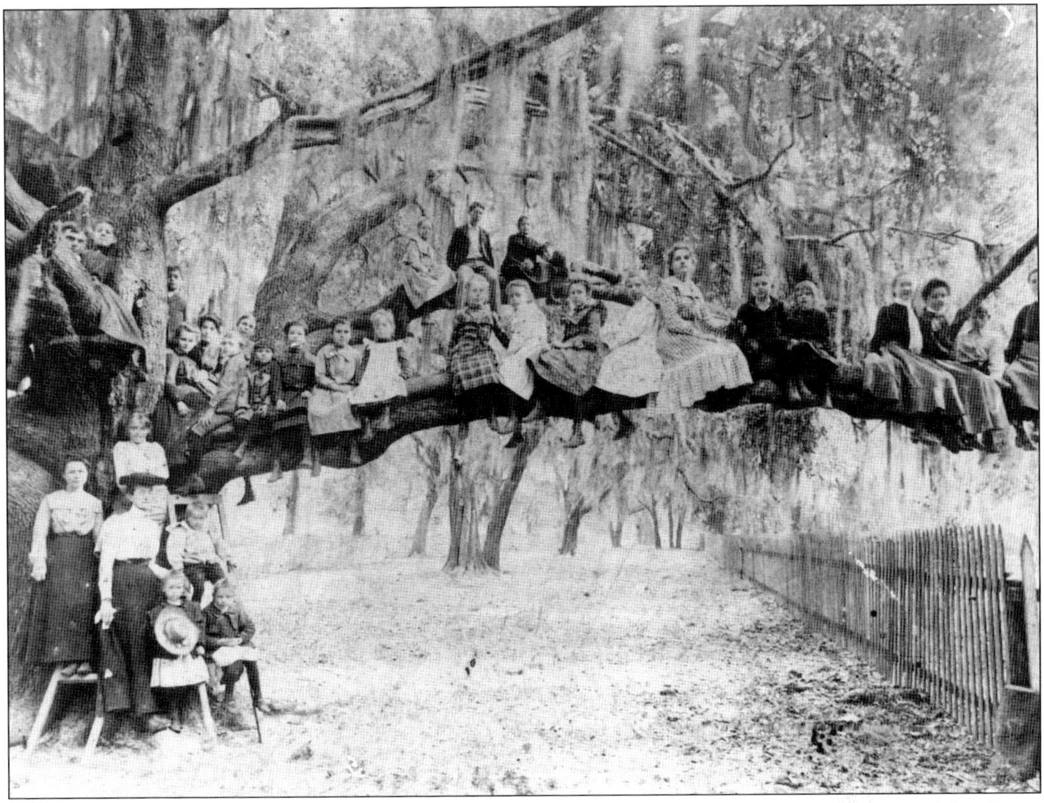

The Mandarin School on Mandarin Road (the current Mandarin Community Club building) was funded with the help of Harriet Beecher Stowe in 1872. It served Black and White children at first, but eventually it served an all-White student body. In the early 1920s, the children transitioned to Loretto School. This tree was in front of the building and served as a wonderful photo opportunity.

The St. Joseph's School began in 1868 when two Sisters of St. Joseph arrived in Mandarin to teach in a little wooden building in the area of Loretto. They taught both White and Black children but separately. The Sisters continued teaching, even for a short time, to public school students. As the St. Joseph's Church continued to grow, the school grew to include an academy with male boarding students until 1963. The academy buildings were torn down in 1967.

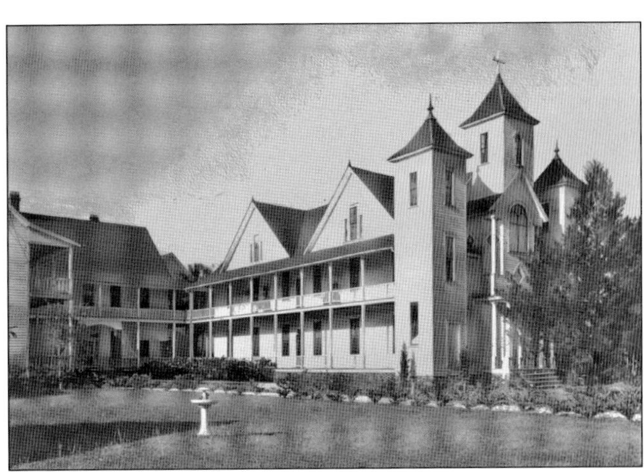

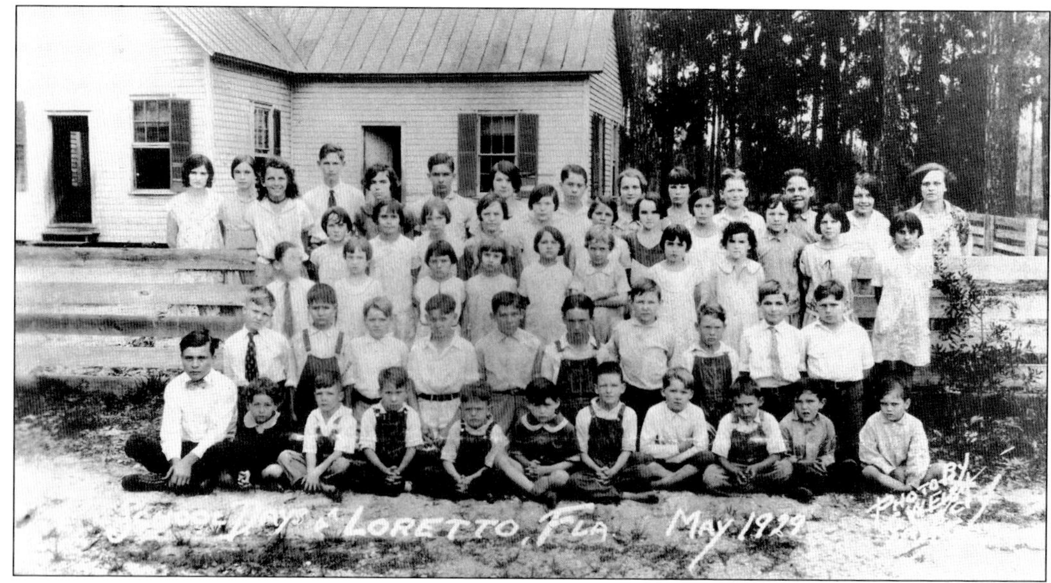

In 1929, Loretto school No. 30, a three-room wooden building was opened at the present location on Loretto Road. By this time, the school had a principal and five teachers (Prof. M.C. Hood, Mrs. Webb, Thelma Williams, J. Wing, Mrs. Jones, and Kate Monson) but still no electricity or running water. By 1943, more land was acquired from the George Hartley estate, and a new six-room brick building was erected.

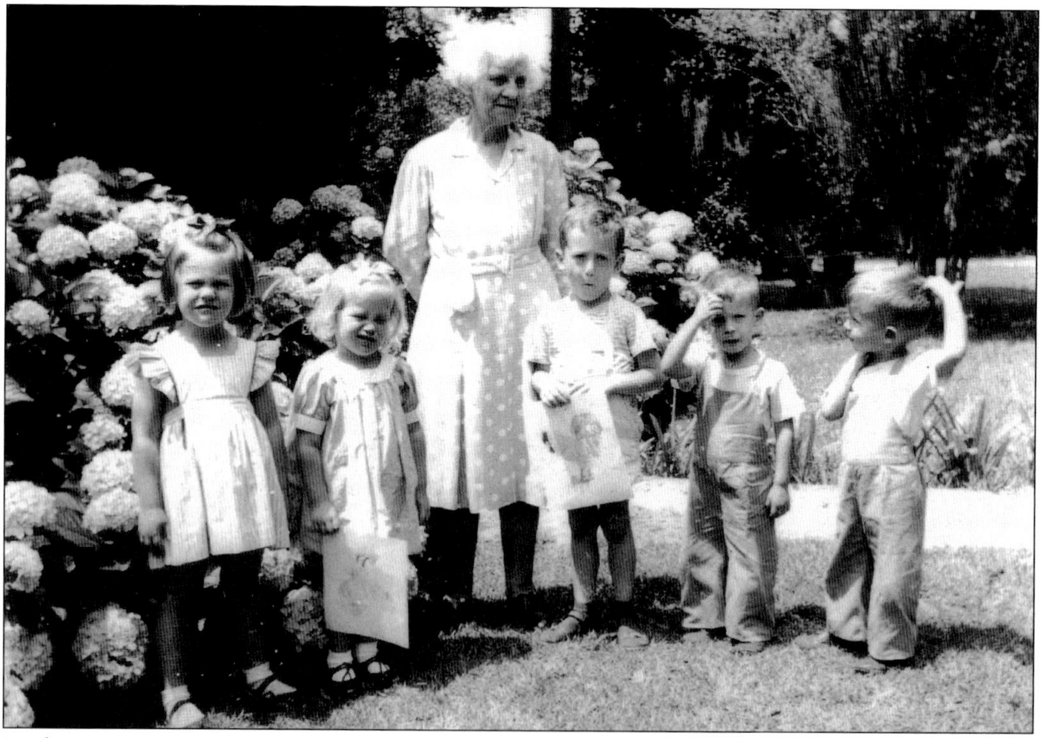

In the 1950s, Kate, or "Miss Katie," Monson, after her retirement from many years of teaching public school, had a private preschool at her home. She is seen here with students, from left to right, Shannon Jeter, Judy Walsh, Joe Walsh, Bill Morrow, and Cary Morrow.

Ten

The Beauty of Mandarin

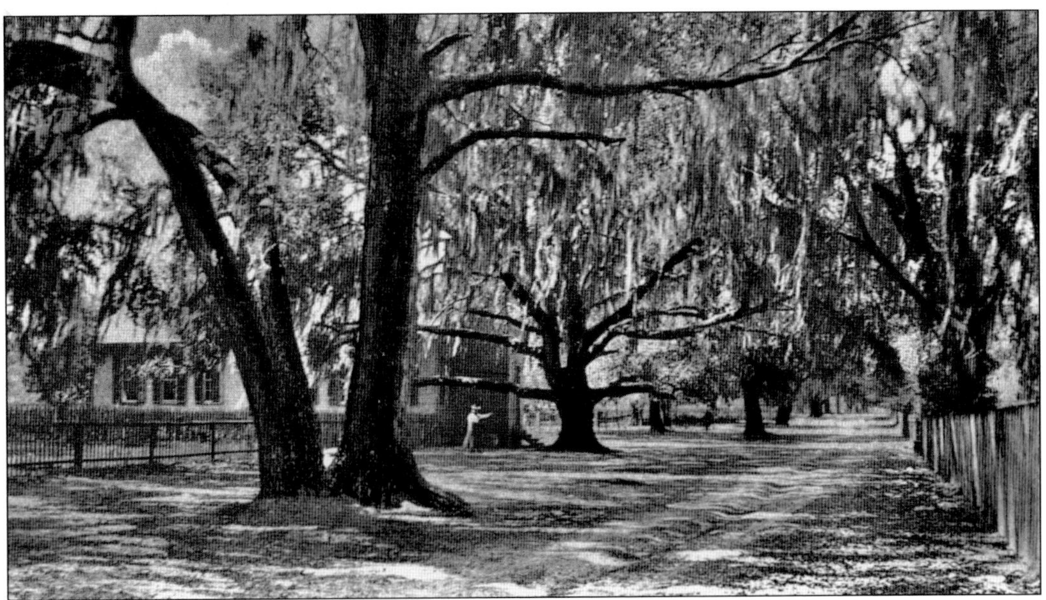

Mandarin has always drawn people because of the inherent beauty of the landscape, climate, and natural resources. Harriet Beecher Stowe encouraged northerners to move here to avoid the cold and dreary winters. She wrote of water lilies, moss blowing in the wind, the magnificent live oaks and magnolias, the scent of the orange blossoms, and the beauty of the river. Residents have worked hard to protect these things that make Mandarin beautiful for over a century. The Mandarin School is seen on the left in this photograph.

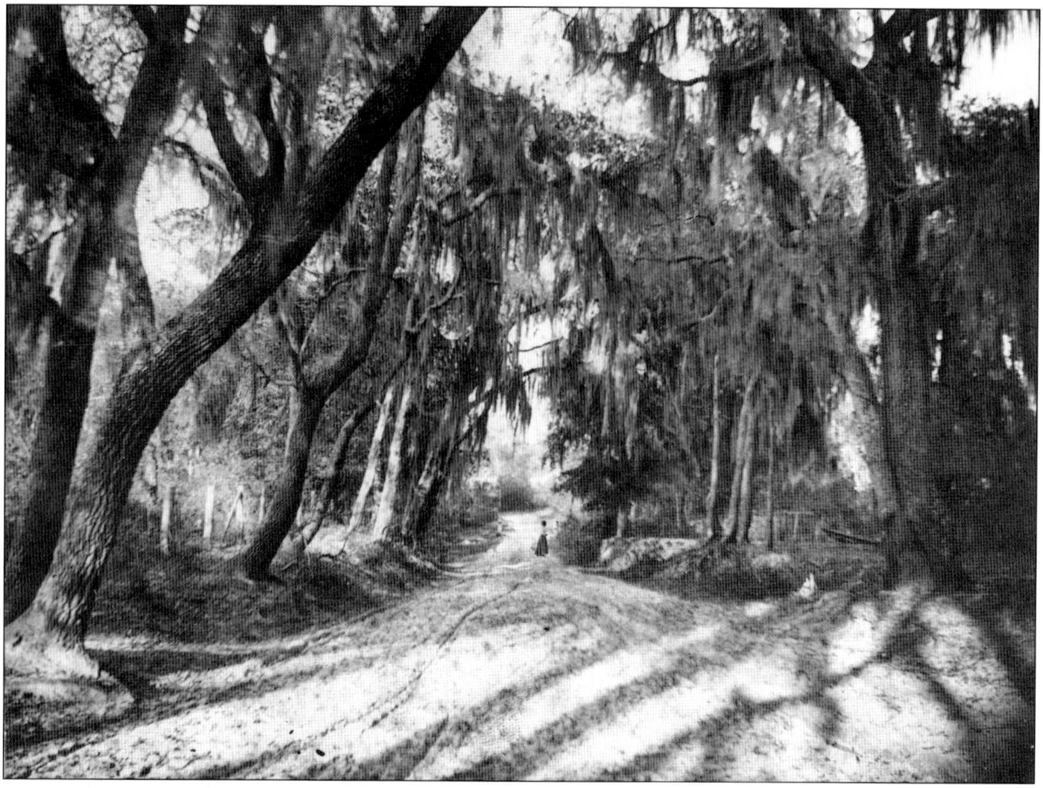

Pictured is unpaved future Mandarin Road, with the canopy of live oaks in the late 19th century. A woman walking in a long dress is seen in the distance.

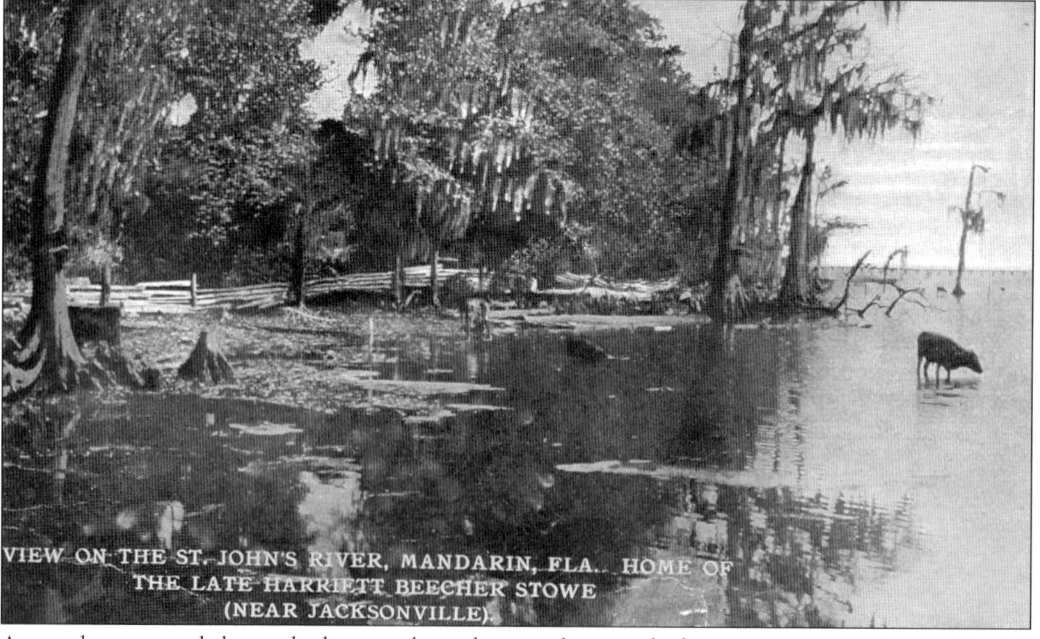

A popular postcard shows the beauty along the riverfront with the cypress trees. The fences were meant to keep the cattle out of peoples' yards.

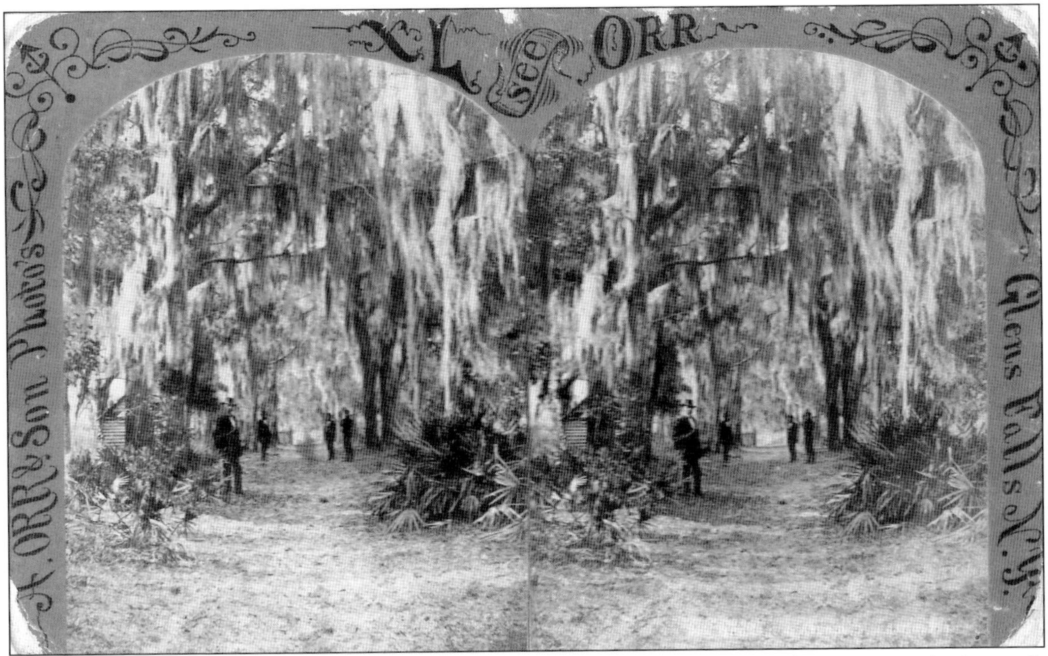

This stereoview shows men standing along Huntington Avenue near Mandarin Point. The Spanish moss and live oak trees were always a key feature of Mandarin's beauty.

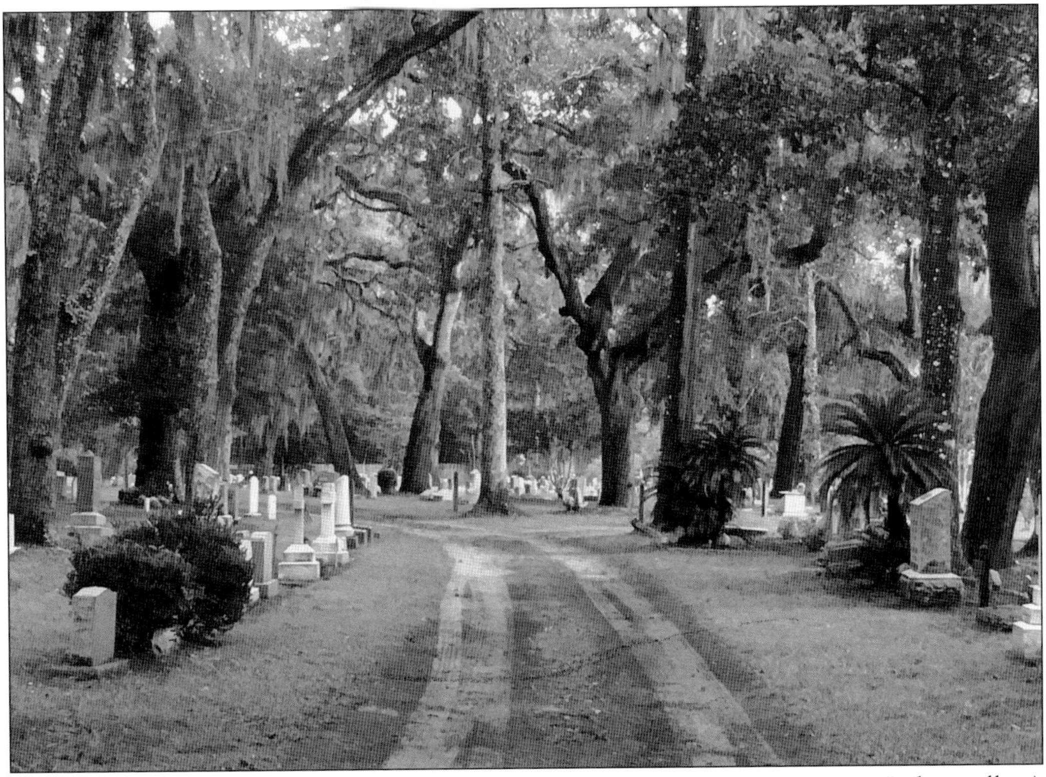

Mandarin Cemetery, founded in 1836, is one of the most beautiful cemeteries in Jacksonville. A brochure is available at the gate for a walking tour of 10 interesting residents of the past.

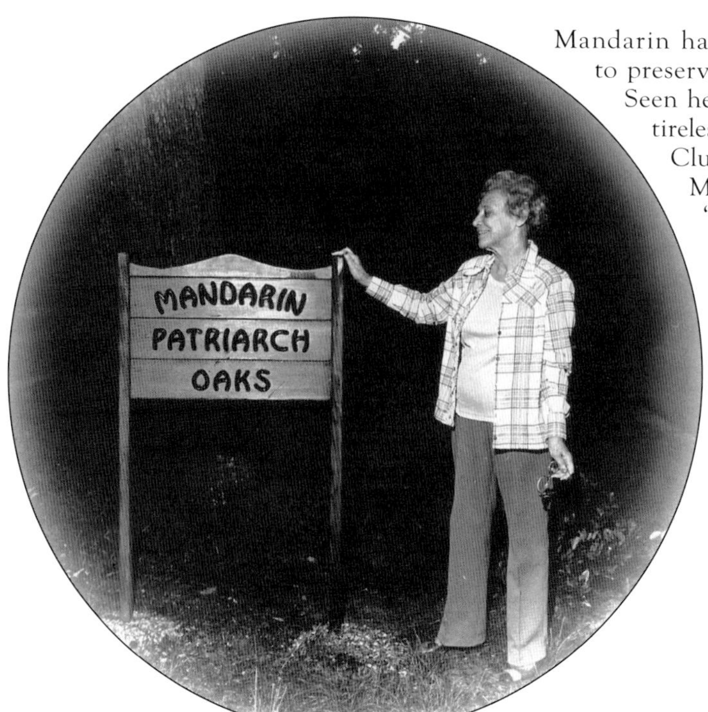

Mandarin has always had people working to preserve its character and its beauty. Seen here is Janet Jones, who worked tirelessly with the Mandarin Garden Club to have the live oaks along Mandarin Road designated as "Patriarch Oaks" in 1987. These trees still today give Mandarin its signature appearance with islands of oaks winding along Mandarin Road. (Photograph by Horace Glass.)

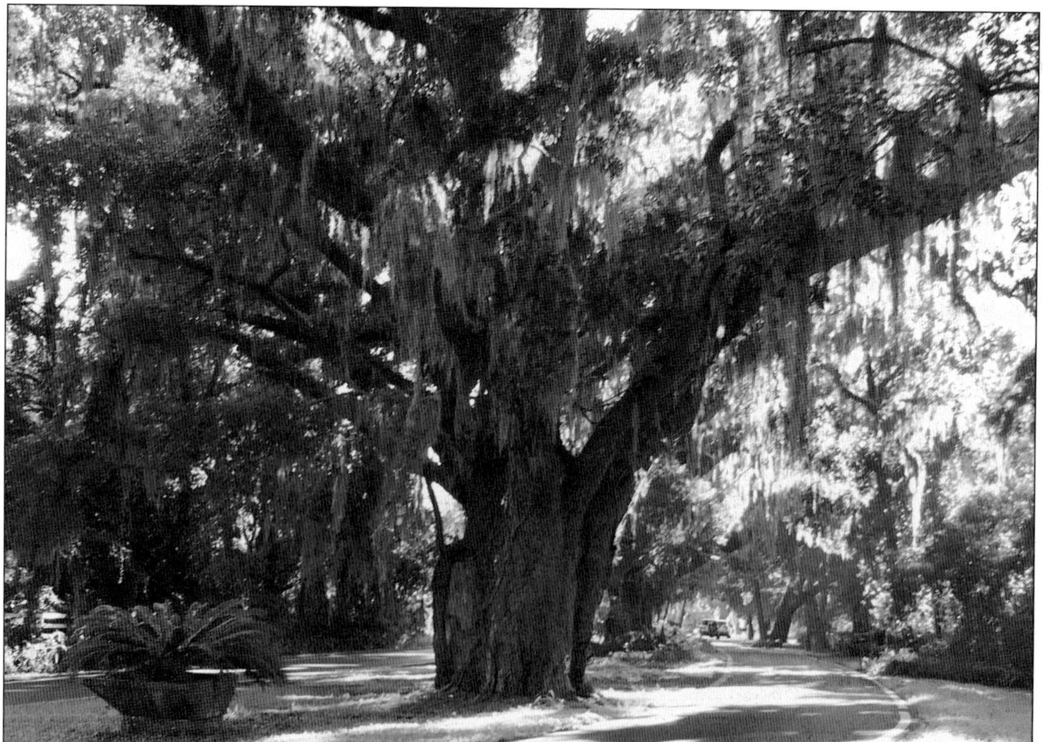

This view of Mandarin Road shows 21st-century cars passing a 19th-century concrete horse watering trough (lower-left corner).

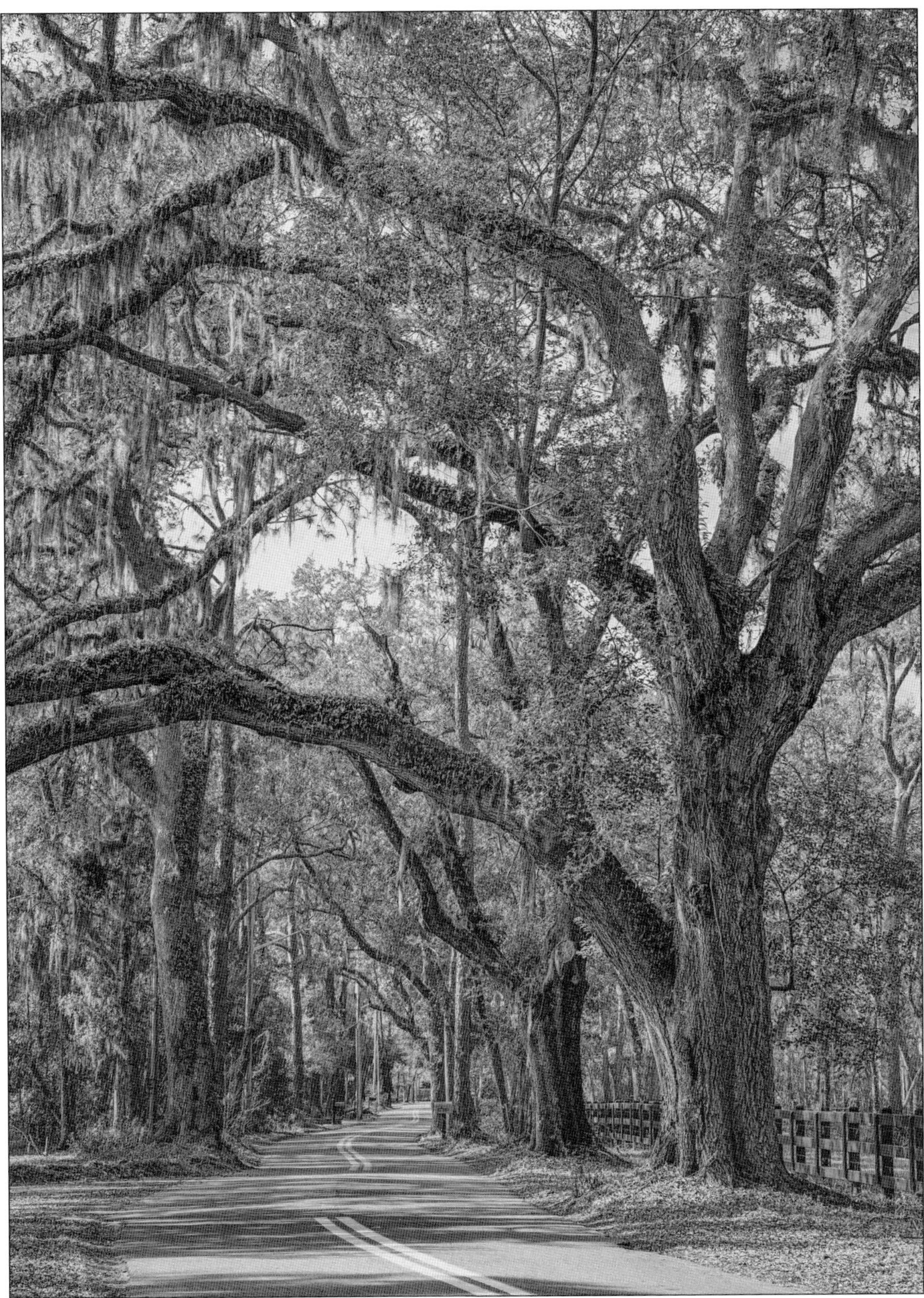

Mandarin, surrounded by the natural beauty of the St. Johns River, its live oaks and magnolias, and a rich history, will take you back to Old Florida. All are invited to discover the "Mandarin Experience." (Courtesy of Olis Garber.)

Always the River

First, the river; then came men. Only guesses guide our thoughts:
Did they come through quiet woodlands, a trail begun, Indian-wise?
Or did a dugout, slicing by, send the heron flying high, warning all with rasping cry?
They came. And after them, the Spanish; low-voiced priests' intoning
    reinforced with armor's clank.
The French too, paused on moss-hung bank, and left a legacy of words when their swords failed.
The English gave a language to this land. Back and forth in dizzying sequence
    the nations came and changed;
Mandarin names, till now, record the origins of its men; Ireland, England, Poland, Spain.
They came. And farms, lumber, turpentine and gracious homes were theirs,
Until the rending grief of war.

Weary and heartsore with wounds in flesh and purse, the immigrants came.
England's Victoria on the throne nodded approval to her sons and bade them come
And bring the tropic riches home. Most stayed instead, but remembering home
They built a church in England's mold.
Axles creaked. Sawmills whined. Farmlands glowed, scarlet, green and gold;
    Gold of fruit – and prosperity.
Oceanbound ships, dozens a day, loaded and sailed, until tragedy.

The climate-borne economy wilted, as the flattened grovelands perished.
Families fled. Hardly an axe rang, hardly a boat paused at the old landings.
Mourning, moss-veiled, Mandarin heard only birdsong and the water lapping.

Gradually, there was a new sound, hesitant, sputtering, the loud, insistent, smooth and confident.
Like the prince awak'ning the sleeping beauty, the auto brought life to Mandarin again.
White ribbons of roads, the handsome skeletons of bridges, and the humming motors
Brought new eyes to enjoy and new hearts to thrill to towering trees, massed flowers, and the
river – Always the river.

Change comes to Mandarin from the river, gold, the aims of the future soar.
A great bridge arcs from shore to shore, bringing action, bringing more.
The Indian quiet long has gone: Planes go shrieking through the sky
And power saws add a chilling cry. Bulldozers bite the harried land; No tree, no bush
    is left to stand. Without a restraining, healing hand
Will the river bathe a desert view?

The vision's bold. Is the vision true?

Jean K. Morrow, 1969

Mandarin native Jean Kennedy Morrow (1909–2004), considered by many to be "Mandarin's historian," wrote this poem about the St. Johns River in 1969.

About the Mandarin Museum & Historical Society

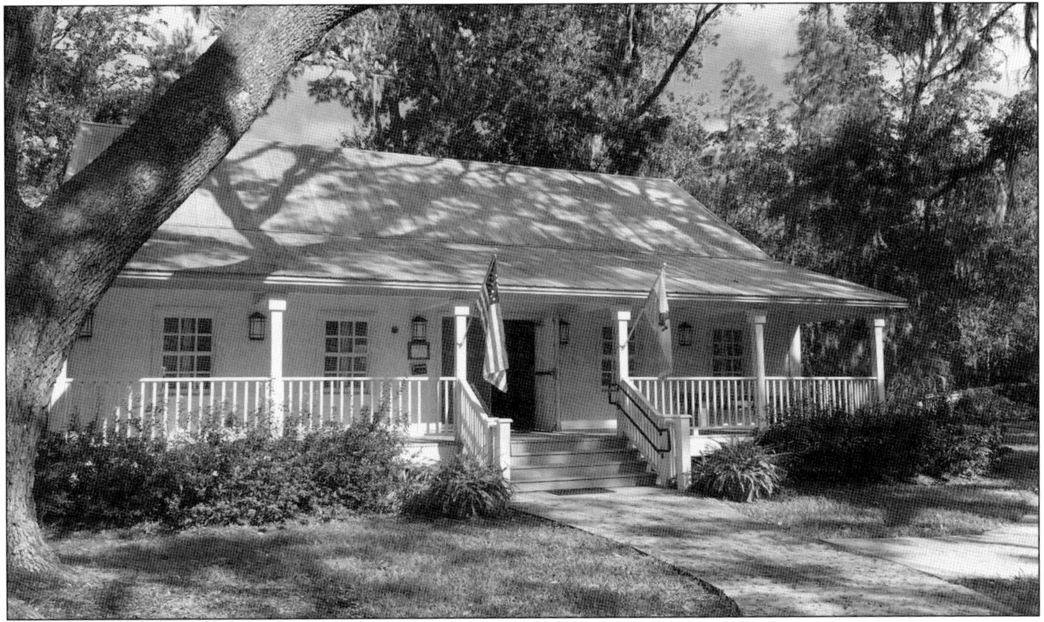

The Mandarin Museum & Historical Society (MMHS) was founded in 1989 by a group of citizens concerned with the loss of historical structures in Mandarin and interested in preserving and celebrating the rich heritage and history of the area. It is a nonprofit 501c3 organization.

The first major project conducted by the organization was restoring the historic 1911 Mandarin Post Office and Walter Jones General Store, which served as the heart of the community until it closed in 1964. In 2001, after renovation, the building was listed in the National Register of Historic Places and earned a designation as a local landmark by the Jacksonville Historic Preservation Commission. The building is owned by the Mandarin Community Club and managed and maintained by MMHS through a generous lease agreement.

An even greater opportunity for MMHS to preserve the local heritage began in 2000 when the City of Jacksonville (COJ) and Florida Communities Trust created the 10-acre Walter Jones Historical Park, which became home to MMHS. This partnership with the City of Jacksonville allows MMHS to manage the historic property and buildings owned by them, providing interpretive exhibits and educational programs in six exhibit areas: the Mandarin Museum, the 1898 St. Joseph's Mission Schoolhouse for African American Children, the 1875 Webb Farmhouse, the 1876 barn, the 1890s Losco Winery, and the Wheeler Sawmill.

The Mandarin Museum features exhibits related to Harriet Beecher Stowe, the *Maple Leaf*, the Untold Stories of Black Mandarin, steamboats, and a variety of general historical topics, as well as an art gallery.